SEX EDUCATION

THE FINAL PLAGUE

SEX EDUCATION
THE FINAL PLAGUE

By
Randy Engel

"But he that shall scandalize one of these little ones that believe in me, it were better for him that a millstone should be hanged about his neck, and that he should be drowned in the depth of the sea."
—*Words of Our Lord*
(Matthew 18:6)

TAN BOOKS AND PUBLISHERS, INC.
Rockford, Illinois 61105

First published in 1989 by Human Life International, Gaithersburg, Maryland. Reprinted by HLI in 1992. Retypeset and republished with corrections in 1993 by TAN Books and Publishers, Inc.

ISBN: 0-89555-471-2

Library of Congress Catalog Card Number: 92-60958

Printed and bound in the United States of America.

TAN BOOKS AND PUBLISHERS, INC.
P.O. Box 424
Rockford, Illinois 61105

1993

To Our Lady of Fatima.

"Far too common is the error of those who, with dangerous assurance and under an ugly term, propagate a so-called 'sex education,' falsely imagining they can forearm youth against the dangers of sensuality by means purely natural, such as a foolhardy initiation and precautionary instruction for all indiscriminately, even in public; and, worse still, by exposing them at an early age to the occasions [of sin], in order to accustom them, so it is argued, and as it were to harden them against such dangers. . ."

—Pope Pius XI
Encyclical *Divini Illius Magistri*
"On Christian Education of Youth"
December 31, 1929
(See page 50 herein.)

Sex Education is "the teaching of explicit sexual matters as a formal matter of classroom instruction, either as a separate curriculum or as an integrated part of legitimate courses of study at the elementary or secondary grade level."

—See page 206.

"We protest in the strongest possible terms against the introduction of sex instruction into the schools!"

—Catholic Bishops of the United States
November 17, 1950
(See page 51 herein.)

"It bears repeating, over and over, that Pope Pius XII's prescription of *PROPER TIME, PROPER MEASURE,* and *PROPER PRECAUTIONS* can *never* be carried out in *any* classroom setting or with *any* group program. . ."

—See page 134.

Instruction with regard to the Sixth Commandment (sexual morality) requires "great caution and prudence" and should be carried out in a manner which stresses "brevity rather than copiousness of exposition," lest, even unintentionally, such instruction may treat of "subjects which, instead of extinguishing, usually serve rather to inflame corrupt passion."

—Material quoted from
The Catechism of the Council of Trent
(See page 133 herein.)

Acknowledgments

With profound humility and gratitude, I wish to acknowledge the special contributions of the following men and women whose good counsel and advice, technical support and encouragement helped make this book a reality:

To my dear friend and colleague, Dick Lloyd, Vice President of the National Coalition of Clergy and Laity, whose suggestion that I write a "one-page critique" of the Mast *Love and Life* program led to this two-year project, covering the entire scope of sex education. Thanks, Dick!

To my three fellow musketeers: Marie Zaccaria of Parents Roundtable, Marjorie Garvey of Our Lady and St. Joseph in Search of the Lost Child (an Ad Hoc Alliance in Defense of the Fourth Commandment) and Suzanne Rini, author and translator extraordinaire. D'Artagnan could not have found better companions anywhere!

To Monsignor Charles Moss and Father Clifton Hill for their spiritual counsel and example of faithfulness to Holy Mother Church.

To Herbert Ratner, M.D., Melvin Anchell, M.D. and Father William Smith for their special insights into family life, latency and Catholic moral theology respectively.

To *The Wanderer* and Keep the Faith for running this book in serial and audio format, and to Father Paul Marx of Human Life International for his continuous encouragement in my writings.

To Frank Spahitz, Josepha M. Vollmer and Diane C. Illis for their technical comments and corrections, and especially Donna B. Marks of Tri-Mark Communications, who was responsible for the typing of the many drafts of this manuscript.

To my parents, Sebastian and Mary Vignone, for passing on to me the Catholic Faith and a love for truth and charity.

To my children, Dawn, Terry, David, Regina and Tricia and their spouses and our grandchildren—Kristina, Katlin, Tony and Jessica—who ever serve to remind me that nothing is more important in the world than God's gift of children and family.

And last, to my dear husband, Tom, who will be happy to know his temporary widowhood, caused by having a writer for a wife, is over—temporarily!

Table of Contents

Publisher's Preface

In writing *Sex Education—The Final Plague,* author Randy Engel has made a tremendous contribution both to the Catholic world and to society at large. For she has rightly called modern classroom Sex Education *"The Final Plague."* It is the *final* plague because ultimately it spells the end of our society—if not totally (which is conceivable), then at least of our society as we have known it—as one with traditional Christian moral customs.

Although in writing this book the author has not specifically stated her Catholic presuppositions regarding illicit sexual activity, they are present nonetheless as unstated theses underlying her entire theme, and therefore, I believe it is essential to state them openly, especially for those non-Catholic readers who may not be entirely familiar with the Catholic moral teaching on sex.

Fundamental to the traditional Catholic view on sex are some nine basic points: 1) Morally considered, sexual activity is allowed only within marriage and only between a validly married husband and wife, and then only in the natural manner that is left open to the procreation of children. *All other sexual activity—whether alone or with others—is forbidden both by the Natural Law and by divine positive law (Revelation).* 2) All purposely willed sexual sins are mortal sins, i.e., sins which, should a person die with one unrepented on his or her soul, will send that person to Hell. 3) A habit of sexual sin is very easy to contract (because of man's natural curiosity about himself, because sexuality is built into human nature by our Creator (carrying a pleasurable experience) and because man—though fundamentally good—is nonetheless inclined to evil, due to the Fall of Adam and Eve. Sexual sins soon become habitual and are thereafter very difficult to discontinue. 4) Sexual sins blind a person to the seriousness of these sins, probably quicker and more profoundly than any other type of sin, thereby prolonging a person's indulgence in them beyond what he might otherwise tolerate with other types of sin. 5) People are naturally ashamed of their sexual sins and therefore generally remain secretive about them, though continuing in them, often thinking that they cannot control themselves because they are just weak—not realizing that *all* people are weak in this regard and that the only way to overcome sexual sins is to *flee* from the near occasion of them and to call upon Our Lord and especially Our Blessed Lady to drive away the temptations to them, rather than to fight them. 6) Those who engage in sexual activity previous to marriage often fall into "an alternate lifestyle" and have less inclination to marry and assume the difficulties and responsibilities of marriage. 7) Sexual activity before marriage distorts a person's ability to assess accurately the suitability of the person he or she is involved with as a prospective mate—which suitability should be based on religious, moral, psychological and intellectual grounds more than on physical and emotional ones. 8) When a person has been sexually active before marriage, what will keep him or her from committing these sins *after* marrying, as temptation arises? This more than anything else can jeopardize a marriage and/or destroy it. 9) Sexual activity before marriage causes a person to lose God's blessing in all areas of his or her life, and particularly the blessing of finding a proper spouse; how can God possibly bless a person who is purposely violating His law? The Bible tells us: "But to God the wicked and his wickedness are hateful alike." (*Wisdom* 14:9). And "A good wife is a good portion, she shall be given in the portion of them that fear God, to a man for his good deeds." (*Ecclesiasticus* 26:3).

In other words, and restating the situation vis-a-vis Catholic morality, the sexual faculty was built into human nature by Almighty God, who coupled it with pleasurable experience, for the purpose of procreating children, and it is to be used only within marriage and then only between husband and wife in the natural manner, that must be left open to the conception of children. All other sexual activity is seriously sinful—a mortal sin.

Further, sexual sins easily become habitual and blind the sinner to the seriousness of them.

By not inculcating in young people the correct idea of the purpose of sex as intended by God, our Creator, and by not warning them of the seriously sinful nature of illicit sex, we are leaving them open to all manner of false ideas and sinful practices—especially so where they are subjected to constant exposure to sexual matters by an openly explicit and moral-less classroom discussion.

Under these circumstances, young people, being naturally curious and often weak in this regard, will soon experiment. Of course they will discover the pleasures of sex. But they will be without the proper understanding of its purpose, as created by God. And soon illicit sex will become habitual to them. They will soon view sex as a sort of game, a sport, a recreation they think they have a perfect right to, not realizing the mortally sinful nature of illicit sex, and definitely not seeing its rightful place in the overall life of man.

Sexual sin makes one less ready and less willing to enter marriage. Sexual sin makes it harder for people to stay married—for why would they give up their sins just because they married? Sexual sin, therefore, aside from its ability to send a soul to Hell for eternity (as if this were not bad enough!), can and usually does mess a person up royally in this world. Sexual sin can keep a person from marriage at all, can lead to an unhappy marriage, can lead to divorce, to illegitimate children, to birth control, to abortion, to self-sterilization, to homosexuality (the ultimate sexual blind alley), and to a host of sins and crimes flowing out of all the above. Sexual immorality is therefore a sort of *plague* on mankind, and modern classroom Sex Education is nothing less than full exposure to this plague. If the devil himself had wanted to infect mankind in the most harmful way, with the least amount of effort, inflicting the quickest yet longest range and most permanent damage, he could not have chosen a better instrument than sexual immorality, nor a better method of introducing sexual immorality on the broadest scale than the present classroom Sex Education.

By imposing modern classroom sex education in our schools,

we are introducing children to the temptation to sin sexually, and very likely to form habitually sinful practices that will both jeopardize their eternal salvation and their earthly happiness. This is especially so in public schools where a secular morality is taught, but it is also true in Catholic schools, where the specific Sex Education courses currently available do not teach traditional Catholic sexual morality (such as the Commandments and the Cardinal Virtues). However, as Randy Engel points out so well in this book, *there is no classroom sex education that is proper or correct,* because it is the province of parents to teach their own children about sex, and this privilege, according to Catholic teaching, may not be arrogated by the school or the nuns or the parish priest, or even by the bishop himself. The right to teach children about the facts of life belongs exclusively to the parents of those children. This right, the Catholic Church teaches, belongs to the parents by the Natural Law, for education in sexuality has to be done gradually and as the child matures and is interested in such matters and is able to comprehend. Only parents are in a position to handle this delicate task for their children. For only parents are with their children on an extended basis; only parents know their children intimately and what they know and can handle; and only parents can deal with the matter privately and with the trust and love that this delicate subject requires. And even if they should fail in this particular duty, that fact does not *remove* their primary right in this area—let alone transfer it to the school. If they should depute another—say a teacher or a priest or a trusted friend—to help with some aspect of this instruction, that other person has the right to do only what the parent asks him or her to do and only for that child and for the occasion for which permission is given.

What purpose can possibly be served by today's explicit classroom sex education—which is often conducted from kindergarten through 12th grade—other than to keep sex continually before the minds of young people and to provide a constant temptation for them to experiment? Especially is this obvious when one sees that in Sex Education classes not only is every aspect of natural sex explored, but all the possible human sexual perversions as well. What hope can the child possibly have to emerge from such an extended program without having entered into serious sins of sexuality, particularly where children of both sexes attend class together?

The ostensible arguments given in favor of classroom Sex Education have almost always hinged on the increasing incidence of unmarried teen-age pregnancy, but Sex Education having been with us now for over 20 years, we should have witnessed the decline of unmarried teen-age pregnancy—which obviously we have not, but rather its increase.

Also there are those who speak of "Catholic" Sex Education, but the author thumps that notion soundly by comparing it to "Catholic" fornication (Page 207). In other words, the concept is a contradiction in terms and ideas. There can be no such thing as "Catholic" Sex Education because, morally speaking, there should never be "Catholic" classroom sex education at all—or any other kind in the classroom! Classroom Sex Education is wrong in and of itself.

A corollary to Randy Engel's thesis that modern classroom Sex Education has no place in Catholic schools is the equally cogent (though unstated) thesis that it has no place in public schools either, or in *any* school context whatever. The principle is very simple: We are dealing here with a Natural Law principle, a reality or truth based on the nature of things as God created them, which we all can know with our unaided reason; therefore, the principles involved in Sex Education pertain to and include everyone. Therefore, modern classroom Sex Education is bad for public and private school children, just as it is for Catholic school children. Therefore, it should be discontinued immediately. In public schools, it is even more harmful because it is taught without any reference to traditional Christian morality. Getting rid of classroom Sex Education, therefore, should be the goal of every parent and of everyone interested in the continuance of our society as we have known it. But this, in turn, leads to another important question.

As one reads this book, a certain fact may escape notice, namely, that classroom Sex Education is the outgrowth of the birth control-sexology-homosexual movement, and as such has been many decades gestating and coming to the fore. After penetrating the public schools, it then was infiltrated into the Catholic schools as well, where, as a concept, it stands in direct opposition to the traditional position of the Catholic Church. But no matter! There it is anyway—despite all opposition! The crucial question is just this: "To whom is classroom Sex Education so important that its proponents have been able to break down all barriers and bridge six or seven decades of time in a difficult, protracted campaign to have it ensconced in virtually all schools today?" This accomplishment in itself is a remarkable feat. In the inimitable words of Franklin Roosevelt, "Things don't just happen; they are planned that way." Two logical questions we should all be asking are these: "Who planned classroom Sex Education?" "And what exactly is the agenda of those who have engaged in such a long struggle, brooking no opposition, to have classroom Sex Education accepted everywhere, even in Catholic schools, where it stands diametrically opposed to the official position of the Catholic Church?"

Still another aspect of this dirty business might escape our notice, and that is the *teachers* of sex education. We all know from experience that no one is immune to explicit sexual information. Let us consider now the teacher, who perforce has had to sit through hours of discussion on the various aspects of sex, and has been exposed to all manner of pictures relating to the subject, and who, moreover, is constantly talking about it to his or her classes. If neither age nor maturity nor experience insulates people from the temptations of explicit sexual materials, then why may we not assume that many, if not most of the "qualified," state-certified teachers of classroom Sex Education are not themselves sexually immoral, if not in fact perverted? What high degree of sanctity or immunity could these teachers possibly possess that the rest of us mere mortals do not that would keep them from being corrupted by the very subject they are teaching? The answer is quite simple: They have no such immunity. And thus we have every right to suspect their personal moral integrity. Why therefore should we entrust our children to them?

Many other objections to classroom Sex Education could be brought forward, and Randy Engel does so, all in the process of showing just what classroom Sex Education, as we know it today, truly is and where it came from. Once a person reads this book and understands the motivation and thought of those behind this program, he will see that *it has no place whatsoever in any classroom, Catholic or public!* As the author states, "The major premise of this book. . . is that any formal 'sex education' is an objective evil—a moral plague—most commonly spread by classroom contact" (Page 200), and therefore that it should be done away with.

A reading of *Sex Education—The Final Plague* will be a real awakener for most people, and it should be an equally powerful motivator for all parents—and for everyone who would see our society survive—to have classroom Sex Education, in whatever guise it presents itself, banned in all schools, even by law, if necessary—and return to the right and duty of instructing in this delicate matter to the parents, where it properly belongs.

Thomas A. Nelson
Publisher

Introduction

In their classic work, *Epidemics*,[1] a chronological and historical account of epidemic diseases from ancient to modern times, authors Geoffrey Marks and William K. Beatty define the term epidemic and/or plague in the broad sense: "a communicable disease that affects a large number of people or creates a strikingly noticeable impact on existing societal structures."

From the ancient plagues of the Pharaohs, Thucydides and Justinian, to the Black Death of the Middle Ages and the pandemics of cholera which penetrated almost every part of the habitable globe, the sine qua non of pestilential disease has been

- The destruction of human life on such a scale as to portend extinction, not only to individuals and families, but to the entire human race.
- The disintegration of family institutions.
- The crumbling of governments, and the abandonment of civil authority and moral principles, which borders on lawlessness.
- The breakdown of religious beliefs and practices, accompanied by a mental and spiritual derangement.
- Demographic turmoil, affecting every aspect of human commerce: culture, education, politics, agriculture, national defense.
- A people racked with fear and crazed with unconsolable grief, and human suffering without parallel and beyond description.

Upon such tragic human and material chaos are built the scaffolding of a new social order and the construction of a new faith and code of human behavior.

This present book is about a 20th-century plague, a new type of plague, but a plague nonetheless destructive, nonetheless damaging to humankind, in fact—when considered from every aspect—it is a plague of, in many cases, infinite dimensions. I speak of the plague universally known as Sex Education. The fact that it is an iatrogenic, i.e., a man-made, phenomenon in no way detracts from its legitimate classification as a form of pestilential disease, nor does its unconventional epidemiology and means of transmission diminish its potential for destruction.

That sex education should be identified as the *Final* Plague may at first appear to be needlessly "apocalyptic." However, to those who understand the nature of the beast, the term "apocalyptic" hardly suffices in describing the ultimate reality of this contemporary assault on the human family.

In undertaking the writing of this book on sex education, I have several objectives in mind:

First, to document the origin and epidemiology of the sex education plague in much the same fashion as a medical historian traces the origin and nature of traditional pestilential diseases and to demonstrate how the operations of this modern plague are diametrically opposed to civil order and Western civilization in general and the Roman Catholic Church in particular.

Second, to provide the reader with an historical perspective of the Sex Education Movement during two critical periods of its development, namely, from 1945 to 1965, when the movement underwent a period of forced latency, and from 1966 to 1988, a period characterized by a vigorous reaction and universal contagion.

Third, to trace accurately the evolution of the plague of sex education from its anti-life origins to its incorporation into the Catholic educational system under the direction of the American Church for the purpose of building a New Moral Order for the New Age of the Brave New World.

Fourth, to illustrate the incongruity of efforts to design a "Catholic" sex education program.

And *lastly,* to make a case for a universal ban on classroom sex education to be issued by the Holy See as a first step in the restoration of the Faith and the reclamation of our Catholic heritage for ourselves and our posterity.

—Randy Engel

Chapter 1
The Nature of Sex Education

> The plague. . .was a mixed epidemic comprising several different diseases brought together by the forced wartime migration of peoples who did not ordinarily mingle. Attempts by the Athenian physicians to apply remedies were fruitless because they did not know the nature of the disease. In fact, the doctors themselves were among the first victims because they often came into contact with it.[2]
>
> (From the history of the plague of Thucydides, 431-427 B.C.)

Clearly, understanding the nature of a pestilential disease is essential for its containment and ultimate conquest. Unfortunately, when dealing with sex education, this essential understanding is conspicuous by its absence, even among those actively engaged in battling against the disorder. This ignorance tends not only to increase the strength of the infection, but broadens the range of its potential victims by striking the victims' attending physicians and protectors. Of course, contemplation of epidemiological considerations and the development of strategies implies both recognition and acceptance by both the authorities and the general populace of the lethal nature of the communicable disease and the necessity of halting its advance, no matter what the cost. Here, then, is where we must begin our counteroffensive.

Sex Education Unmasked

Realistically, most Americans do not think seriously about the matter of sex education, if they think about it at all. For some, the concept that sex should be institutionalized as a legitimate and thematic subject of academic pursuit in elementary and secondary classrooms seems absurd. After all, no life forms, from the simple amoeba to the more sophisticated primate, ever had to attend school to learn how to reproduce.[3]

Somehow, humanity has managed to be fruitful and multiply without benefit of formal instruction and endless organ recitals. Indeed, men and women throughout the centuries have managed this task so happily and so well that we now are told that there must be compulsory population control. The fact that this war against propagation is brought to us by the very same people campaigning for compulsory sex education should signal even the most addled brain that something is amiss. For others, it is the sex education controversy itself that is ridiculous. How can any rational person, they ask, oppose classroom instruction in basic human anatomy and male or female physiology?

Unfortunately, it does not occur to these mental lightweights to ask themselves why it takes 13 years of classroom instruction, 45 hours of additional teacher training, and thousands of dollars spent on selected textbooks and visual aids to convey such uncomplicated and straightforward biological facts.

There is yet another segment of the American society, perhaps representing the majority of citizens, who feel uncomfortable with sex education because they perceive it (and correctly so) as an invasion of parental rights, and a public exhibition of something which is by nature intimate and private.

For these persons, man's procreative powers are tied to both the natural and supernatural order of human existence. The belief that spousal union is sacred is so deeply embedded into their hearts and psyches that their instinctive reaction to classroom sex education is one of repulsion and suspicion.

These men and women are by no means sexual prudes, nor are they ignorant of the consequences of human sexual behavior. Indeed, they are usually aware and supportive of civil and ecclesiastical influences and actions taken to protect the common good and promote public virtue.

In this they are of one mind and spirit with Christian, non-Christian and even pagan cultures throughout the world which have sought to influence man's behavior and harness his sexual energies under a plenitude of customs, laws, rituals and taboos. Rather than *contradict* these customs and sanctions, we must *reinforce* the sacred and intimate nature of the sex act. As for the task of transmitting sexual knowledge from one generation to another, as well as the formation of character and conscience, each human community appears to employ a particular mode of communication within the framework of the primary and extended family unit, which is both unique and separate from learning which occurs in more formal educational settings.

At this point the reader may ask himself: if familial-based instructions in matters of human sexuality are the accepted universal norm, why do we need to institutionalize K through 12 sex education as part of any academic curriculum?

The simple answer is we do *not,* because, to borrow a phrase, there is *no need* to be formally educated in doing what comes naturally.

Unfortunately, this kind of reasoning can lead to a mental paralysis because it incorrectly assumes that the ultimate objectives of informal home instruction and those of classroom sex education are one and the same and therefore that the sex education controversy is merely one of debate over methodology and setting.

In reality, nothing could be further from the truth. Although the former is indeed about doing what comes naturally, the latter is about doing what comes unnaturally, because the term unnatural means going against nature. One can now begin to appreciate why it takes thirteen years of classroom instruction (some say a lifetime) for a person to be truly "sexually educated."

The Ultimate Goal of Sex Education

> The next century can be and should be the humanistic century. . . [Preface] We affirm that moral values derive their source from human experience. Ethics is autonomous and situational, needing no theological sanction. . . [Ethics]
>
> . . . In the area of sexuality, we believe that intolerant attitudes, often cultivated by orthodox religion and puritanical

> cultures, unduly repress sexual conduct. The right to birth control, abortion and divorce should be recognized.
>
> While we do not approve of exploitive [sic], denigrating forms of sexual expression, neither do we wish to prohibit, by law or social sanction, sexual behavior between consenting adults. The many varieties of sexual exploration should not in themselves be considered "evil."
>
> Without countenancing mindless permissiveness or unbridled promiscuity, a civilized society should be a tolerant one. Short of harming others or compelling them to do likewise, individuals should be permitted to express their sexual proclivities and pursue their life-styles as they desire.
>
> We wish to cultivate the development of a responsible attitude toward sexuality, in which humans are not exploited as sexual objects, and in which intimacy, sensitivity, respect and honesty in interpersonal relations are encouraged. Moral education for children and adults is an important way of developing awareness and sexual maturity. *("The Individual")*
>
> To enhance freedom and dignity, the individual must experience a full range of civil liberties in all societies.
>
> It [i.e. this freedom] includes a recognition of an individual's right to die with dignity, euthanasia, and the right to suicide. . . ["Democratic Society"][4]
>
> (Excerpts from the *Humanist Manifesto II*)

It is important to note that except for a generic reference to "The Human Family," the 3,000-word Humanist Credo makes no mention of words normally associated with human sexuality, such as marriage, family, or procreation, but does include references to such "necessities" as birth control, abortion, divorce, euthanasia, suicide and varieties of sexual expressions.

Advancing the Sexual Revolution

When the late Alan Guttmacher, M.D., former president of Planned Parenthood and a signatory of the *Humanist Manifesto II,* was asked how the Supreme Court abortion decision of January 22, 1973 could be made absolutely secure, once and for all, he responded with two words: "Sex education."[5]

Actually, the sly old fox was being too modest. The "right" of a woman to kill her unborn is but one of the many inalienable "rights" which sex education desires to guarantee, including:

- The "right" to contracept.
- The "right" to sterilize oneself and the retarded.
- The "right" to commit adultery, and to trial marriage and divorce.
- The "right" to eugenic breeding, i.e., artificial insemination and surrogate motherhood.
- The "right" to suicide, i.e., to kill oneself.
- The "right" to euthanasia, i.e., to kill others who are ill.
- The "right" to infanticide, i.e., to kill the mentally and physically handicapped.
- The "right" to eugenic abortion, i.e., to kill the mentally and physically handicapped pre-born child.
- The "right" to free access to pornography.
- The "right" to all forms of sexual expression, including masturbation, sodomy, bestiality, and sado-masochism.
- The "right" to pedophilia, so infants and children can engage in "creative" sexuality.
- The "right" to commercial sex (i.e., prostitution), as well as heterosexual, homosexual and surrogate sex therapy.
- The "right" of the State to implement programs of population control, both voluntary and compulsory.

This baker's dozen of sexual "rights" clearly reveals the nature of the beast.

Sex Education...

- is not about fecundity; it is about sterility.
- is not about the facts of life; it is about death and killing.
- is not about virtue; it is about vice.
- is not about love; it is about genital stimulation.
- is not about honor; it is about infidelity.
- is not about God; it is about sexual idolatry.
- is not about chastity; it is about the cannibalism of innocence and purity.
- is not about morality; it is about immorality.

In truth, *sex education is not education at all; rather, it is a legalized form of child seduction and molestation.*

The Advantages of the Classroom

At this point, one begins to see the necessity and obvious advantages to the Humanists of their institutionalizing sex education into a K through 12 school curriculum. Being true to its pestilential nature, it must seek out a massive, vulnerable population to infect, and the classroom provides the perfect medium for the contraction and transmission of the disease.

First, thirteen years of access to a captive audience of immature and non-discriminating children and adolescents present more than sufficient opportunities to arrest *normal* sexual development in the young and *break down* sexual inhibitions and feelings of revulsion which act as natural barriers to premature sexual expression. Essential to this sexual-attitudinal restructuring process is the destruction of the latency period, a matter which will be discussed at length later in this book.

Second, sex education, by making human sexuality *thematic* and *public,* strips the sexual act of its natural, intimate and sacred nature. Once the child comes to the understanding that human intercourse has all the moral relevancy of emptying one's bladder and he or she can openly recite to his or her classmates a litany of sexually stimulating techniques (as well as the meaning of Freudian pan-sexualism) with the ease of an eight-year-old rattling off his times tables—and with as much passion—then the battle *against* sex education is all but lost.

Third, tax-supported institutions carry the weight of legitimacy, which also extends to the teaching authority of the instructor. Thus, armed with newly acquired respectability, *the teacher-turned-sexologist can with immunity devalue and undermine both parental direction and religious influence.* It should be understood that the sex educators *know* that their views go against traditional sexual norms and that they will be rejected by parents who instinctively act to protect their children from harm. Hence, the importance of an instruction environment *apart* from the home.

And *fourth,* since public schools must remain morally neutral, classroom instruction must be morally neutered, and human sexuality is thereafter studied without reference to the Natural Law, the Ten Commandments or any moral absolutes. This separation of human sexuality from traditional and religious morality is instrumental in the deformation and desensitization of the tender young conscience, and in the assassination of character and virtue.

Lastly, sex education has a number of fellow-travelers, which cling like barnacles on a dry-docked ship: These include values clarification, role-playing activities, peer counseling, school-based contraceptive dispensaries and abortion-referral services, to name but a few.

The Cradling of Sex Education

As with the study of the more traditional plagues which have ravaged the human race since the beginning of time, invaluable insights into the true nature of a pestilence may be discovered by examining its origin and point of entry. For example, the Plague of Justinian began in the vicinity of Pelusium, along the eastern border of the Nile. It then spread to the east over Syria, Persia and the Indies and finally reached westward to the continent of Europe via the coast of Africa.[6] The origin of the Black Plague was central Asia, and it gradually spread eastward to China, south to India and finally westward to the borders of Europe, following the routes of the great Caravans.[7]

Likewise, the origins of the contemporary plague of Sex Education are well known. While philosophically rooted in one of the most ancient of gnostic heresies, Manicheanism, the movement only gained ascendency in the early part of the twentieth century as a synthesis of Malthusianism, Eugenics and Sexual Reform Movements, all of which had their origins in the late 1800's and early 1900's in England and Scandinavia. On the European Continent, with the exception of the Netherlands, Belgium and Germany, the plague fell on rocky ground, so deeply embedded were Europe's religious ties to Christianity. Its pestilential path spread westward to the Americas, however, which proved to be more fertile ground, and it was here that the plague eventually would gather its deadliest harvest.

Sex Education and the Anarchists

The earliest reference to formalized public sex instruction for children in America that I have found is an essay entitled "Moral Evolution in America" by Sidney Ditzion, Ph.D. This essay, along with other important works on sex education which I shall cite during the course of this study, appear in *The Encyclopedia of Sexual Behavior*.[8] This encyclopedia was edited by Robert Ellis, Ph.D., the father of sexology, and his associate Albert Brandt Abarbanel, Ph.D., a pioneer in psychotherapy and a prolific author on the merits of "scientific sex."

The Ditzion essay highlights the early anti-marriage and anti-propagation sentiments prevalent among Free Thinkers, Socialists and Anarchists during the mid 1800's, many of whom were immigrants to the United States from England.

Prominent among the Socialist innovators was Robert Owen, whose utopian community of New Harmony became a safe harbor for anti-marriage theorists, feminists, divorce-law reformers and birth-control advocates.

An early convert to the Malthusian-Eugenic-Sexual-Reform cause was Robert Owen's son, whose columns in the *New Harmony Gazette* and *The Free Thinker* spoke of the need for formalized sexual instruction of the young to 1) relieve their anxieties and 2) to give knowledge in the area of human sexuality.

The younger Owen, a disciple of the Neo-Malthusians and Eugenics, also enthusiastically embraced birth control as an answer to the working man's economic plight, a means of checking the transmission of hereditary diseases, and to relieve women of the health hazards of overbreeding and self-induced abortion. Robert Dale Owen's cry for sexual freedom and reform was echoed by American anarchists like Stephen Pearl Andrews, Ezra Harvey Heywood and Moses Harmon. Their ultimate goal was summarized on the masthead of the anarchist periodical, *The Word,* as "Free Land, Free Labor, and Free Love."[9]

World League for Sexual Reform

Developing side-by-side with the Neo-Malthusian Leagues and the Social Hygiene Movement for race betterment through scientific breeding, were the National and World Leagues for Sexual Reform, all precursors of Planned Parenthood and SIECUS.

A study of the Sex Reform Movement of the early 1900's continues to provide the reader with additional documents on the anti-life origins of classroom sex education.

According to Robert Wood, former editor of the *Journal of Sex Education,* the modern demand for sexual reform was "a new attitude born for the most part out of the new science of sexology." However, Wood was quick to point out that "both in Europe and America there was a negative mythology of sex that provided the foundation of a repressive and antibiological morality," and that *"the first step in sexual education was to undermine the authority of this morality."*[10] (Emphasis added).

Central to the platform of the National and World Sex Reform Leagues were:

- The repeal of laws making sodomy a crime and the acceptance of homosexuality as a legitimate and alternative form of sexual expression.
- The legalization of prostitution, accompanied by state registration and medical inspection of brothel facilities and inhabitants.
- The legalization and promotion of anti-conception techniques and the dissemination of prophylactics to curb the spread of venereal disease.
- The establishment of Sexual Counseling Centers to promote birth control and eugenic enlightenment.
- The liberation of marriage and the expansion of grounds for divorce.
- The repeal of all restrictions on induced abortions.
- The repeal of all obscene libel laws, which were seen as impediments to the work of the sexual educator.
- And finally, systematic and scientific sexual education for both the young and adults.[11]

According to Wilhelm Reich, the World League for Sexual Reform, founded by Dr. Magnus Hirschfeld, an *avowed* homosexual, in Berlin in 1928, was "comprised [of] the most progressive sexologists and sex reformers in the world," including Sigmund Freud, Bertrand and Dora Russell, Dr. Abraham Stone and Judge Benn Lindsey.[12]

At the start of World War II, while many of the Sex Reform Leagues had disbanded, their agendas had already been picked up by the birth-control activists. The policies advocated by Margaret Sanger in the United States and Marie Stopes in England were eventually absorbed into the directives of the International Federation of Birth Control Leagues, which included groups such as the U.S.-based Society for the Scientific Study of Sex and the English-based Sex Education Society.

Perhaps one of the most important spin-offs of the World League for Sex Reform, however, was the Swedish-based *Riksforbundet und Sexuell Upplisning* (National League for Sex Education—RFSU) founded in 1933 by the Norwegian-born Mrs. Elise Ottensen-Jensen. A member of the World Sex Reform League, and later President of the International Planned Parenthood Federation (IPPF), Ottensen-Jensen is considered by many to be the mother of Sex Education world-wide. It was largely through her efforts that, as early as 1942, a Royal Proclamation called for the introduction of sex education in all schools throughout Sweden. In 1955, following the promulgation of an official handbook on sex education by the Royal Board of Education of Sweden, sex education became compulsory in the schools.[13] It should be carefully noted that Ottensen-Jensen was an ardent proselytizer for medically induced abortions on demand, both in Europe and throughout the world as a member of the IPPF Governing Board.

The Eugenics Movement

The epidemiology of sex education will be completed by a brief account of the fusion between the Eugenics-and-Racial-Hygiene Movement, on the one hand, and the precepts of Social Darwinism enunciated at the turn of the century, on the other.

The first Eugenics working society was established by Francis Galton, the Father of Eugenics, at University College in London in 1904. One year later, Dr. Alfred Ploetz founded the German Society for Racial Hygiene, which emphasized particularly the drive for racial betterment through scientific breeding and the elimination of the unfit, and which attracted an ever-increasing number of supporters and adherents.

Closely allied with the theoreticians and practitioners of eugenics were the mental hygienists, who, on the whole, supported the eugenic principles of the elimination of the unfit by means of separatist colonies and institutions, by the prohibition of procreation, and by the castration and sterilization of defectives.

In the classic study *Geheime Reichssage* (*The Men Behind Hitler*), translated from the German by H. R. Martindale, writer Bernard Schreiber makes the following observation:

> As the original supposed purpose of the mental hygiene movement was improved care of the mentally ill, it is strikingly odd that the first laws passed on the international basis at the instigation of the mental hygiene movement were laws to sterilize the mentally ill and prevent them from reproducing.[14]

With the publication in 1922 of *Die Freigabe Der Vernichtung Lebensumwerten Lebens* (*The Release of the Destruction of Life Devoid of Value*) by Jurist Karl Binding and prominent psychiatrist Alfred Hoche, physical, mental, moral and cultural defectives were awarded the subsequent "benefit" of euthanasia or mercy killing.[15]

According to Schreiber, under the Third Reich, the common denominator of non-Aryan religious and ideological minorities, including gypsies, Freemasons, Jehovah's Witnesses, Jews and Christians, was "that all strongly believed in something spiritual and mental and oriented their lives according to this belief. They were unlikely to respond to a psychiatric dream-world and therefore found no place in the psychiatric view of life."[16]

This was in stark contrast to the predisposition of the sex reformers and sex educators of the time who fitted *perfectly* into the psychiatric dream-world of the Eugenic-Racial-Hygiene Movement.

Sex Education—A Synthesis of Anti-Life Philosophies

Thus it was that, *from the very beginning,* the fates of the Neo-Malthusians and Sex Reformers, including leaders of the Radical Feminist Movement, Homosexual Movement, the Darwinists and the Eugenicists were joined together in a combined effort that would become known as the *Sex Education Movement.* This is why to them any "authentic" sex education program for the young must include the full gamut of anti-life precepts and practices if it is to be true to its original mission.

Chapter 2
The Evolution of the Plague (1945-1965)

Introduction

The historical evidence presented thus far, documenting the origin and goals of the Sex Reform/Sex Education Movement, is, I believe, incontrovertible.

So manifestly clear was the existence of the blood-bond between the Eugenicists, the Neo-Malthusians, the Social Anarchists and the Sex Reform/Sex Education Movement from the mid-1800's to the early 1900's, that when the former were forced to go underground during the post World War II era, the latter quickly followed. It was take cover or perish!

The simple truth was that in the United States and Europe, particularly among the intelligentsia, who were always agreeably amused and titillated by the irreverent ravings of the new barbarians, the seemingly harmless-sounding and pseudo-scientific abstract phrases, such as, "useless eaters" and "life devoid of value" had taken on a new and sinister meaning when faced with the realities of the Soviet concentration camps of Treblinka, Sobibor, Chelmno, and Pelzec.

Condemned by the circumstances of "guilt by association" to a relatively long period of quiescence and obscurity—a kind of forced "latency period," one might say—the proponents of sex reform/sex education devoted their time, energies and monies to the arduous task of re-organizing, networking and revitalizing their respective pet causes.

Essential to their rebirth was the development of innovative and effective judicial, political and mass-media strategies, which were intended to

- influence public opinion in the matter of sexual mores and practices,
- change or eliminate "antiquated" laws and prohibitions regarding marriage, family, etc., and
- eliminate, or at least neutralize, the opposition that was and still is Western Civilization in general and the Roman Catholic Church in particular.

In 1935, shortly before his death, World League for Sexual Reform founder Magnus Hirschfeld spelled it all out. He envisioned the coming of the new "sexual sociology," which would encompass "sexual ethics, sexual criminal law and sexual statesmanship."[17]

According to Hirschfeld, this new wave of societal reform would involve "the provision of a sexual code dealing not only with marriage and divorce, but all sexual relations, including those of unmarried persons, the difficult problem of prostitution and above all *the scientific regulation of birth.*"[18] (Emphasis added).

It should be noted that Hirschfeld put particular emphasis on the last of these because he believed, and correctly so, that no sexual revolution could take place unless sex could be completely divorced from procreation, by means of contraception, sterilization, and induced abortion, and unless scientific breeding and selection of the fittest by artificial insemination and other eugenic techniques could be implemented.[19]

Reorganizing for the Sexual Revolution

The fact that this "sexual mafia" was to be enormously successful in completing its task is evident by the partial listing of the private, governmental, medical, educational, political, scientific, social, religious, judicial and economic network they managed to build during the four decades following World War II.

Chart I

The Sex Reform/Sex Education Network from 1940-1980 (Partial Listing)

Sex Information and Educational Council of the United States (SIECUS)

American Association of Sex Educators and Counselors (AASEC)
National Association of Sex Education (NASE)
Planned Parenthood Federation of America (PPFA)
Worchester Foundation for Experimental Biology
Institute for Sex Researchers (ISR)
Reproductive Biology Research Foundation (RBRF) (Masters and Johnson)
National Sex and Drug Reform
Playboy Foundation
Abortion Reform Association
Society for Humane Abortion
Association for the Study of Abortion (ASA)
National Abortion Rights Action League (NARAL)
National Association for Repeal of Abortion Laws (NARAL)
Association for Voluntary Sterilization (AVS)
Catholics for a Free Choice
Clergy Counseling Services
Victor Bostrum Population Fund
Hugh Moore Fund
Population Reference
Population Crisis Committee (PCC)
Population Council (PC)
Zero Population Growth (ZPG)
Pathfinder Fund
Negative Population Growth (NPG)
Concern for the Dying
Euthanasia Society of America
Euthanasia Educational Council
American Public Health Association
American Medical Association (AMA)
American Academy of Pediatrics (AAP)
American College of Obstetrics and Gynecology (ACOG)
American Social Hygiene Association (ASHA)
Institute of Advanced Study in Rational Psychotherapy (IASRP)
American Association of Planned Parenthood Physicians (AAPPP)
Family Source Association of America (FSAA)

American Association of Marriage Counselors (AAMC)
American Eugenics Society
National Education Association (NEA)
National Catholic Education Association
American School Health Association (ASHA)
U.S. Agency for International Development, Department of State (AID)
Department of Health, Education and Welfare (HEW) later Health and Human Services (HHS)
National Institute of Health
Office of Population Affairs, Department of Health, Education and Welfare (HEW)
Office of Economic Opportunity (OEO)
UNICEF, UNESCO, WHO (United Nations Agencies)
Board of Church and Society, United Methodist Church
National Council of Churches of Christ in the United States (NCC)
Metropolitan Community Church
American Humanist Association (AHA)
Young Men's Christian Association (YMCA)
United States Catholic Conference (USCC)
Rockefeller Foundation
Ford Foundation
American Civil Liberties Union (ACLU)
National Organization for Women (NOW)
North American Man/Boy Love Association (NAMBLA) (established for the promotion of pedophilia)
Gay Teachers Caucus of the National Education Association
Gay Caucus, American Bar Association
Gay Caucus of Public Health Workers
Gay Caucus of the American Psychiatric Association
Dignity (Pro-Homosexual "Catholic" Organization)
Lesbian and Gay Associated Engineers and Scientists
Churchill Films, Los Angeles
Contemporary McGraw Hill Films, New York
Guidance Associates, New York
Perennial Education, Illinois
Unitarian-Universalist Association, Maine

Multi-Media Resource Center, California
William C. Brown Co., Iowa

From Private Vice to Public Virtue[20]

It is true that turning *private vice* (i.e., divorce, sodomy, abortion, contraception, fornication, adultery, sterilization, prostitution, etc.) into *public virtue*—and thus a national mandate—is neither a simple nor inexpensive matter. It is also true that seven or eight-digit organizational budgets and the influence of powerful political family dynasties, like the Rockefellers, McCormicks, and Gambles, can go a long way in eliminating *almost any* obstacles to success. I say *almost* any, however, because there was one thing money and power could not buy, at least not directly, and that was *respectability!*

The entire anti-life coterie needed extensive cosmetic surgery before resurfacing again. The object was to change the external features while still retaining their true nature, or to put it another way, to put on a new face while keeping their tail intact.

Somehow the negative image of the Eugenic/Neo-Malthusian/Sexual Reform/Sex Education Movement which most Americans held until the second half of the twentieth century had to be changed if their policies and programs were to be universally accepted. No longer could their activities be viewed in the public eye as anti-marriage, anti-family and anti-baby, or tied to illicit sex and prostitution.

The problem, as they quickly saw it, boiled down to proper marketing techniques and improved packaging. The art of using euphemism and the "heart appeal" of the "hard case" was honed to a razor's edge.

Almost overnight, *birth control* was out and *family planning* was in, since the latter term conveyed no psychological animus against large families[21] and would link, at least subconsciously, contra-conceptive measures with marriage and babies, instead of whoredom and illicit sexual alliances.

References to family planning could *now* be legitimately discussed in polite society within the context of basic human rights and civil liberty.

Similarly, Margaret Sanger's Birth Control Federation of America became Planned Parenthood of America, a title Sanger despised whole-heartedly until Dr. Alan Guttmacher convinced her that the new name was necessary "to neutralize the highly negative image offered to the public by the term 'birth control' and a single clinical service, *the prevention of pregnancy.*'"[22] (Emphasis added).

Malthusian and eugenic propaganda, slightly tarnished by the Nazi experience, was now couched in the language of the social sciences, giving a pseudo-academic imprimatur to concepts such as the "population explosion" and "population control." The use of *eugenics* was changed to *genetics*.

Techniques of artificial insemination, once reserved for the stockyard, were brought into the American boudoir and now referred to simply as A.I. (artificial insemination) or A.I.D. (artificial insemination: using donor's sperm).

The vomitive phrase "alternative life style" was brought into vogue to sanction all types of human sexual experiences, whether with man, beast or thing, including masturbation, sodomy, incest and bestiality.

Induced abortion and voluntary sterilization—euphemistically referred to as "post-conceptive family planning" and "surgical contraception"—were pleaded for the "hard case," that is, for rape, incest and eugenic reasons, but were quickly expanded to include contraceptive failure or failure to *use* contraceptives.

The physiological difference between *contra*-conceptive techniques and *abortion* having been successfully blurred thereafter, abortifacient devices as well as abortifacient drugs, such as the IUD and the birth control pill (the latter employs a triple mechanism—including early abortion—to insure no births), could be pawned off on the American woman, who was already suffering from attacks by the new women's liberation ideology, as well as on women in Third World countries.

Abortion and contraceptive referral agencies and clinics, which had been operating outside the law, were now reincorporated under new titles such as Parents' Aid Societies or Parents' Information Centers.

Then the case of "Griswald v. Connecticut" (in favor of birth control), followed by "Roe v. Wade" (in favor of abortion), destroyed much of the legal protection which the American family and its members—born and unborn—had enjoyed since the founding of the nation.

And last, but certainly not least, the reconstituted anti-life forces formally baptized sex education with a new name: "Family Life Education," and sought to integrate their "new creation" into the American public and private school systems, as well as institutions of higher learning.

This particular strategy deserves further explanation if we are to appreciate fully its implications.

From "Sex Education" to "Family Life Education"

Thanks to Beryl Suitters, a former librarian in the London office of the International Planned Parenthood Federation, activities of the IPPF during its formative years were chronicled in a book entitled *Be Brave and Angry,* which was published on the occasion of the 21st anniversary of the federation. In this book, readers are afforded a close-up and personal glimpse of the bitter internal struggle that raged within the IPPF during the 1950's and 1960's concerning the discontinuance of the term "sex education" in favor of the more ambiguous term "family life education."[23]

The European IPPF leadership favored the change in terminology as a strategic maneuver. They blamed the "emotional resistance" of Europeans to family planning on their deep-rooted cultural, religious and political conservatism, and they also believed that their organization was the victim of harassment by Catholic organizations, as well as residual fascist legislation. According to Suitters, "family life education" would be more acceptable because Europeans favored large families and were strongly influenced by their religious beliefs.[24]

The Dutch IPPF affiliates, upset with what was perceived to be an American obsession "with worldwide information about attacking population problems, and *especially those of colored people*'' (emphasis added), were themselves charged with being obsessed with sex education, however it was packaged. The Dutch argued that "from experience they knew that the problems of organizing birth control could not be solved until programs of sex education had been followed through and people made conscious of sexuality as something of special importance and *separate from reproduction*."[25] (Emphasis added).

The IPPF Asian representatives argued in favor of the new title because it was more comprehensive and less threatening and would therefore meet with less resistance, since the general population continued to associate negatively sex education with the practice of birth control.[26]

The Africans followed suit by stating that their efforts to promote "family planning" were hindered by native tradition, prejudice and ignorance, but the new title would be more readily accepted.[27]

The hardline opposition favoring the retention of the term "sex education" was dominated by the United States and Swedish IPPF affiliates, led by Margaret Sanger and Mrs. Elise Ottensen-Jensen, respectively. They argued that their direct and confrontational approach to promoting the goals of sexual reform were more open and honest. They expressed fear that sex education would be emasculated if it were renamed and absorbed into a family-life curriculum. Further, they said, the new strategy betrayed the cause and was counter-productive, since it merely enforced the belief that sex was related to marriage, family and babies—a belief that they had spent a lifetime trying to destroy. Lastly, they warned that teachers would be ill-trained and backward about teaching explicit sexual details in the classroom and would instead stick to "safe" topics, such as budgets and dating, to basic biological reproductive facts and a rehash of conventional morality.

"Ottar," as Mrs. Ottensen-Jensen was affectionately called by her co-workers, was adamant that compulsory sex education, beginning in first grade, was a universal necessity. Her comments on parental resistance to sex education, made while she was President of the IPPF, are very enlightening. "We are well aware that it was *inevitable* that there would be *conflicts between the home and the school, once a sex education programme started,* and that it was vital to make every effort to teach parents to face up to the difficulties and to prepare them for what lay ahead."[28] (Emphasis added).

In the end, the debate whether to call their program "sex education" or "family-life education" proved to be purely academic, if for no other reason than there was not a chance at all for the hardline strategy to survive in post-war Europe or the United States, and certainly not in Third World Nations. The Sex Reform/Sex Education Movement, as it stood in the late 1940's, was simply an anathema to most of the world's adult population.

"Family Life Education," on the other hand, if correctly packaged, would have universal appeal and would in time "have the advantage of moving sex education toward a realistic recognition of the problems of human sexual behavior, rather than focusing on sterile knowledge, unrelated to the conduct of relationships."[29]

This process is described in detail and praised in Lester Kirkendall's 1967 essay, "Education for Marriage and Family Living." According to Kirkendall—a professor of Family Life at the School of Economics at Oregon State University and a founder of the Sex Information and Education Council (SIECUS) in 1964 as well as a signatory to the *Humanist Manifesto II* in 1973—"Family Life Education" was less threatening to parents and teachers and, in the end, "would lead to *more* not *less* sex education."[30]

Thus it was that the use of the term "sex education" was temporarily abandoned in favor of "family life education," the latter being integrated into various formal programs of instruction, including home economics, social studies and biology. By the mid-1960's, most secondary schools, colleges and universities in the United States carried "family life education" courses as part of their standard curriculum. There also was a plenitude of organizations—like the Child Study Association of America, the National PTA and American Social Health Agency—dedicated to the advancement of these programs.

At this point, the sex education picture becomes somewhat blurred. While the leadership of the Sex Reform/Sex Education

Movement saw family life education programs as a vehicle to salvage and eventually bring their cause to fruition, their opponents, specifically the Roman Catholic Church, envisioned these programs as a vehicle for transmitting traditional Christian sexual morality and promoting the sacred institutions of marriage and the family, in the form of formal academic courses in parochial schools, Catholic colleges and universities and Cana and Pre-Cana instructions for engaged or married couples. This latter view was supported by the American population at large, including parents, clergy and teachers.

It is important to note, however, that classroom sex education in the form of reproductive instruction and health hygiene for boys and girls was accepted as part of the formal curriculum by both public and parochial schools by the 1960's.

Even the sexual radicals, chronically irritated by the diluted and almost unrecognizable attempts at teaching sex education in the classroom, had to appreciate the strategy which bought them the time so clearly needed to reorganize, and which served as a foot in the schoolroom door for that time when they were ready to move once again onto the scene.

This confusion over the nature and purpose of family life education programs, as we shall see, would work to the definite *advantage* of the anti-life forces and to the distinct *disadvantage* of the pro-family forces when the sex education controversy would erupt once again in the U.S. in the late 1960's.

To wrap up this period of the evolution of sex education in America, I have prepared a chronological listing of important events related to the movement from 1900 to 1973, including important papal documents and counter-developments in the Sex Education/Sex Reform Movement. I will be referring to Charts I and II in the next chapter, which deals with the reactivation of the sex education plague and its spread into the public and parochial schools of the United States.

Chart II

Important Events Related to the Sex Reform/Sex Education Movement from 1900 through 1973

1900 International Neo-Malthusian League formed in Paris.

1905 Second International Neo-Malthusian Congress in Liege.

1905 American Society for Sanitary and Moral Prophylaxis formed in the U.S.A.

1912 National Education Association begins push for training of teachers in sex education and sex hygiene.

1921 Marie Stopes establishes first birth control clinic in England.
First International Congress for Sexual Reform in Berlin.

1922 Birth Control League incorporated in New York State by Margaret Sanger.

1923 Birth Control Clinical Research Bureau founded by Margaret Sanger.

1928 World League for Sexual Reform (WLSR) founded in Copenhagen.
Graenberg IUD introduced.

1929 Pope Pius XI issues the Encyclical letter *Christian Education of Youth,* condemning naturalistic and public sex education programs.

1930 Anglican Lambeth Conference adopts Resolution 15, which sanctions artificial contraception for hard cases.
Seventh and last International Neo-Malthusian Congress in Zurich.
Pope Pius XI issues *Casti Connubii,* upholding traditional Catholic sexual morality and condemning birth control practices.

1931 Health Committee of the League of Nations officially recognizes "child spacing" as a health problem.

1932 Ogino in Japan establishes scientific basis for the "rhythm method."

1938 Alfred C. Kinsey begins sexology studies at Indiana University. (See "The Kinsey Myth" by Edward Eichel, Parents Roundtable Seminar 2/11/89. Audio tape available from Arthur Assoc., Dorien, CT).

1939 N.Y.C. Board of Education institutes 15-week sex education training program for public school teachers.

1942 Birth Control Federation of America becomes Planned Parenthood Federation of America.

1945 Sweden institutes compulsory sex education in schools.

1949 Pope Pius XII condemns artificial insemination on September 29. (Reaffirmed in 1951 and 1956).
British Royal Commission on Population endorses birth control as public policy.

1952 John D. Rockefeller III establishes Population Council.

1953 International Planned Parenthood Federation founded in London.

1958 Anglican Lambeth Conference endorses contraception as a positive good, opening the door to induced abortion and sterilization.

1959 American Law Institute pushes for legalized abortion.

1960 American Medical Association (AMA) adopts liberalized induced abortion guidelines.

1963 John Rock, M.D. publishes *The Time Has Come,* a book which erroneously introduces the birth control pill as being "safe, natural and physiologic."
Planned Parenthood Federation of America merges with the World Population Emergency Campaign to become Planned Parenthood World Population.

1964 UNESCO sponsors an International Symposium on Health Education, *Sex Education* and Education for Home and Family Living in West Germany.
Sex Information and Education Council for the United States (SIECUS) founded by Planned Parenthood leadership.

1965 Griswald v. Connecticut—the U.S. Supreme Court strikes down anti-contraception statutes under the constitutional fiction of "the right to privacy."

1965-1966 U.S. Senate Hearings on S. 1676—historical landmark hearings conducted by Senator Gruening (D-Alaska), paving the way for massive federal birth control programs at home and abroad under Title X of the Public Health Service Act and Title X of the Foreign Assistance Act.

1966 U.S. Department of Health, Education and Welfare announces vigorous support of birth control programs.
U.S. Bishops condemn all federal programs of birth control and population control.

1967 *United States Catholic Conference (USCC) replaces National Catholic Welfare Conference and reverses NCWC policies condemning governmental birth control and sex education programs.*
American Association of Sex Educators and Counselors (AASEC) established by SIECUS leadership.
National Committee of Maternal Health absorbed into the Rockefeller Population Council.
United Nations Fund for Population Activities (UNFPA) founded in New York.

1968 National/Interfaith statement promoting universal sex education is signed by representatives of U.S. Catholic Conference, National Council of Churches and Synagogue Council of America.
Pope Paul VI issues *Humanae Vitae* and controversy over the Church's stand on birth control explodes.
Human Life Foundation established in Washington, D.C.
National Foundation/March of Dimes begins eugenic policies and programs.

1969 Full-page advertisement for universal sex education appears in October 16, 1969 issue of the *New York Times,* sponsored by SIECUS.
Right-to-Life Movement begins to take shape.
National Education Association, American Medical Association, and American School Health Association call for sexuality training programs.

1970 Congress rewrites Comstock Act, removing contraceptive information and appliances from obscene list.
Presidential Commission on Population Growth and the American Future, J. D. Rockefeller III, Chairman, begins its study.
U.S. Catholic Conference representative testifies before House Subcommittee on Public Health and Welfare, endorsing universal sex education.

Congress passes Title X of the Public Health Service Act—the first five-year plan for governmental birth control.

1971 White House Conference on Youth endorses universal sex education mandate for elementary and secondary schools. U.S. Senate holds hearings on S.J. Resolution 108, proposing to establish U.S. population stabilization policy.

1972 Eisenstadt v. Baird—Supreme Court upholds the right of unmarried persons to birth control.

1973 Roe v. Wade—Supreme Court strikes down all anti-abortion statutes under "right-to-privacy" invocation.

1973 *Humanist Manifesto II* issued.

Chapter 3
The Reactivation of the Plague

Introduction

In this chapter of the anti-life saga of sex education, we will examine some important developments, starting at the end of its "latency period" in the early 1960's, and continuing through the early 1970's. This period was marked by phenomenal organizational growth, favorable judicial decisions and highly successful public relations initiatives. Above all, it was a period of reactivation, identified by a major paradigm shift, i.e., a transformation of the plague from its state of forced inactivity following World War II—when it lived the life of a hybrid known as "Family Life Education"—to a more virulent strain of the disease that was true to its nature and more identifiable with its radical Eugenic and Malthusian roots.

When in 1981 I critiqued the U.S.C.C. Sex Education "Guidelines," entitled *Education in Human Sexuality for Christians,* for *The Wanderer,* I put a great deal of emphasis on the significance of the paradigm shift that took place in sex education in the mid-1960's, as well as on the tactical and strategic implications of that shift. It is an emphasis which bears repeating.

A paradigm can be best described as a well-defined pattern or framework of thought or behavior which is held in common by a group, or a society as a whole. The term "paradigm shift" indicates a transformation from a traditional set of beliefs and practices to a new and different way of perceiving and acting on ideas—a process which obviously does not happen overnight.

When a new paradigm is introduced into society, it may first be met with hostility, or outright rejection. In the case of sex education, as I have documented, the early ideas of the radical sex reformers, Eugenicists and Neo-Malthusians were largely ignored or rejected by most Americans and Europeans, up to and including the post-World War II era.

The sexual revolution was put on hold because the United States, Europe, and most nations of the civilized world were not ready to accept a totally new Manichean* approach to human sexuality, marriage and family. Furthermore, it was absolutely clear that *no* acceptance would ever be forthcoming unless the sex education and reform advocates, in league with their natural allies, could manipulate and gain control of public opinion and secure the endorsement of influential and moneyed elements of society, including government leaders, members of the legal and medical professions, powerful foundations, and especially the *mass media*.

This last was essential, as attorney William Ball pointed out in his brilliant 1968 study, *Population Control—Civil and Constitutional Concerns:* "It is not Orwellian fictionalizing to point to the near certainty of conditional reflex which modern communication techniques are able to stimulate and measure."[31]

Ball cites a quote from Jacques Ellul's *The Technological Society* (1964) which illuminates his point, "The tendency toward psychological collectivization is the 'sine qua non' of technical action. . .the problem is to get the individual's consent artificially through depth psychology, since he will not give it of his own free will, but the decision to give consent must appear to be spontaneous."[32]

If we re-examine Chart II—"Important Events Related to the Sex Reform/Sex Education Movement from 1900 through 1973" (see the end of Chapter 2), we can see that by the early 1970's most of the major mechanisms needed to secure the institutionalization of a new societal sexual paradigm shift, or transformation, were in place.

First and foremost was the growing acceptance of the term "family planning," the new euphemism for "birth control" which appeared on the American scene. As Father Cahal Daly noted in his essay on contraception in *Morals, Law and Life,*

*(Mani, a Persian sage [died A.D. 276], taught that there were two opposing absolutes, God and matter. Since matter was the source of all evil, all contact with nature was repugnant—women and children being especially abhorrent.)

by the late 1950's the nation's moral conscience on the matter of contraception had been sufficiently anesthetized by heavy anti-natalist artillery, which lacked only an aura of religious sanction. He continues, "Until August, 1958, almost the only argument *not* yet used for contraception was that it had deep religious and Christian value. The Lambeth Conference of that date has tragically been the means of supplying the missing motivation."[33]

It should also be noted that the ambiguously worded report of the Conference's Committee on the Family in Contemporary Society held the door open not only to contraceptive practices, but also to induced abortion, abortifacients, and sterilization, as well as governmentally sponsored programs of population control.[34]

It is a truism that the "contraceptive society" is also an "abortion society" and that contraception and abortion are both mutually stimulating and mutually competitive, i.e., they are fruits from the same tree.

It is not surprising that only eight years after Griswald v. Connecticut (1965), when the Supreme Court struck down an "uncommonly silly law that prohibited contraceptive practice,"[35] the same court should move to strike down the nation's anti-abortion statutes under Roe v. Wade (1973), and that *both* decisions were made under the legal fiction of an alleged constitutionally protected "right to privacy."

Second, the new paradigm shift was moved inextricably forward by the reorganization of old and the founding of new organizations dedicated to the advancement of sex education and sexual reform, such as the International Planned Parenthood Federation (IPPF) and its American affiliate, Planned Parenthood Federation of America (PPFA), Sex Information and Education Council of the United States (SIECUS), and the American Association of Sex Educators and Counselors (AASEC).

The Neo-Malthusian mantle was handed down to organizations such as John D. Rockefeller III's Population Council, the Population Reference Bureau and Zero Population Growth. The Eugenics mantle was given over to the National Foundation/ March of Dimes, which by 1967 was experiencing its own paradigm shift in favor of eugenic killing of pre-born affected children, as well as to a wide variety of well-funded pro-abortion and pro-euthanasia organizations, the most important of which are listed in Chart I, The Sex Reform/Sex Education Network (see page 14).

The shift was apparent even among the more traditional professional organizations, such as the American Medical Association (AMA), which in 1967 adopted a policy broadening the medical and eugenic indications for abortion,[36] as well as among many main-line Protestant denominations and the Reform Judaism Leadership.

A third factor in the success of the new paradigm shift, which catapulted sex education into the mainstream of the American consciousness, was the fateful decision of the Federal Government to move into the Birth Control/Eugenics/Malthusian area, thereby committing billions of tax dollars and an entire federal bureaucracy to the fueling of the sex revolution. This included the promotion and funding of contraception, abortion, sterilization, population control and a universal mandate for sex education.

The details of this shameful episode in our nation's history have been well documented by the United States Coalition for Life in its own *Pro-Life Reporter,* and in its reprint series on foreign and domestic population control programs funded by the Federal Government from the early 1960's to the present day. Since this documentation is already available elsewhere, I will not burden the reader with further references to the governmental promotion of anti-life activities, although I shall touch upon them briefly when I discuss the role of the U.S. Catholic Conference in promoting the new sexual paradigm shift.

Before examining this most important aspect of the new paradigm shift, that is, the destruction and/or neutralization of opposition forces, I think it would be helpful to highlight the content, goals and methodology of the new sex education resulting from the ascendancy of the new sexual paradigm, as well as the decline of traditional values and beliefs related to human sexuality, marriage and the family.

I use the term "new sex education"* only because this is the

---

*Also referred to as "sexuality education"—a more comprehensive term, which combines the biological facts with sexual attitudes, values, etc.

label which its proponents have chosen to distinguish it from the old family-life programs of the post-war period. The reader, however, will want to keep in mind that the new sex education is really the old or original sex education in Madison Avenue advertising attire. The family life format of the '40's and '50's was merely viewed as a temporary measure designed to keep the sex education ship afloat while the old leadership reorganized and consolidated its efforts.

A Profile of the New Sex Education

Happily, one does not have to guess what the new sex education is all about, because its architects have spelled it out in clear, concise English in the sex educator's resource book published in 1978.

Entitled *The New Sex Education,* the text is a series of original contributions by twenty-eight of the nation's leading sex educators, and edited by sexologist Herbert Otto. According to Otto, the book's purpose is to explain "the new concepts, ideas, approaches and programs coming to the fore in the burgeoning field of sex education," and it "can be expected to establish standards for years to come."[37]

The biographical data of the contributors provided in the book reads like an anti-life *Who's Who* directory:

William P. Brown, Ph.D.—SIECUS Board member.
Derek L. Burleson, Ed. D.—SIECUS Director.
Mary C. Calderone, M.D., M.P.H.—SIECUS co-founder; Medical Director of PPFA.*†
Albert Ellis, Ph.D.—Sexologist, AASECT; SIECUS Editorial Board.*†
Sol Gordon, Ph.D.—Sexologist, AASECT Advisory Committee.*
Winifred Kempton, M.S.W., A.C.S.W.—PPFA.
Joseph F. Kennedy, M.C.—AASECT.
Lester A. Kirkendall, Ph.D.—SIECUS co-founder; PPFA.*
Herbert A. Otto, Ph.D.—Pioneer in Human Potential Movement.

Patricia Schiller, M.A., J.D.—Executive Director and Founder of AASECT.
Leon Smith, B.D., Ed.D.—Director of Marriage and Family, United Methodist Church; SIECUS.
Alan P. Bell, Ph.D.—SIECUS official.*

*Signers of the Humanist Manifesto II.
†Humanist of the Year award recipient.

Chart III is a comparison between the "old" sex education and the "new" sex education, as viewed by Otto in his introductory remarks regarding the expanding frontier of sex education. It first appeared in my 1981 *Critique on the U.S.C.C. Sex Education Guidelines,* and I elected to put the information in this particular format because it seemed to simplify the meaning of the new sex education paradigm.

My critique also highlighted three of the twenty-five essays found in the resource book, including:

- Leon Smith's "Sex Education in the Churches."
- Lester A. Kirkendall's "Values and Sex Education."
- Herbert A. Otto's "Neglected Aspects and Priorities in the New Sex Education."

These essays had been selected with deliberation on my part due to their relevancy to the United States Catholic Conference Sex Education Guidelines of 1981.

Dr. Smith describes the new sexuality paradigm shift as follows: "The old rules for sexual behavior have been rejected by many church members and most of the society. New guidelines have not emerged. . .churches are re-evaluating their stands on human sexuality. They are turning away from their mistakes of the past and are looking for ways to help people appreciate sex as a gift from God."[38]

His essay is full of SIECUS tripe—

- All persons are "sexual beings."
- Sexual relations with "significant others," as opposed to the terms "spouse" or "married couple."

Chart III
An Overview of the Paradigm Shift in Sex Education

1945-65
SEX EDUCATION

1) Restricted to a specific body of knowledge related to human sexuality, with special emphasis on the acquisition of biological information on human reproduction, the process and mechanics of fertilization, gestation, embryonic development and birth. Separate classes for boys and girls, involving instruction on changes associated with the onset of puberty (menstruation, nocturnal emission, secondary sex characteristics). Basic information on venereal disease.

2) Teaching format includes formal lectures, use of such visual aids as schematic diagrams, animated drawings or slides, and anatomical medical charts of male and female internal reproductive organs and various reproductive processes.

3) Use of regular reproductive biology terminology. Vigorous avoidance of slang and offensive four-letter words.

4) Reproductive information tied to procreation within the context of marriage and the family.

5) Recognition and acceptance of the meaning and implications for teaching of "the latency period" in the normal sexual development of the child.

6) Birth control information and instruction omitted from curriculum. Such sexual matters involving morals and faith left to the discretion of parents and churches.

1966-89
SEX EDUCATION

1) A holistic, scientific, and values approach in the teaching of sex education. Unrestricted information on all aspects of human sexuality, including the full range of psycho-sexual deviations. Special emphasis on the restructuring of student attitudes and behavioral goals, ordered toward the acceptance of masturbation, homosexuality, and abortion. Reproductive biology occupies a relatively minor part of the total curriculum. Basic instruction on anatomy and physiology tied to use of contraceptive techniques, venereal disease, and the rudiments of erotic stimulation. Co-ed classes.

2) Informal teaching setting using open-ended group discussion, values clarification techniques, and exploration of principles involved in ethical decision-making. Use of sexually explicit visuals on all aspects of sex including intercourse, masturbation, and homosexual acts.

3) Full range of explicit sexual terminology, including medical terms, street talk, and obscenities—all used to "desensitize" students.

4) Sex act linked to the development of interpersonal relationships and personal gratification and fulfillment. Emphasis on the separation of sexual intercourse for pleasure and mutual satisfaction of partners from the procreation of children—both within and without the married state.

5) "Latency period" labeled a myth. Emphasis on the lifetime sex education of the total person beginning with parental erotic stimulation of infants and acceptance of mutual sexual experience by young children, including brothers and sisters.

6) Explicit information on all forms of birth control including abortion, contraception and sterilization as an absolute requirement of any total sex education program. Materials also provide for referrals for such services to minor children without parental knowledge and/or consent.

- Religious reaffirmation of the right to legalized abortion under medical supervision.
- Religious affirmation of masturbation as a healthy form of sexual expression for all ages.
- The necessity of redefining pornography, and legitimizing sexually explicit materials and films for sex education purposes.
- The acceptance of homosexual lifestyles and practices as *variant,* rather than *deviant* behavior.
- The acceptance of homosexual marriage as a "holy union."
- The merits of new scientific sexual behavior-modification programs such as SARS (Sexual Attitude Reassessment Seminars).
- Sex as a personal and relationally fulfilling act.[39]

Smith's essay is proof positive that you can openly peddle any perversion in religious circles, as long as you smother it in sufficient "God language." It is also interesting, but *not* coincidental, that many of Smith's concepts are found *almost verbatim* in the United States Catholic Conference *Sex Education Guidelines,* published just a few years later.

The Kirkendall essay, "Values and Sex Education," begins with a slightly different variation on the same theme used by Smith; namely, the traditional value framework for human sexuality, "which has rested heavily upon religion, with its transcendental aura, as well as upon long-existing social customs," is no longer functional. The scientific and the rational are replacing the mysterious and the abstract, he warns, and sexual taboos and forbidden sexual practices must give way to a new affirmative, one-world values system.[40]

Kirkendall makes a plea for a values system which is "person," not "act"-oriented and that is relational in nature—one where the basic need for "love" and "caring" has top priority. His conclusions are obvious: ". . .Might those who can participate in both heterosexuality and homosexuality experiences find even more life-affirming experiences than those who follow one pattern only?" and in regard to masturbation ". . .can it be used to obtain the optimal effect in healthful living?"[41]

The author's love affair with situation ethics is obvious. The same love affair is equally obvious with the 1981 U.S.C.C. *Sex Education Guidelines,* Goals and Objectives for Formal Education (pages 15-18), which state, for example:

- "The learner will...understand and evaluate the biological and psycho-sexual processes of different sexual lifestyles, commitments or noncommitments, and evaluate them accordingly."
- "The learner will...understand the means of and reasons for family planning, *both natural and artificial,* and understand and appreciate the church's (sic) teaching on this matter."
- "The learner will...understand some of the pitfalls and social problems caused by *inappropriate expressions of sexuality* (e.g., venereal disease, *rape, incest,* and *sexual abuse of children*)."[42] (Emphasis added).

The fact that the authors consider criminal acts such as rape and child molestation to be mere manifestations of "inappropriate expressions of sexuality" is a fascinating concept—in keeping with the new sex education mandate, as elucidated by editor Otto in his essay, "Neglected Aspects and Priorities in the New Sex Education."[43]

Highest priority, according to Otto, must be given to teaching the teachers; that is, to putting prospective sex educators through sexual attitudinal restructuring (SAR) and AASECT certification training programs.

Quoting Teilhard de Chardin, "Joy is the most infallible sign of the presence of God," Otto cites the need to integrate liberal theological Judeo-Christian and Eastern-Oriental spiritual values into a holistic approach to sex education.[44]

Points 6 and 7 of Otto's holistic approach include the "awareness and acceptance of childhood sexuality." Children as well as adults are "sexual beings" and are capable of relating "to another person in an erotically intimate manner...long before puberty, and have the potential for extensive sexual experimentation."[45]

"Who is being harmed (other than the prejudices of parents) when children engage in sex play," Otto asks. *"Perhaps more sexual censure and nonsense are currently being perpetrated,*

using as justification the preservation of the innocence and purity of children, than for any other stated cause.''[46] (Emphasis added).

In Point 7, Otto presses for the expansion of sexual frontiers by promoting sex as a form of play, to be enhanced by the use of sex games, sex toys, sex manuals and pornography. The new sex education will go one step beyond—teaching children and adults that masturbation is not harmful and promoting self-stimulation as an aid to maintaining sexual health.[47] Listed in Otto's Resource Addendum is the San Francisco porno house known as Multi-Media (producers of SAR pornographic films) and Richard Farson's *Birthrights,* heralding the new sexual rights of children.[48]

As I stated in Chapter 1 of this book, sex education is not education at all; rather, *it is a legalized form of child seduction and molestation.* The Otto essay clearly validates this accusation in a language so simple and direct that its meaning cannot be open to question. Neither can the meaning of the remaining twenty-two essays, *not* reviewed here for lack of space, be interpreted as anything less than a total, all-out declaration of war against Christianity, as well as against the fundamental moral and ethical foundations of Western Civilization.

Securing the New Sex Education Paradigm—The Special Role of SIECUS and AASECT

No discussion of the new sexual paradigm and the content and the pedagogy of the new sex education would be complete without some background material on the two organizations which were instrumental in advancing their cause: the Sex Information and Educational Council of the United States (SIECUS), and the American Association of Sex Educators, Counselors and Therapists (AASECT).

The relationship that existed between the Planned Parenthood Federation of America (also called simply Planned Parenthood) and the formation of SIECUS in 1964, and the formation of AASECT by the SIECUS leadership in 1967, is a matter of historical fact:

"SIECUS came into being in 1964 to help people live their total lives as whole human beings, neither sex machines nor repressed hermits, neither sexual exploiters nor sexually exploited."[49]

The creation of SIECUS was the brainchild of Dr. Mary Steichen Calderone, often called "Typhoid Mary" by her critics. Mary served as the SIECUS Executive Director from 1964 to 1975, at which time she assumed the role of President. Mary Calderone is credited with the primary structuring of the organization and development of its standards and goals.

A Quaker by birth and a humanist fellow traveler by desire, she graduated from Vassar in 1925 and earned her M.D. at the University of Rochester in 1939. In 1953, she became Medical Director of Planned Parenthood, a position she held for eleven years, until the founding of SIECUS. This position propelled her into the inner sanctum of the abortion referral and legislative repeal programs of Planned Parenthood, as explained by George Langmyhr, M.D., who also served a term as Medical Director of Planned Parenthood:

> It goes without saying that Planned Parenthood affiliates have long been involved in programs of abortion information, counseling and referral. Before the recent change in abortion laws, these activities were necessarily unpublicized. Thus, we generally do not know the results of these early counseling and referral programs.[50]
>
> . . . I think it is fair to say that most professionals and volunteers associated with Planned Parenthood have accepted, for a long time, the necessity of abortion as an integral part of any complete or total family planning program. The dilemma of a woman who has a legitimate method failure, or any type of unwanted pregnancy, cannot be avoided by Planned Parenthood clinic personnel.[51]
>
> . . . As a non-profit, tax exempt agency, "Planned Parenthood is specifically unable to lobby or overtly attempt to achieve legislative reform. However, there are many dedicated volunteers and professionals from Planned Parenthood affiliates who have been effective in working with other concerned citizens and reform groups. . . Planned Parenthood helped prepare various legal briefs which have been presented to the

> courts as a means of effecting change."[52]
>
> In summary, Planned Parenthood hopes that abortion will become even more available, and it supports the efforts of others in seeking reform and repeal of outdated abortion laws.[53]
>
> Excerpts from *The Role of Planned Parenthood-World Population in Abortion*
> by Dr. George Langmyhr (1971)

Actually, 1964 must have been quite a year for Planned Parenthood. While its Medical Director was busy rounding up her cohorts for SIECUS, its president, Alan Guttmacher, M.D., was meeting with his old abortion cronies, Allan Barnes, Robert Hall, Joseph Fletcher and Christopher Tietze, to set up the Association for the Study of Abortion, whose *raison d'etre* was the nullification of all restrictive state abortion laws.

There is some evidence that the incorporation of SIECUS as a tax-free foundation was connected with a United Nations Educational, Scientific and Cultural Organization (UNESCO) symposium on Sex Education and Family Life held in West Germany four months prior to the incorporation of SIECUS.[54]

The philosophy and purpose of UNESCO was itself heavily influenced by its first Director General, Humanist/Eugenicist/Darwinist/Malthusian Julian Huxley. Sir Julian Huxley viewed sex education primarily in terms of eugenic breeding and population control, viewpoints which were shared by its incorporators and which were integrated into SIECUS's total philosophy and its programs.

Its initial organizer, as I have already indicated, was Planned Parenthood's Dr. Calderone. In researching her background, I found two particularly interesting articles on her views about human sexuality: The first was in the April, 1970 issue of *Playboy,* and the second was a 5-page interview in the *U.S. Catholic,* October, 1982. All things being equal, the *Playboy* article was typical; whereas, the *U.S. Catholic* interview, entitled "Why Parents Can't Say Enough About Sex," was absolutely incredible, both from what Dr. Calderone *said* and what she and the editor *did not say!* The editor gave Dr. Calderone's credentials as follows:

- she was 78 years old and a mother,
- a Quaker by birth,
- a co-founder and past president of SIECUS, and
- the co-author of two family books on sexuality.

Apparently, the editors of the *U.S. Catholic* did not think Mary's eleven years of employment by the nation's number one baby-killing agency, Planned Parenthood/World Population, was significant enough to mention in their introduction, although Dr. Calderone mentions the fact several times in her own response to such probing questions as, "How did you get into the sex business?"

Her answer to this particular question was interesting. She told *U.S. Catholic* about the death of her first child, her ensuing divorce, and the recommendation of her psychoanalyst to take an aptitude test; this in turn eventually led to a career in public health and to her job with Planned Parenthood.

Later in the interview, she explained how she promoted the rhythm method and warned Planned Parenthood Affiliates not to "subvert Catholic women" by saying the method was not effective. Planned Parenthood, however, if we are willing to take Langmyhr's word on it, did not mind "subverting Catholic women" by helping them to kill their babies in the womb.[55]

Asked about how parents can avoid passing their sexual hang-ups on to their children, Mary explained that she too had sexual hang-ups, particularly about homosexuality, until she went through a SAR (Sexual Attitudinal Reassessment) program. In this program, she viewed a homosexual couple keeping house and then engaging in lovemaking (i.e., mutual masturbation and sodomy). "I went out walking on air, because now I knew what homosexuals did, and they did all the same things that I like to do, and it was fine. I felt good about them from that moment on."[56]

On the matter of founding SIECUS, Mary said that she had an interest in dysfunctional sex and problems of human sexuality in general, and SIECUS was established to help people deal with their sexuality in a correct way, including the aging, children and infants, the last producing orgasms "with a great deal of vigor."[57]

In passing, she also mentioned the fact that "two of the earliest members of the board were Roman Catholics, Father George Hagmaier, C.S.P., and Father John L. Thomas, S.J.,"[58] a sociologist and SIECUS director who distinguished himself by having been the first priest ever to attend an annual Planned Parenthood Banquet.

At least three Catholic priests were known to have served on the SIECUS Board, including Father George Hagmaier, C.S.P., Ed.D., Associate Director of the Paulist Institute for Religious Research in New York; Father John L. Thomas, S.J., Ph.D., Cambridge Center for Social Studies, Cambridge, MA; and Father Walter S. Imbiorski, Cana Conference of Chicago and editor for Benziger's "Becoming A Person Program," which originated as a sex education pilot project of the Cana Conference. Before his death, Imbiorski had left the priesthood and married the book's co-author, Miss Frances Marzec.

As I said before, the Calderone interview in the *U.S. Catholic* was absolutely incredible, more perhaps because of what it revealed about the editors and their selection of Mary Calderone as an authority on sex instruction of the young, than about the woman and the organization she was representing.

But enough about Mary Calderone. Let us now discuss her associates at SIECUS in those embryonic years of the organization's foundation: Lester Kirkendall (family life), William H. Genne (religion), Wallace Fulton (health education), Harriet Pilpel (law) and Clark Vincent (sociology).

The credentials and humanist philosophy of one of SIECUS's founding fathers, Lester Kirkendall, have already been highlighted earlier in this book in connection with the new sex education. In addition, I would like to note an important document drafted by Kirkendall, entitled, "A New Bill of Sexual Rights and Responsibilities," which appeared in the January/February, 1976 issue of *The Humanist* and which was intended to supplement the section on sexuality found in the *Humanist Manifesto II*. The document is a sex educator's dream, a societal *carte blanche* for sexual perversion and vice.

The individual credited with the incorporation of various modes of psychotherapy and sensitivity-training techniques into the SIECUS training program for teachers and students was Clark Vincent, former director of the Behavioral Science Center at the Bowman Gray School of Medicine, Winston-Salem, NC.[59] Prominent among these techniques are role-playing and group criticism, which are commonly employed by the sex educator to "desensitize" the student and prepare him for the process of sexual attitudinal restructuring.

Adding the "health education" component to the SIECUS program was Wallace Fulton, Community Service and Health Educator. Fulton played an important role in the development of a purely humanistic "health" curriculum, popularly known as SHES (School Health Education Study), which, in addition to promoting the *Humanist Manifesto II* sexual agenda, also promotes the use and legalization of marijuana.

Perhaps the best known of SIECUS's founding board of directors was Harriet Pilpel, a senior partner in the law firm of Greenbaum, Wolff and Ernst, which assisted in the incorporation of SIECUS, while also providing legal services to Planned Parenthood/World Population.

An abortion zealot, Pilpel served as general counsel to a large number of anti-life agencies besides SIECUS, including Guttmacher's Association for the Study of Abortion and the Association for Voluntary Sterilization.

In the *Case for Legalized Abortion Now,* published in 1967 and edited by Alan F. Guttmacher, Harriet F. Pilpel is identified as vice-chairman of the National Board of Directors of the American Civil Liberties Union, a New York attorney and author. In her essay, "The Abortion Crisis," Pilpel discusses two routes to abortion "sanity," the first being judicial liberalization or invalidation, and the second, legislative reform.[60] She does quite a bit of Catholic baiting, stating the Church's well-known opposition to induced abortion, but claiming that the Catholic Church has no right to force its belief on others in the form of laws.[61] (This, as we all know, is a privilege granted only to the humanist.)

Last but certainly not least among the SIECUS founders was the Reverend William H. Genne, Director of the National Council of Churches' Commission on Marriage and Family Life, who, like Kirkendall, is identified in the new sex education exposé. His prime directive within the SIECUS structure was to attract religious support, particularly among the Catholic clergy, for the organization's philosophy, policies and programs. Like a number of other SIECUS Board members, Genne served as a board consultant to the scurrilous publication, *Sexology,* which in its December, 1968 issue featured Genne's editorial proposal: "Let's Celebrate the First Menstruation" (like a Bar Mitzvah).[62]

In 1968, Genne joined Rabbi Mordecai Brill and Father James T. McHugh of the United States Catholic Conference in issuing an Interfaith Statement on Sex Education, a matter which will be discussed in greater detail later in this book.

Given the humanist mind-set of its founders and the large anti-life coterie that was eventually attracted to the SIECUS Board of Directors, officers and staff, the following beliefs and position-statements come as little or no surprise.

> ...Sex Education, at any age, cannot be effective as long as it occurs in a society which, in many of its aspects, inhibits rational assessment of sexuality as a central force in human behavior. SIECUS's role is to identify and publicize social policies which perpetuate unhealthy attitudes about sexuality and foster alienation from self and others.
>
> ...Free access to full and accurate information on *all aspects of sexuality* is a basic right for everyone, children as well as adults.
>
> ...It is the right of all persons to enter into a relationship with others, *regardless of their gender,* and to engage in such sexual behaviors as are satisfying and non-exploitive...
>
> ...Sexual self-pleasuring (masturbation) is a natural part of sexual behavior for individuals of all ages...[it] helps to relieve tension...develop a sense of one's self as a fully functioning human being.
>
> ...Contraceptive services should be available to all, including minors...
>
> ...Explicit sexual materials should be available to adults who wish to have them.[63]
>
> (From SIECUS Position Paper, 1978).

SIECUS Report, the organization's bi-monthly newsletter, the *SIECUS Study Guides Numbers 1-14* on various sexually related topics and selected bibliography, and SIECUS' special publications and resource listings reflect the full measure of SIECUS' anti-life commitment.

For example, SIECUS' *Legal Briefs,* prepared by Ralph Slovenki, LL. B., Ph.D., promote tax-funded induced abortions for all, including the poor and minors, without parental consent.[64]

SIECUS Study Guide Number 2, "Homosexuality," by Alan P. Bell, Ph.D., views the practice of sodomy within the context of an alternative lifestyle and condemns "negative" and "discriminatory" attitudes towards the practice and its practitioners.

The SIECUS Reprint Series includes the 1970 Calderone interview with *Playboy Magazine; The War on Sex Education: A Survival Kit for School Boards* by Joanne Zazzaro, which instructs school boards on dealing with critics of sex education; and other articles, covering the wide range of SIECUS interests, primarily from a humanist perspective.

Of particular interest are two reprints found in SIECUS' 1971 listings.

The first is reprint No. 049, "How Not to Teach Children About Sex," by E. James Lieberman, M.D., published by the National Council of Catholic Women, March, 1968.

Dr. Lieberman, a former director of SIECUS, a member of NARAL's medical committee, and an organizer of one of the nation's most lucrative chains of abortion clinics, states in *Abortion and the Unwanted Child:*

> . . .the prevention of unwanted pregnancy, including abortion when necessary, is more than prevention. It is an enhancement of life, and it supports the right of every child to be reared by someone who cares. . .no one has the right to impose his religious views on anyone else. . .the owner of the womb has the right to decide whether it shall bear fruit. No child should be compelled to enter the lives of unwilling parents, much less the corridors of understaffed, over-crowded institutions.[65]

Question! How did Dr. Lieberman, a SIECUS director and well-known pro-abortionist, manage to be published in a National

Council of Catholic Women's publication?

The second reprint, No. 056, is another interview by Dr. Calderone, this time on *The Catholic Hour,* May 26, 1968, entitled "Sex Education—Helping Children Understand Their Masculine and Feminine Identities." This interview, which was *rebroadcast* on September 1, 1968, concludes with a warning to parents, "One of the great roles fathers and mothers can play is not to stand in the way of their children and of the efforts of their schools and their churches in the provision of this kind of preparation, of education for mature, responsible, creative sexuality."[66]

Again, question! How did SIECUS founder Calderone gain access to the *Catholic Hour,* sponsored by the National Association of Catholic Men? Why was her eleven-year association with Planned Parenthood not mentioned at the beginning of the broadcast?

The answers to these rather provocative questions, unfortunately, will have to wait until our next two chapters, which document the history of the New Sex Education Movement within the Catholic Church in America from 1967 to the present day.

Teaching the Teacher

The story of the New Sexual Education Movement and the paradigm shift in general, and of SIECUS in particular, however, would not be complete without mentioning AASEC(T), the American Association of Sex Educators, Counselors and (later to include) Therapists.

As SIECUS was created by Planned Parenthood and company in 1964 to promote the new sex education, so AASEC(T) was created by SIECUS and company in 1967, for the stated purpose of training and accrediting educators, health personnel and other "helping" professionals in the area of human sexuality and the dissemination of sex research findings as directed at sexual enlightenment.

The question of who would teach the teachers has always been a pressing problem. As SIECUS co-founder Kirkendall noted as far back as 1944, teacher training institutions were needed to meet the challenge of training competent sex educators. According to Kirkendall, who in addition to his ties with SIECUS was also a member of Planned Parenthood of Oregon: "A situation existed where many of those who participated in sex education programs were unprepared intellectually and emotionally to handle problems they met; in fact, they were unprepared even to recognize them."[67]

In 1955, the National Association of Secondary School Principals announced that teacher preparation institutions would soon be offering separate degrees for those qualified as sex educators. The NASSP was echoing the earlier concerns of the National Education Association and the American Medical Association, calling for sex educators who were "perceptive and qualified instructors. . .and aware of the impact of their own values on the students."[68]

The founding of AASEC(T), under the control of SIECUS, solved the dilemma of not only *who* would train and accredit sex educators, but also *how* that training would take place and *what* would be taught in teacher preparation courses.

SIECUS officials who also served as official advisors to AASEC(T) included Warren Johnson, Lester Kirkendall, David Mace, Isador Rubin, Philip Sarrel, Sophia Kleegman, Elizabeth Koontz, Harold Lief, James Peterson and Gilbert Shimmel. At least nine members of AASEC(T)'s Advisory Committee served on the staff of *Sexology* or contributed articles to it.[69]

Patricia Schiller, M.A., J.B., was one of AASEC(T)'s founders and served as its first Executive Director. In Otto's *The New Sex Education,* she described the AASEC(T) indoctrination program in detail.

According to Ms. Schiller,

> Today AASEC(T) is recognized as the single national interdisciplinary interest group whose central concern is the training, standards and certification of sex educators, counselors and therapists. This organization has developed model training programs and curricula for sex educators which have influenced the policies and training programs of the World Health Organization, Geneva, Switzerland, leading U.S.

public school systems, the National Association of Independent Schools and graduate in-service training programs at leading universities and teacher training institutions.[70]

The incorporation of the New Sex Education into the school curriculum required more than the mere transmission of reproductive facts. Ms. Schiller pontificates,

> AASEC(T), at its national and regional sex workshops and institutes, includes sensitivity sessions of sixteen hours, ten hours and eight hours, geared toward awareness in human sexuality. Films, attitude inventory tests, role-playing, case presentations, psychodrama, are all among the methods which may be used to develop sexual awareness. . . SAR, a multimedia form of sex attitude reassessment, is used by many.[71]
>
> Attitudes toward nudity, adolescent pregnancy, masturbation, abortion, homosexuality, contraception, divorce, group sex and extramarital sex relations are of major significance in the effectiveness of the sex education and counseling process. These are the realities of human sexuality.[72]

She also explains the purpose of a Graffiti Board for use as an ice breaker for opening up verbal discussions of particular "dirty words"[73] and to desensitize participants of SAR programs.

A trained and qualified sex educator, says Ms. Schiller, must possess a broad range of sexual knowledge dealing with reproduction, abortion, contraception, population control, sexual development and functioning, sexual deviations, sexual dysfunctions, sexual values and behavior, sex and gender, marriage, family and interpersonal relationships, sexual diseases, sexual anxieties and neuroses, and a history of sexual beliefs and attitudes, as well as information in the latest findings of sexual scientific research (Ellis, Freud, Kinsey, Masters and Johnson).[74]

AASEC(T)'s job is to provide this information to the sex educator, train him in the psychotherapy techniques necessary to communicate this knowledge to others, and restructure his sexual attitudes and values so as to equip him to expand his students' tolerance and acceptance of variant sexual practices and lifestyles.

I think it is quite clear, after reading Ms. Schiller's description of the AASEC(T) program, particularly her reference to SAR, which includes having participants view pornographic films of homosexual, lesbian and heterosexual acts, as well as masturbation, that students are not the *only* victims of the new sex educational paradigm, but it includes the teachers as well. Further, her explanation of AASEC(T)'s virtual monopoly in the field of training accreditation of sex educators reveals how the new sexual paradigm was able to gain such a strong hold on the American educational system in such a brief span of time.

AASEC(T)'s Standing Committee on teacher certification was initially headed by sexologist Dr. Albert Ellis, and by 1973 had approved over 450 applications for certification.

In the spring of 1973, at the sixth Annual Institute of AASEC(T), Dr. Ellis spoke on the matter of childhood sexual influences. Despite the sacrilegiousness and vulgarity of his words, I believe they should be quoted here:

> . . .Then a lot of the early influences are still very bigoted, narrow-minded, absolutistic. . .such as the doctrine which still holds. . .some of the most powerful groups in America, including officially the Catholic Church—but nobody believes in the Catholic Church anymore, but people do go to the goddamn church (laughter), and it does officially say that premarital sex is invariably bad, especially if it includes intercourse and, technically even, any kind of petting. And the Orthodox Jews say the same thing. Now we better fight this horseshit! It is not good at all, that early influence.[75]

This concludes our study of the rise of the new sex education within the public school system of the United States during the mid-1960's and into the 1970's and '80's, highlighting the key roles of SIECUS and AASEC(T) in moving the New Sex Education paradigm inextricably forward.

How the leadership of the sex education movement was able to penetrate the parochial educational system and bring its Trojan Horse into the Roman Catholic Church is the subject of our next two chapters.

Chapter 4
The Collapse of The Opposition

Introduction

Until the mid-1960's the teachings of the Magisterium of the Roman Catholic Church that bear on so-called "sex education" in the classroom were clear and unequivocal: It is to be forbidden and condemned.[76]

Further, the Church has exhorted parents and their allies to be at the forefront of the battle and to act "without human timidity or respect"[77] in opposing by every legitimate means the propagation of classroom sex education—by giving sound instruction to their own children by word and by example, and by storming the gates of Heaven with frequent and fervent prayers, especially to Our Lady, for the grace of a final victory.[78]

Because the nature of man has not changed, it is obvious that the Catholic Church's condemnation of public, explicit and naturalistic instruction in human sexuality is as valid today as it was more than a half-century ago; and that the traditional norms established in 1929 by Pope Pius XI[79]*—who issued the first official condemnation of school sex education—have never been nullified or abrogated; and that therefore they remain in effect to the present day.*

The following chronological exposition of the Church's teachings on human sexuality, marriage and the family—which are inextricably tied to the Church's teachings on the nature of man and his divine destiny—has been prepared with a view toward framing the controversy of sex education in Catholic schools in a more workable historical format than has heretofore been available to the public. The chronology also lists some important events related to the advancement of the Sex Education/Sex Reform movement as they relate to the Church. Since the roots of the Sex Education Movement in the U.S. and Europe can be traced back to the latter part of the nineteenth century, I have begun this chronology in 1880 with Pope Leo XIII's encyclical *Arcanum Divinae Sapientiae,* which reiterates the sacramental, unitive and procreative aspects of marriage and the indissolubility of the marriage bond. For purpose of comparison, readers may find it helpful to refer once again to Chart II, "Important Events Related to the Sex Reform/Sex Education Movement from 1900-1973," found on page 23 of this book.

Chart IV-A

Key Documents and Events Related to Catholic Teachings On Human Sexuality, Marriage and Family—1880-1966.

1880 Encyclical *Arcanum Divinae Sapientiae.* Pope Leo XIII reiterates the traditional Church teachings on marriage, including divorce as being against Divine Law.

1907 Pope St. Pius X issues a sweeping condemnation of the doctrines of the Modernists in *Lamentabili Sane* and *Pascendi Dominici Gregis.*

1929 Encyclical letter of Pope Pius XI on *The Christian Education of Youth (Divini Illius Magistri),* the first official condemnation of school sex education in this century:

"...every form of pedagogic naturalism which in any way excludes or weakens supernatural Christian formation in the teaching of youth, is false. Every method of education, if founded, wholly or in part, on the denial or forgetfulness of Original Sin and of grace, and relying on the sole powers of human nature, is unsound...

"...so today we see strange sights indeed, educators and philosophers who spend their lives in searching for a universal moral code of education, as if there existed no Decalogue, no Gospel law, no law even of nature stamped by God on the heart of man, promulgated by right reason, and codified in positive Revelation by God Himself in the Ten Commandments...

"Such men are miserably deluded in their claim to

emancipate, as they say, the child, while in reality, they are making him the slave of his own blind pride and of his own blind disorderly affections."

[On the matter of sex instruction]:

"Another very grave danger is that of naturalism, which nowadays invades the field of education in that most delicate matter of purity of morals. Far too common is the error of those who with dangerous assurance and under an ugly term propagate a so-called sex education, falsely imagining they can forearm youth against the dangers of sensuality by means purely natural, such as a foolhardy initiation and precautionary instruction for all indiscriminately, even in public; and, worse still, by exposing them at an early age to the occasions [of sin], in order to accustom them, so it is argued, and as it were to harden them against such dangers...

"In this extremely delicate matter, if, all things considered, some private instruction is found necessary and opportune, from those who hold from God the commission to teach and who have the grace of state, every precaution must be taken...

"Speaking generally, during the period of childhood it suffices to employ those remedies which produce the double effect of opening the door to the virtue of purity and closing the door upon vice."

1930 Encyclical *Casti Connubii.* Pope Pius XI, in this most eloquent and comprehensive statement on marriage in the entire history of the Church, reiterates the classic tripartite value of Christian marriage and attacks modern errors which deny the sacramental nature of marriage and its divine purpose.

1930 Development of Cana and Pre-Cana Movements.

1931 American bishops create the Family Life Bureau in the National Catholic Welfare Conference.

Decree of March 21, 1931, Congregation of the Holy Office, forbidding sex education as follows:

Question: "May the method called 'sex education' or even 'sex initiation' be approved?"

Answer: "No. In the education of youth the method to be followed is that hitherto observed by the Church and the Saints as recommended by His Holiness the Pope in the encyclical dealing with the Christian education of youth, promulgated in December 31, 1929...

"... Hence, no approbation whatever can be given to the advocacy of the new method, even as taken up recently by some Catholic authors and set before the public in printed publications."

1946 The International Committee for Sex and Marriage, the precursor of the International Planned Parenthood Federation, is established in London. The Committee declares the Roman Catholic Church is a major obstacle to its advances in promoting birth control and sex education.

1950 Bishops of the United States issue a Statement of November 17, 1950, regarding the role of parents in the instruction of children on matters relating to sex, and on the *absolute prohibition of classroom sex education:*

"Fathers and mothers have a natural competence to instruct their children with regard to sex. False modesty should not deter them from doing their duty in this regard. Sex is one of God's endowments. It should not be ignored or treated as something bad. If sex instruction is properly carried out in the home, a deep reverence will be developed in the child and he will be spared the shameful inferences which he often makes when he is left to himself to find out about sex. *We protest in the strongest possible terms against the introduction of sex instruction into the schools!!!*"

1951 Pope Pius XII, Address to the French Fathers of Families on September 18, 1951, on the matter of sex initiation and propaganda, as follows:

"There is one field in which the work of educating public opinion and correcting it imposes itself with tragic urgency. . .

"We here wish to refer to writings, books and articles concerning sex initiation, which today very often obtain enormous editorial successes and flood the whole world . . .

"It is the case really to ask oneself if the dividing line is still sufficiently visible between this initiation, which is said to be Catholic, and the press which with erotic and obscene illustrations purposely and deliberately aims at corruption and shamefully exploits, for vile gain, the lowest instincts of fallen nature.

". . .Such propaganda also threatens Catholic people with a double scourge, not to use a stronger expression.

"First of all, it greatly exaggerates the importance and range of the sexual element of life. . .It makes the real and primordial aim of marriage to be lost sight of, that is, procreation and education of children and the serious duty of the married couples with regard to this end, which the writings in question leave obscure.

"Secondly, this literature, if such it could be called, does not seem in any way to take into account, based as it is on nature, the general experience of all times, whether it be that of today or yesterday, which attests that in moral education, neither initiation nor instruction offers any advantage of itself. Rather, it becomes seriously unwholesome and prejudicial when not closely allied with constant discipline, with vigorous self-control, and above all with the use of the supernatural forces of prayer and the sacraments. . .

". . .Even the principles so wisely illustrated by Our Predecessor Pius XI in the encyclical *Divini Illius Magistri* ["On Christian Education of Youth"] on sex education and questions connected thereto are set aside—a sad sign of the times! With a smile of compassion they say: Pius XI wrote twenty years ago, for his times! Great progress has been made since then!

"Fathers of families here present! Unite. . .under the direction of your Bishops certainly. . .call to your aid all Catholic women and mothers. . .in order to fight together. . .to stop and curtail these movements under whatever name or under whatever patronage they conceal themselves or are patronized."

1951 Pope Pius XII, *Allocution to Midwives,* condemned the practice of contraception.

1953 Pope Pius XII, in his address of April 13, 1953, states that personal sex instruction of children and youth in the home should place special stress "upon self-mastery and religious training." He reminded his audience that "The Holy See published certain rules in this connection shortly after the encyclical of Pius XI on Christian Marriage. *These rules have not been rescinded, either expressly or via facti.*" (Emphasis added).

1959 *Explosion or Backfire?* A statement condemning governmental promotion of birth control practices and population control propaganda issued by the bishops of the United States. The Catholic hierarchy denounces the promotion of birth prevention as a disastrous approach to population issues and a violation of God's law.

Catholic members of the American Public Health Association are actively solicited to promote birth prevention services by American Public Health Association leaders.

1960 Planned Parenthood and the national and international anti-life network begin a concerted campaign to neutralize and/or destroy Catholic resistance to birth control and government population-control efforts.

1961 Mary Calderone, Medical Director of Planned Parenthood/World Population, lectures on the role of churches in promoting sex education before the first North American Conference on Church and Family, which she formed as a precursor to SIECUS.

1959- Pope John XXIII announces his plan to convoke the
1965 Church's Twenty-first Ecumenical Council, the first since Vatican I of 1869-70. The Council opened on October 11, 1962, and concluded its final session on December 8, 1965. *The Declaration on Christian Education* was promulgated on October 28, 1965, and *The Pastoral Constitution on the Church in the Modern World* on December 7, during the last Council meeting.

In Vatican II's *Declaration on Christian Education,* we read that, "parents. . .have the first and the inalienable duty and right to educate their children." (N. 6). And again, "parents must be acknowledged as the first and foremost educators of their children." (N. 3). (Cf. Pius XI, encyclical letter *Divini Illius Magistri,* p. 59ff.)

It should be noted that the Council document has 13 footnote references to Pope Pius XI's encyclical on *The Christian Education of Youth*.

The Council document makes a single and curt reference to "sexual education" or "matters related to sex," depending on which translation one uses.

The edition of *Documents of Vatican II* by Walter M. Abbott, S.J., published by American Press, Associated Press in 1966, contains the wording, "as they [i.e., children and young people] advance in years, they should be given positive and prudent sexual education." (pg. 639).

The Austin Flannery, O.P., version published by Costello Publishing, N.Y. in 1975 reads as follows:

"As they grow older, they should receive a positive and prudent education in matters related to sex." (pg. 727, 1981 edition).

In the *Pastoral Constitution on the Church in the Modern World,* the Council Fathers reaffirm with simple clarity that the place for "positive and prudent" education in matters related to sex is in the family, *not* in the classroom:

"Especially in the heart of their own families, *young people should be aptly and seasonably instructed about the dignity, duty, and expression of married love. Trained thus in the cultivation of chastity, they will be able at a suitable age to enter a marriage of their own after an honorable courtship.''* (N. 49). (Emphasis added).

This statement, taken from the document's chapter on "The Dignity of Marriage and the Family," is but one of many references to the Church's traditional teachings on marriage, family and the education of offspring, including:

"Marriage and married love are by nature ordered to the procreation and education of children. Indeed children are the supreme gift of marriage and greatly contribute to the good of the parents themselves. . .Whenever Christian spouses in a spirit of sacrifice and trust in divine providence carry out their duties of procreation with generous human and Christian responsibility, they glorify the Creator and perfect themselves in Christ. Among the married couples who thus fulfill their God-given mission, special mention should be made of those who after prudent reflection and common decision courageously undertake the proper upbringing of a large number of children. . .The Church wishes to emphasize that there can be no conflict between the divine laws governing the transmission of life and the fostering of authentic married love. God, the Lord of life, has entrusted to men the noble mission of safeguarding life, and men must carry it out in a manner worthy of themselves. Life must be protected with the utmost care from the moment of conception: abortion and infanticide are abominable crimes. Man's sexuality and the faculty of reproduction wondrously surpass the endowments of lower forms of life; therefore the acts proper to married life are to be ordered according to authentic human dignity and must be honored with the greatest reverence. . .Thus, in the footsteps of Christ, the principle of life, they [married people] will bear witness by their faithful love in the joys and sacrifices of their calling, to that mystery of love which the Lord revealed to the world by his death and resurrection."

1964-1965 Pope Paul VI, through the channels of the National Catholic Welfare Conference (NCWC—an agency of the U.S. Bishops), canvasses the bishops of the world on contraception, reserving to himself, as Supreme Pontiff, final judgment on the matter.

Pope Paul VI decides to reconvene the Papal Birth Control Commission, established by his predecessor Pope John XXIII, to investigate the role of steroids, as well as to review other types of data and scientific developments related to the regulation of births.

Pope Paul VI reminds the Ecumenical Council that any Vatican II statements relating to the matter of contraception are to take note explicitly of statements made by his Predecessors, Pius XI and Pius XII, on the issue of birth control, and that the norms enunciated in *Casti Connubii* remain in effect.

1965-1966 Attorney William Ball testifies on behalf of the National Catholic Welfare Conference (NCWC) *in opposition to governmental advances in the field of birth control and population control* before Senate hearings on S. #1676—the first major federal effort to institutionalize the Sangerite philosophy and its birth-control practices into public policy.[80] (The Gruening hearings were dominated by representatives of almost every major anti-life group in the United States, including Senator Gruening himself.)

Office of Economic Opportunity and Department of Health, Education and Welfare announce plans to begin a push for birth control for the poor and adolescents who were "sexually active."

1966 United States Catholic Bishops issue their *final* statement in opposition to governmental programs of birth control and population limitation at home and abroad, under the auspices of the National Catholic Welfare Conference, one month before the NCWC is disassembled and replaced by the bureaucracy called the United States Catholic Conference, Inc. (USCC).*

William Ball recounts the tragedy that followed the failure of the American bishops and their new bureaucracy to "call out the troops" in order actively to oppose governmental birth-control programs:

"It can at any rate now be concluded that the default of the Catholic Church (or of Church staff officers whose duty it is to carry forward policy) on the subject of governmental birth control programming may prove to have been of historic moment because the Catholic Church alone, among all bodies in the American Society, probably possessed the means to bring government birth control into public question and to cause its proponents to attempt to make their case for it.[81]

"...The position on governmental birth control activity expressed by the American Catholic bishops brings ultimately into focus...fundamental questions respecting the nature of the human being, of human liberty, of the role of the state, of the poor, and of the Providence of God. It is an historic misfortune that, prior to setting the nation's course in the direction of population control, discussion was not had of such course in terms of these questions. Even as unfortunate was the failure of the largest Church of the world's most powerful nation to do more, in terms of discussion of these questions, than to issue a statement.[82]

"This statement (of November 14, 1966, of the Catholic bishops) was an argument, complete in itself, but by virtue of its assertions, it plainly opened the door to do a national debate. This debate was never forthcoming...the public—and the specially exhorted Catholic public—having been called to 'oppose vigorously and by every democratic means' state and federal promotion of birth control, were left with nothing but the dying echo of the trumpet call. Far from being provided with any sort of

---

*The United States Catholic Conference, Inc. (USCC) is the civil-religious service agency of the National Council of Catholic Bishops (NCCB); the USCC's purpose is to carry out the Church's social mission. The NCCB and USCC have identical directors.

detailed information on the issues by the statement's authors who had raised them, or guidelines to the action sought, *the Catholic laity of the United States never heard another word about the whole subject.*''[83]

Chart IV-B

Key Documents and Events Related to the Neutralization and/or Destruction of Catholic Teachings on Human Sexuality, Marriage and the Family—1967-1988.

1967 The United States Catholic Conference (USCC), under the presidency of Archbishop John F. Dearden, replaces the old National Catholic Welfare Conference (NCWC), to provide a formal organizational structure and policy resource center for the promotion and financing of the agenda of the emerging "New American Church."

Monsignor James T. McHugh, an Advisory Board Member of the American Association of Sex Educators, Counselors and Therapists—AASEC(T)—assumes the directorship of the Family Life Division of the United States Catholic Conference, with influence and authority over more than 130 Catholic dioceses across the United States. McHugh begins promotion of SIECUS and AASEC(T) programs and policies, while attacking opponents of classroom sex education.

The New Jersey Department of Education (Division of Curriculum and Instruction, Office of Health, Safety and Physical Education) publishes SIECUS-based "Guidelines for Developing School Programs in Sex Education" and suggests that schools obtain the services of SIECUS as "consultant for additional sights." (See Claire Chambers' *SIECUS Circle* for additional details.)

(These guidelines would eventually form the basis for a Sex Education Program adopted by the New Jersey State Board of Education and endorsed by the Bishops of New Jersey in March of 1981.)

1967 *National Catholic Reporter* publishes drafts of both

majority and minority conclusions of the Papal Birth Control Commission, which were "leaked" to the press in April of 1967.

For a detailed profile of the Commission, and its disastrous effect on traditional Catholic sexual morality, see *Honest Love and Human Life—Is the Pope Right About Contraception* by Christopher Derrick (Coward-McCann, Inc., Publishers, N.Y., 1969).

1968 Interfaith Statement endorsing classroom sex education is issued in June, 1968, by:

*Monsignor James McHugh, for the Family Life Bureau of the U.S. Catholic Conference.

†Reverend William Genne, for the Commission on Marriage and the Family of the National Council of Churches; Rabbi Mordecai Brill, for the Committee on Family of the Synagogue Council of America.

*Advisory Board Member of AASEC(T).
†SIECUS founder, Advisory Board Member to AASEC(T).

(Note: This pamphlet, *An Interfaith Statement on Sex Education,* claims to represent "the common affirmations of the major faith groups of our country" and has been widely distributed by Catholic, Protestant and Jewish advocates of classroom sex education. This statement bears the indelible AASEC(T)-SIECUS imprint, i.e., situation ethics, denial of moral absolutes, and emphasis on the "relational" aspects of sex in marriage, *apart* from procreation.)[84]

The *U.S. Catholic,* a media precursor for the "American Church," publishes a special eleven-page report on birth control, claiming the traditional prohibition against contraception is in doubt and no longer applicable.

1968 Pope Paul VI issues his prophetic encyclical *Humanae Vitae (On the Transmission of Human Life)* on July 25, 1968. This was published by the USCC under the title "The Regulation of Birth."

(For a brilliant analysis of the battle over the authentic

Magisterium of the papacy and the right of the Church to teach with absolute authority in matters of Faith and morals, see Anne Roche Muggeridge's *The Desolate City—Revolution in the Catholic Church* [Harper and Row, Publishers, 1986]. Also, "Catholic War on the Potomac" by Reverend Monsignor George A. Kelly in *Human Sexuality in Our Time—What the Church Teaches* [St. Paul Editions, 1979].)

1968 Cardinal O'Boyle of Washington, D.C. establishes the Human Life Foundation to promote the teachings of *Humanae Vitae* and investigate scientific advances in periodic abstinence, based on natural body rhythms.

1968 In November 1968, six months after endorsing the Interfaith Statement on Sex Education, U.S. Catholic Bishops issue the pastoral *Human Life In Our Day,* which makes classroom sex education programs *obligatory* in parochial school and CCD curriculums. The text pertaining to Sex Education follows:

"...We are under a *grave obligation,* in part arising from the new circumstances of modern culture and communications, to assist the family in its efforts to provide such training. *This obligation can be met either by systematic provisions of such education in the Diocesan school curriculum or the inauguration of acceptable education programs under other diocesan auspices, including the Confraternity of Christian Doctrine.*" (Emphasis added).

(Note: Almost simultaneous with the tragic decision of the National Conference of Catholic Bishops and its new bureaucratic arm, the U.S. Catholic Conference, to drop all official opposition to governmental birth control programs was the attempt to institutionalize a systematic and formal program of sex education into the Church's parochial and CCD educational system. That the authors of the pastoral *authorized* and *rationalized* this blatant attack on parental rights and openly defied the historic Catholic prohibition against classroom sex education programs—basing themselves on Vatican II's single reference to "a positive and prudent education in matters related to sex"—is an issue which will be examined in greater detail later in this book. The important point to make here, however, is that both decisions, one to *drop* universal opposition to population control and the other to *initiate* universal sex education, *were developed and carried out almost simultaneously under circumstances which deliberately precluded any real or open debate as to the correctness or wisdom of those decisions.*)

1969 The move to institutionalize sex education in Catholic Schools and CCD classes swings into high gear in the United States under the leadership of the Family Life Division (FLD) of the USCC and the National Catholic Education Association (NCEA).

■ The FLD/USCC, under the direction of Monsignor McHugh, and the NCEA issue a joint statement, *Sex Education: A Guide for Parents and Educators.*

■ NC News Service carries an FLD/USCC press release entitled, "Dioceses Accepting Sex Education Idea," by Monsignor McHugh.

■ Sex Education Guidelines promoted by FLD/USCC at NCEA 66th Annual Convention in Detroit.

■ USCC issues a school supplement, "Sex Education—A Guide for Teachers," by Monsignor McHugh; it is sent to all Catholic school superintendents by Very Reverend Monsignor James C. Donohue, the Director of the Division of Elementary and Secondary Education, Christian Formation Department, USCC. The packet contains a cover letter asking for the materials promoting classroom sex education to be publicized in diocesan publications and newsletters.

The above-mentioned USCC documents and news releases by Monsignor McHugh *promote* the anti-life organization SIECUS and condemn opponents of classroom sex education. The following endorsement issued of SIECUS is found in Monsignor McHugh's 1969 NC News Service Release:

"During this past year a somewhat negative reaction to sex education set in throughout the country. Inspired by ultra-conservative pressure groups, it was largely directed at. . .SIECUS, a private, non-profit organization which supplies information and materials to encourage the development of sex education programs in local communities.

"But it also had some effect in the Catholic community through the overall confusion it generated. In most instances, however, the clear directives of the pastoral letter and the patient planning of school administrators *offset the reaction.*" (Emphasis added).

Monsignor McHugh, who failed to state publicly his association with the SIECUS-founded and -controlled AASEC(T), also fails to mention the "negative reaction" of Pope Pius XI and Pope Pius XII to classroom sex education and their condemnation of such instruction outside the home.

In the USCC supplement, "Sex Education—A Guide for Teachers," editor McHugh permits Dr. William Zeller to promote the SIECUS-AASEC(T) complex as a resource center for Catholic educators, as follows: "Within the past few years, a number of national organizations have done pioneering work in this field. Among the organizations would be the Sex Information and Education Council of the United States (SIECUS), the American Association of Sex Educators (AASEC(T)) and the Interfaith Commission on Marriage and Family. . .These undertakings deserve the support and participation of parents, teachers and clergymen. . ."[85]

1969 The SIECUS ad for universal sex education, placed in the *New York Times* (10/16/69) by the National Committee for Responsible Family Life and Sex Education, contains the signatures of 200 members, including prominent "Catholics" such as Reverend Charles Curran, Reverend Dexter Hanley, S.J., Reverend Theodore Hesburgh and John Rock, M.D. The ad reaffirms that "enlightened

Americans support the concepts of SIECUS: that sex education and family life training are a community trust and are essential to self-awareness and human development."[86]

1969 Pope Paul VI and the Catholic Bishops are attacked with ads in the *New York Times* for their stand against birth control and population control with headlines that read: "Pope denounces birth control as millions starve" and "Catholic Bishops assail birth control as millions face starvation," which were paid for and sponsored by the campaign to check the Population Explosion, a front group for Planned Parenthood and the Hugh Moore Fund. (For reproductions of the original Hugh Moore ads and information on the Planned Parenthood World Population Agenda, see *Breeding Ourselves to Death* by leading abortion advocate Lawrence Lader, Baltimore Books, N.Y., 1971.)

The 138 signatures to the various Hugh Moore ads include those of:

Eugene Black (World Bank).
Dr. William V. D'Antonio (Notre Dame University).
General William H. Draper, Jr. (U.S. Representative to NATO).
Dr. Louis Dupre (Georgetown University).
Robert McNamara (World Bank).
Dr. Linus Pauling.
Drs. Gregory Pincus and John Rock.
Drs. Albert B. Sabin and Jonas Salk.
Rt. Reverend Henry Knox Sherrill (World Council of Churches).
Bishop John Wesley Lord (Methodist Church).
Mrs. Fifield Workum (Margaret Sanger Research Bureau).
Reverend Carl J. Westman (Unitarian-Universalist Church).
U.S. Senator Ernest Gruening (D-Alaska, Chairman of the U.S. Senate Population Assembly).
Rabbi Wolfe Kelman (Rabbinical Assembly).

Mrs. Eleanor Roosevelt.
Mrs. Robert M. Ferguson (International Planned Parenthood Federation).
Reverend Harry Emerson Fosdick (Riverside Church).
Reverend Eugene Carson Blake (United Presbyterian Church, U.S.A.).
Reverend Robert McAfee Brown (Stanford University).

(In *The Documents of Vatican II With Notes and Comments by Catholic, Protestant and Orthodox Authorities,* edited by Walter M. Abott, S.J.—Reverend Robert McAfee Brown, a signer of the vicious Hugh Moore ads, gives the "Response" to *Gaudium et spes,* "The Pastoral Constitution on the Church in the Modern World"—pp. 309-316. After taking a swipe at the Church's teaching on procreation as the primary end of marriage, and while applauding the Council's "modest victory" at deliberately leaving the matter of birth control "open," Brown states, "The Protestant commentator cannot underscore too strongly that the matter needs resolution, since not only Roman Catholics are affected by the matter, but other persons as well, *for whom the denial of birth control information to non-Catholics desiring to have it constitutes a serious moral as well as a social problem.*"—pg. 315, emphasis added.)

1969 Federal Agencies, particularly the U.S. Department of Health, Education and Welfare (HEW) and the Agency for International Development (US-AID) push for major birth control programs at home and abroad and universal sex education curriculums for elementary and secondary schools, linked to promotion of small family norms and the education of youth in the practice of contraception, sterilization, abortifacients and surgical abortion.

Planned Parenthood in the U.S. and abroad increases efforts to neutralize the Church's opposition to birth control and sponsors governmental programs of population limitation.

Planned Parenthood had two important links to the U.S.

Catholic Conference, via first Father Imbiorski of the Cana Conference, who was serving as a Director of SIECUS and advisor to AASEC(T) while serving on the Advisory Board of the USCC's Family Life Division, and second Monsignor McHugh, who, as an Advisory Board Member to AASEC(T) and also the Family Life Director at the USCC, used his position to promote the programs and policies of SIECUS at the international level.

The IPPF sends Planned Parenthood representatives to the Vatican to open up a "dialogue" on "family planning" while soft-pedalling sterilization and abortion, which the IPPF was vigorously pushing behind the scenes.

Dr. Van Emde Boas of the Netherlands, a founder of the International Planned Parenthood Federation (IPPF), explains the strategy against the Church's position on birth control as follows:

"Do not let us, family planners, fight the rhythm method in spite of all its drawbacks. . .It might turn out to be the lever by which we could in the not too distant future break the opposition against family planning that until now has been put forward by the church hierarchy in individual cases as well as on a national and international scale. Let us therefore study and improve the method by all available means. In the near future it will then turn out to be true that even the most refined rhythm method retains its drawbacks. And what then? I am not quite sure, but it might be not too audacious to conclude by venturing: 'From Ogino to Pincus: *il n'y a qu'un pas*.'"[87] ("There is only one step.")

1970 Catholic Diocese of Newark Family Life Apostolate co-sponsors Human Sexuality workshop at Montclair State College (N.J.) on June 17, 1970. Speakers include Dr. Alan Guttmacher, President of Planned Parenthood/World Population, Vice President of the Association for the Study of Abortion and Advisor to the Euthanasia Educational Council, who discusses the "need" for abortion law repeal. Honored at the workshop for the achievements in the field of sex education and human sexuality are SIECUS Directors Frederick Margolia, Wardell Pomeroy and Ira Reiss. (See Claire Chambers *SIECUS Circle*, pg. 307 for further details.)

1970 *Total collapse* of Catholic Bishops' long-standing absolute opposition to federal and state birth control programs is witnessed in public testimony of Monsignor McHugh in August, 1970, before the House Subcommittee on Public Health and Welfare, holding hearings on Title X of HEW's multi-billion dollar first five-year plan for "population research" and "birth control."

Note: At the hearings, the USCC traded off its opposition to governmental population control programs for a toothless and nearly worthless anti-abortion clause known as the Dingell Amendment. At the same time, Monsignor McHugh, representing the USCC/FLD, called for a stepped-up campaign of universal sex education programs from birth to maturity. His testimony is as follows:

"When you ask what might happen to people who need some knowledge of the reproductive cycle, I would hope that we will be able to construct good, value-oriented programs of sex education reflecting the best scientific knowledge, the best anthropological and sociological knowledge, and a real concern for religious values and religious teachings, so that in time we will be able to raise another generation of Americans who will have a positive attitude toward their own sexuality and considerably more information about it than most of us were benefitted with as we passed from adolescence to adulthood. I think this is a priority."[88]

1970 The World Council of Churches sponsors the Symposium on Family Life and Sex Education in Geneva. There churches are urged to support universal sex education.

1971 Pope Paul VI issues explicit public condemnation of aberrations in classroom sex education programs, which is repeated in his address of September 13, 1972, condemning contemporary sexual errors as follows: "On the scientific plane, psychoanalysis; on the pedagogical plane, sex education; on the literary plane, obligatory eroticism; on the plane of entertainment, indecent exhibition, straining towards the obscene. . ."

1971 The Education Committee of the U.S. Catholic Conference issues the pastoral letter, *To Teach as Jesus Did,* which advocates classroom sex education in Catholic Schools and CCD programs and warns parents against interfering with the execution of such programs.

Having removed the iron fist from the velvet glove, the USCC Education Department, in cooperation with the Family Life Division, comes down hard on parents who allow their anxiety "to be translated into indiscriminate opposition to all forms of classroom education in sexuality. *Such opposition should be contrary to the teachings of Vatican II and the Pastoral policy of the American bishops.* Also, to the extent that it might disrupt responsible efforts to provide formal education in sexuality for the young, it would violate the right of other, no less conscientious parents who ask for such instruction for their own children." (No. 57, emphasis added).

Thus parents, who only twenty years before were exhorted by Pope Pius XII to band together to *fight* the evils of sex education, are now condemned, intimidated and cowed into silence by the U.S. Catholic Conference, with the approval of the American bishops. Second only to the incredible title of the document is the statement that parents "have the right to be informed about the content of such programs and to be assured that diocesan-approved textbooks and other instructional materials meet the requirements of propriety." Propriety!!! For goodness sake!!! What about the *primary and inalienable right of parents to educate their children* as re-stated in Vatican II's *Declaration on Christian Education?* And how about the *RIGHTS OF CHILDREN* to receive sound doctrinal instruction in matters of faith and morals? What about the obligation of parents to protect their children from "occasions of sin" in the form of USCC-FLD promoted programs such as "Becoming a Person" (BAP), or the Fox program "Life Education: A New Series of Correlated Lessons," or the Rochester Program "Education in Love"—all of which were operational in various Catholic dioceses throughout the United States at the time *To Teach as Jesus Did* was issued.

Occasions of sin for youth? Too strong language? Not so. For example: *Life Education* gives detailed instruction to 8th grade boys and girls on how to masturbate to climax.[89] If this be "propriety," then propriety be damned! All three programs bear the SIECUS and AASEC(T) "imprimatur," which is not surprising, since Father Imbiorski of SIECUS-AASEC(T) designed the BAP program; Dr. Gerald Guerinot of the Rochester diocese and a member of the National Catholic Conference of Bishops' Task Force on Sex Education and an AASEC(T) Training and Standards Committeeman designed the original text for "Education in Love"; and Drs. James and Marie Fox, devotees of SIECUS situation ethics, explicit sexual instruction and sensitivity training, created the "Life Education" curriculum.

1971 In April of 1971, Father Imbiorski addresses Catholic educators at the NCEA annual convention on the value of sex education and tells audiences that opponents of SIECUS "are going to have to answer before God" for "slander" against SIECUS.[90]

1973-1978 U.S. Catholic Conference undergoes major reorganization and personnel changes:

Monsignor McHugh is transferred from the Family Life Department to head the Bishops' Committee on Prolife Affairs.

The USCC replaces the Family Life Division with a new Ad Hoc Commission on Marriage and Family, which later becomes the Committee on Marriage and Family under the direction of Father Donald Conroy. The USCC

Department of Education announces a major shift in the development of Catechesis related to human sexuality education in the classroom.

1977 Daniel Dolesh, S.T.D. joins the staff of the USCC Ad Hoc Commission on Marriage and Family, and in 1977 becomes the Chairman of three key USCC Department of Education posts related to the promotion of classroom sex education:

- The Family Centered Religious Education National Committee,
- the National Parenting Committee and
- the National Committee for Human Sexuality Education, which would draw up the USCC Sex Education Guidelines, "Education in Human Sexuality for Christians."

Note: The appointment of Daniel Dolesh secured the SIECUS-AASEC(T)-Planned Parenthood foothold at the U.S. Catholic Conference. An AASEC(T) member, like Monsignor McHugh, Dolesh enjoyed a litany of anti-life memberships in the National Forum for Sex Education, the Metropolitan Sex Education Coalition (a clearinghouse for Planned Parenthood and Lutheran Social Services), the U.S. Council of the International Council of Sex Education and Parenthood, and he was a promoter of Sexual Attitudinal Reassessment (SAR) seminars.

1974 The Wingspread Conference on Adolescent Sexuality and Health Care is held in April 1974 and features Reverend William Genne of the National Council of Churches. The Conference issues a plan of action and a Manifesto on the Sexual Adolescent, as a follow-up to the USCC-approved *Interfaith Statement on Sex Education,* urging churches to join with secular societal forces to clarify traditional values and assumptions related to human sexuality.

1975 The Vatican's Committee for the Family issues its report, *The Marriage Sacrament—The Church's Answer to the*

Appeals of the Family, a three-year study of the fundamental teachings of the Church on marriage as a divine institution, and the divine mission of the family.

1975 The Vatican's *Declaration on Certain Questions Concerning Sexual Ethics* is published with the approval of Pope Paul VI and signed by Franjo Cardinal Seper, Prefect of the Sacred Congregation for the Doctrine of the Faith, and Archbishop Jerome Hamer, its secretary.

This document confirms traditional Catholic teaching on the sinfulness of fornication, adultery, homosexuality and masturbation, and advises bishops of their mission "to see that a sound doctrine enlightened by faith and directed by the Magisterium of the Church is taught in facilities of theology and in seminaries" and "that confessors enlighten people's conscience and that catechetical instruction is given in perfect fidelity to Catholic doctrine."

Note: In sharp contrast to the SIECUS-AASEC(T) philosophy of sexual permissiveness, the Declaration reaffirms Catholic teaching on the existence of the Natural Law, of moral absolutes and of eternal, objective and universal norms of human behavior which are impressed on the human conscience and the human heart by God and are binding on all men.

1976 The Call-to-Action Committee of Detroit: Resolutions 25, 36, 39 and 40 support universal classroom sex education programs.

1977 Paulist Press publishes *Human Sexuality—New Directions in American Catholic Thought,* a study commissioned by the Catholic Theological Society of America and edited by Anthony Kosnik.

Note: Reverend Monsignor Eugene Kevane, visiting Professor of Catechetics at the Angelicum in Rome, makes this observation of the nature of the Kosnik study: "this 'study'. . . rationalizes the acceptability of actions which have been consistently branded as *the way of death* throughout the entire course of Sacred History from *Genesis* down to the present period of Church history.

"This 'study' stands in quite *explicit contestation* with the living Magisterium, with the documents of the Magisterium throughout the Twentieth Century and in particular with the *Declaration of Sexual Ethics* issued December 29, 1975...This self-styled 'study' is in conflict with the entire immense dimension of Divine Revelation and as such stands in opposition to the Creator from the beginning of the universe to the present moment on His ongoing Creative Activity."[91] (Emphasis added).

Monsignor Kevane notes two aspects of the CTSA "study" which are deserving of special attention:

First, its "deceptiveness" at a number of different levels, including the abusive treatment of Sacred Scripture, "the abusive treatment of Doctrine," "the slanted use made of empirical sciences," "the distortion of Vatican II, particularly, *Gaudium et spes*," and the most devious deception of all, that of using "an alien philosophy in the *Doctrina Sacra* of the Catholic Church, thus producing a mental construct which has the surface appearance of theology but which is actually an exercise in philosophy of religion."[92]

The second peculiar aspect cited by Monsignor Kevane is "...the element of surprise for the laity that such a doctrine could be presented within the Church as if it were authentic Catholic Christianity for modern man... especially by persons of the Catholic cloth."[93]

"It's simply another milestone in the record of this unfortunate intellectual disobedience...Always it is stubborn desire to introduce existentialist phenomenology (and now Marxist Hegelianism as well) as preferable to Christian Philosophy for use in *Doctrina Sacra*,'"[94] Monsignor Kevane concludes.

Kevane's critical analysis of the Kosnick study has been deliberately quoted here at length, because only four years later the USCC Department of Education would publish a "kindergarten" version of the CTSA sexuality "study," entitled *Education in Human Sexuality for Christians,* that was destined to create the same moral havoc at the elementary and secondary levels as the Kosnik study wrought in Catholic seminaries and institutions of higher learning.

1977 The USCC/NCCB Commission on Marriage and Family Life proposes the formulation of a catechesis for human sexuality and family life, including the development of guidelines, curriculum and resource materials, as well as catechetical training programs for educators, religious and family life ministers. (Proposals No. 1, 17, and 24). This event marks the beginning of the history of the USCC Sex Education "Guidelines."

1978 Bishop Bernard D. Stewart, D.D., of Sandhurst, Australia issues his "Pastoral Statement on Formation in Chastity of Children and School Pupils" on February 2, 1978. Defending parents as the natural and competent teachers of their children in the delicate matter of conscience formation and the transmission of sexual knowledge, Bishop Stewart condemns open and public sex education classes, especially the kind of "education" which promotes " 'letting children make up their own mind' about sex; or asking school children to debate for or against the certain moral code of the Church; or raising doubts for children and not resolving them; or by telling them 'what theologians say' against Church teaching without telling them that 'what those theologians say' is of no value at all and cannot be followed in conscience."[95]

Bishop Stewart's interpretation of the role of the school in helping parents fulfill their role as the primary educators of their children is in stark contrast to that of the American Bishops, as evidenced by the following admonition by Bishop Stewart:

"...The school is to foster an atmosphere of modesty, purity and chastity...Teachers are to instruct pupils systematically and properly in the moral doctrine of the

Church concerning the nature and role of conscience, personal behavior, marriage and the transmission of life... and to instruct their students convincingly and without ambiguity in the Fifth, Sixth and Ninth Commandments..."[96]

1978 Daniel Dolesh, of the Family Education and Elementary Grades Section of the USCC Department of Education, issues the USCC memo "State of the Question Regarding Moral Education and Sex Education in the Public School Systems," on November 8, 1978. The memo is distributed to Catholic Conferences across the United States.

Note: As the new SIECUS/AASEC(T) mole in the U.S. Catholic Conference, Dolesh warns opponents of classroom sex education against action which would "polarize and antagonize other elements within the Community."[97] He suggests instead that Catholics develop alternative public school curricula of moral education and sexuality which would reflect a shared "Judeo-Christian" heritage.[98]

1980 Hawaiian State Catholic Conference publicly testifies in opposition to classroom sex education on April 22, 1980 and correctly links the latter with an increase of venereal disease and sexual promiscuity among the young, as well as pornography.[99]

1981 Catholic Bishops of New Jersey mandate sex education in all the state's Catholic schools and endorse the N.J. state Board of Education K-12 sex education curriculum, which includes topics such as sexual intercourse, sexual deviations, self-abuse and all means of birth control.

1981 United States Catholic Bishops announce release of a National Catechetical Directory (NCD), *Sharing the Light of Faith.* The document contains an ambiguous reference to classroom sex education based on Vatican II's single reference to "positive and prudent sexual education."

"Education in sexuality includes all dimensions of the topic: moral, spiritual, psychological, emotional and physical." (NCD Section 11, No. 190). "Even after their [i.e., the parents'] reasonable requirements and specifications have been met, however, some parents may remain anxious about education in sexuality. They should not let their feelings express themselves in indiscriminate opposition to all classroom instruction in sexuality, for that would not be consistent with the position of the Second Vatican Council and the Bishops of the United States. Furthermore, to the extent such opposition might disrupt responsible efforts along these lines, it would violate the rights of others, no less conscientious parents, who desire such instruction for their children." (n. 191).

1981 Pope John Paul II's *Familiaris Consortio* is issued by the Vatican on November 22, 1981.

Note: This document will be discussed later in this book in conjunction with the "Charter on the Rights of the Family" released on October 22, 1983, and "Educational Guidance in Human Love" issued on November 1, 1983 by the USCC.

1981 Bishop Thomas C. Kelly, O.P., General Secretary of the USCC, announces the release of the USCC Department of Education "Guidelines for Sex Education," entitled *Education in Human Sexuality for Christians,* formulated by the National Committee for Human Sexuality Education.

Note: The 1981 USCC "Guidelines" will be compared to Kosnik's "Study" in a special addendum in this book.

1981 The Fellowship of Catholic Scholars (U.S.A.) condemns the USCC Sex Education "Guidelines."

1981 *The National Catholic Reporter* praises the USCC "Guidelines" for the document's new insights into homosexual behavior and its emphasis on relational sex.[100]

Chapter 5
Chronological Addenda

Introduction

Thus far I have identified the origins and nature of the sex education plague in the United States and traced its pestilential path through the secular and parochial educational systems from the post-World War II era to the late 1970's and early 1980's.

As indicated earlier, presenting material in a chronological fashion has the considerable advantage of revealing developmental patterns and trends which are frequently lost in other styles of writing. One disadvantage, however, is the inevitable necessity of telescoping important events and documents into a single sentence or a few brief paragraphs, and in doing so of depriving the reader of additional insights. I trust the following addenda will remedy this literary deficiency.

I. *Addendum on Vatican II and Sex Education*

> In its Declaration on Christian Education the Second Vatican Council said young people should receive a positive and prudent sexual education. (No. 3) [sic]. Although this was not the first and certainly not the last official endorsement by the Church, it represents the highest level of support which the Church is capable of giving to the idea and practice of education in human sexuality which respects Christian moral values.[101]
>
> —The Foreword to *Education in Human Sexuality for Christians,* USCC Sex Education Guidelines

Since the *Declaration on Christian Education* is the document most often cited to justify the introduction of mandatory classroom sex education in formal Catholic curricula, a brief examination of its genesis and history and its relation to other schemata promulgated by Vatican Council II, as well as to the traditional Magisterium of the Church, appears in order.

In his commentary on the *Declaration on Christian Education,* Reverend Mark J. Hurley, who served as a "peritus," or expert, on the Commission on Education, illustrates the tortuous history of this schema from its original classification as a "constitution" to its reduction to a "votum" and thence a series of propositions and finally its re-elevation as a "declaration" promulgated by Paul VI on October 28, 1965.[102] Readers should keep in mind that "no text or document of the Council was really ever finished or completed before the final ballot" and there was always "the possibility of amendment, modification and change. To this, the text on education was no exception."[103]

On June 12-13, 1962, the first draft of the Education Preparatory Commission, which combined two Council schema on Catholic schools, universities and seminaries, was rejected as being too "legalistic" and "negative," especially with reference to "co-education."[104] One month later, the secretary of the Commission resubmitted the amended document for Conciliar action, which covered a two-year period of heated debate among the Council Fathers and a multitude of "periti" (experts) who had grafted themselves onto the various educational subcommissions.

The first text of the educational schema was presented to the Council Fathers on April 17, 1964 in the form of 17 theses, or propositions, on various universal principles of education. The draft was rejected and sent back for a complete overhaul, including a change of title from "Catholic Schools" to the more inclusive "Christian Education."

Again, on October 6, 1964, another version of the schema, featuring a new reference to parochial school aid (Fair Share), was rejected as unsophisticated and in need of further qualifications.[105]

Finally, in early November, a new 1,000-word text with key provisions for the establishment of a Post-Conciliar Commission on Education, and an Introduction twice the size of the text, was presented for general debate on the floor of St. Peter's.[106]

There were 21 oral interventions and 37 written submissions to the Commission on Education.[107]

The American hierarchy intervened five times on matters of state aid and distributive justice, parental choice in education, the right of the Church to educate and the contribution of Catholic schools to society in general. It is interesting that Bishop Donohoe warned that the text must not overemphasize parental rights to the exclusion of the rights of others with a role in education.[108]

On November 19, the Plenary Commission thanked the Council Fathers for the debate and promised to return with a satisfactorily revised text. This draft was completed by the Spring of 1965, but was not published or distributed to the Bishops of the world until the opening of Vatican Council II's 4th Session in September. Only the members of the Educational Commission received copies of the revised text and modi[109] (new amendments).

When the final text was printed, there was a great deal of confusion because the new texts and amendments were done in standard type and the former text was done in italics,[110] just the reverse of what was normally done. Many Council Fathers argued that there was so little left of the original text that the schema they were being asked to vote on was *not* a revised text but a totally new document.[111]

Readers will note that, thus far, no mention has been made of any Conciliar discussion or debate on the issue of sex education. The reason is quite simple—and of profound importance.

The single mention of education in human sexuality—i.e., "As they grow older, they should receive a positive and prudent education in matters related to sex"[112] (Flannery), or "As they advance in years, they should be given positive and prudent sexual education"[113] (Abbott), was one of three last-minute additions to the final text of the Declaration on Christian Education.[114] Hurley makes no mention of any discussion or spirited debate on this particular addition, although there was lengthy discussion and debate on the addition related to St. Thomas Aquinas.[115]

On October 13, 1965 following a section-by-section vote, the entire schema was approved. The next day the Secretary General presented the document to the Holy Father. On October 28,

1965, Pope Paul VI promulgated *De Educatione Christiana* in the name of the Ecumenical Council, Vatican Council II.

What Vatican II Really Said

Interestingly, Hurley, the Council's best-known recorder of the internal workings of the Commission on Education, quotes not one but two references to sex education found in the Declaration in his commentary on the document.

First, he cites the statement that both parents and teachers should "give due consideration to the difference of sex and the proper ends Divine Providence assigns to each sex in the family and in society. (n. 8)."[116]

It is obvious that the Council Fathers wished to emphasize the fact that God created us male and female and that any attempt to deny or ignore this fundamental fact must be rejected. It is equally obvious why this Conciliar reference is never cited in sex education texts which regard androgynous sex as the norm.

Secondly, Hurley cites the text reference to sexual education of youth (n.1.) and states: "This curt text stands in rather sharp contrast to the four paragraphs on sex education in Pius XI's encyclical on the *Christian Education of Youth, but in no way contradicts the encyclical, whose strictures on naturalism, 'so-called sex education,' early exposure to the occasions of sin and denial of original sin in the matter still stand valid*." (emphasis added).[117]

According to Hurley, the Council Fathers simply changed Pius XI's conditional "if" to the imperative mood, thus in effect saying, ". . . in this extremely delicate matter, all things considered, some private instruction is necessary. . ."[118]

As if anticipating the argument that the Council Fathers intended a radical departure from the norms of Pius XI, or that the mention of sexual education of youth signaled a mandate for programs of formal classroom instruction on delicate sexual matters in Catholic schools or CCD classes, Hurley points out that the members of the Commission on Education were acutely aware of the relationship of their work to Pius XI's encyclical. Indeed, the Council document has 13 footnoted references to Pius XI!

Readers may also keep in mind that the term "education," when used in Magisterial statements, which reflect the universal mind of the Church, *"refers first and foremost to education by parents,* informal and interpersonal," while in the American experience, "education" is virtually synonymous with formal classroom instruction.[119] In the matter of classroom sex education, this ambiguity of the definitions of education has permitted the American Church to steamroll over legitimate opposition to such instruction, all in the "spirit of aggiornamento" of Vatican II.

However, as the actual Council record of the Declaration on Education clearly demonstrates, the claim that Vatican II mandated formal classroom sex education is absolute fiction.

II. *Addendum on the New Sexual Catechetics*

A stinging indictment by Monsignor Eugene Kevane of the Catholic Theological Society of America's commissioned "Study," *Human Sexuality: New Directions in American Catholic Thought,* edited by Reverend Anthony Kosnik, was presented earlier in this book (pp. 70-71).

In this addendum, the Kosnik "Study," which was highly vaunted at the time of publication in 1977 as representing the New American Catholic Magisterium and an updated "sexual catechesis" for consenting Catholic adults, will be examined side by side with the USCC Department of Education Sex Education Guidelines, *Education in Human Sexuality for Christians,* which was published in 1981 by *The Wanderer* and likewise vaunted by the American church as the new "sexual catechesis" for Catholic children and youth. I will also compare the reaction of the U.S. hierarchy and the Vatican to both these documents and update readers as to the "future" of the Guidelines, which are being revised by the USCC-DOE Task Force on Human Sexuality for presentation to the United States Bishops.*

*A modified version of the Guidelines was approved as a USCC Department of Education document at the NCCB-USCC meeting in Washington, D.C. in November, 1991.

A Second Look at the Kosnik "Study"

According to Msgr. Eugene Kevane in his article, "Catechesis and Sexuality: What the Church Teaches," which was published in *Human Sexuality in Our Time,* "Catechetics is a field of study constituted in its material and formal aspects by the Articles of Faith: What they are in themselves, and how they are handed on effectively to others by teaching." (Kevane).[120]

In the moral order, Holy Mother Church, from the time of the Apostles, has communicated—to all men, of all nations, for all times—*the Way of Life,* which constitutes human actions that conform to the Law of God and lead to eternal salvation, and *the Way of Death,* which constitutes human actions that disregard God and His laws and lead to eternal damnation.

As Monsignor Kevane points out in his critique of the Kosnik "Study," not only does this "Study" seek to catechize the Faithful in the Way of Death, but it attempts to present the latter as an "updated" and "enlightened" Christianity. Having relegated "the once-cherished Way of Life to an intellectually and culturally outmoded past, and after a paradigm whispered originally in the Garden of Eden," the "Study" declares "the Way of Death, not only quite harmless, but also the Positive and mature Way of Creative Growth and Integration."[121]

Since *New Directions* is not a theological study at all, but rather "a philosophically based advocacy" in "atheistic existentialism,"[122] it is not surprising to find that the authors of the "Study" have replaced Sacred Scripture and Sacred Tradition and the Magisterium with a more "dynamic" and "relational" yardstick of human behavior. Modern man is henceforth "released" from the shackles of the natural law and moral absolutes, and "free" to seek his salvation through "creative growth toward integration, which is the basic finality of sexuality" and "the essence of Christian Life."[123]

According to the "Study," "...critical biblical scholarship finds it impossible on the basis of empirical data to approve or reject categorically any particular sexual act outside of its contextual circumstances and intention."[124] "As in the Old Testament, every statement in the New Testament regarding human sexuality is historically occasioned and conditioned."[125] "It must be said at this time that the behavioral sciences have not identified any sexual expression that can be empirically demonstrated to be, of itself, in a culture-free way, detrimental to full human existence."[126]

Seven values that are singled out as being conducive to creative growth and integration are: 1) self-liberating, 2) other-enriching, 3) honest, 4) faithful, 5) socially responsible and 6) life-serving and, finally 7) joyous.[127] "Where such qualities prevail, one can be reasonably sure that the sexual behavior that has brought them forth is wholesome and moral."[128]

Since we are assured by the "Study" that there are no acts which are intrinsically evil, all forms of sexual expression—including homosexuality, wife-swapping, masturbation, premarital sex, "swinging" and adultery, etc.—can be morally justified if they are "creative and integrative." There are no sexual perversions, only "sexual variants."[129]

Consider the matter of bestiality. According to the "Study," "The lack of adequate heterosexual opportunities in many isolated farm areas appears to be the major reason for the substitution of animals for sexual purposes. . .Where the individual prefers sexual relations with animals where heterosexual outlets are available, the condition is regarded as pathological."[130] Presumably having sex with a female bovine is not "pathological" if the individual would have *preferred* the farmer's daughter to the heifer, but circumstances were such that the former was not available for servicing and the latter was!

Here are other intellectual "gems" gleaned from the Kosnik "Study":

▪ On surrogate sex: "Since it is not at all clear that the use of surrogates are necessary, even to achieve the limited objective of erotic arousal and may be counterproductive. . .the use of stand-ins does not seem morally justified at this time."[131]

▪ Categorized masturbation: Listed by category, for "pastoral" purposes, are "Adolescent Masturbation; Compensatory Masturbation; Masturbation of Necessity; Pathological Masturbation; Medically Indicated Masturbation; and Hedonistic

Masturbation."[132]

- On marital variants: "...the complete control of conception has made extramarital activity practically safe and secure for men and women alike."[133]
- On "co-marital [threesome] sexual relations" and "mate-swapping [a foursome, or two couples]": "...while remaining open to further evidence from the empirical sciences, we would urge the greatest caution in all such matters, lest they compromise the growth and integration so necessary in all human activity."[134]
- On contraception: "...such an interpretation of the teaching of Vatican II (i.e., person, not act-oriented values) on marriage recognizes that there are times when the decision to use artificial methods of contraception is both morally responsible and justified."[135]

In better days, of course, anyone who would have tried to pawn off this patently dishonest intellectual drivel as having anything whatsoever to do with authentic Catholic thought would have summarily been ridden out of town on a rail amidst an avalanche of academic hoots and hollers. The idea that one needed only a 180-word esoteric footnote on the Baal cycle[136] to explain away Old Testament strictures against sexual fetishes and intercourse with animals would have sent clergy and laity alike rolling in the aisles with fits of uncontrollable laughter. But not so with the Kosnik "Study."

Prior to being formally "received" on October 15, 1976 by the Catholic Theological Society of America Board of Directors, which expressed its "gratitude to the committee for its theological effort" while at the same time hedging its bets by adding a disclaimer as to "the approval or disapproval by the Society or its Board" of the contents of the report,[137] there were two drafts of the "Study" which were farmed out to twenty-five theologians and other experts for their review and criticism. In June of 1976, at the Board's request, three additional theologians (unrelated to the previous consultations) reviewed the "Study" and made additional recommendations. Consultants to the "Study" included Fr. Gregory Baum, Fr. Charles E. Curran,

Richard A. McCormick and Cornelius J. Van der Poel, C.S.Sp. Finally, according to Chairman Kosnik, "the final product. . .was acceptable to every member of the committee,"[138] which was composed of three priests, one religious sister, and a layman, and was often referred to by its critics with delicious irreverence as "the Gang of Five".[139]

Sex Education and the Formation of the Young

Of particular import to this book was the "Study's" foursquare support of "the systematic programming of sex education, based on the findings of studies in the human sciences and presented through group instruction outside the family."[140] While recognizing such programs are a "new" development in Christianity, the "Study" claims that *formal sexuality instruction of children and adults and people with special needs such as the handicapped and retarded is needed in order to fight "the sexism of contemporary American society; to stem the tide of hedonism and instill wholesome attitudes and values regarding human sexuality"*[141] *and "to supplement and/or correct" home formation.*[142]

"Sex education must grow out of life experiences," and should prepare every human being for an experience of sexuality that fosters "creative growth toward integration, within the framework of a chosen lifestyle,"[143] the "Study" concludes.

Background of the USCC "Guidelines"

Before drawing comparisons between the Kosnik "Study" directed at the sexualization of Catholic adults—clergy, religious, and laity—and the USCC Sex Education "Guidelines," *Education in Human Sexuality for Christians,* directed at the sexualization of Catholic children and youth, some background on the members of the National Committee who drafted the "Guidelines" will, I think, prove both interesting and instructive.

Chairman for the USCC/DOE Sex Education Task Force was Daniel Dolesh, S.T.D., a veteran of a number of family life and religious education committees of the USCC and the NCCB from 1977 to 1981. During this period, Dolesh acquired membership in several anti-life organizations including AASEC(T), the National Forum for Sex Education and the Metropolitan Sex Education Coalition. These associations assured the anti-life triad of continued access to the Catholic educational network, opened a decade earlier by Monsignor James McHugh.[144] Dolesh, who holds a Doctorate in Sacred Theology from Catholic University, is a member of the Catholic Theological Society of America. As a primary architect of the USCC "Guidelines," Dolesh authorized much of that text, including the foreword, introduction and Chapter 4, "Sex Education in the Context of Formal Instruction and the School."

Other task force members included Cornelius Van der Poel, C.S.Sp., a consultant to the Kosnik "Study" and author of Chapter 3 of the "Guidelines"—"The Church Environment and Education for Human Sexuality"—and Dr. David Thomas, a well-known dissenter from *Humanae Vitae* who constructed Chapter 1, "Christian Foundation for Education in Human Sexuality" and Chapter 2, "The Christian Home and Education for Sexuality."

Two auxiliary bishops, now archbishops, sat on the USCC Sex Education Task Force—Daniel E. Pilarczyk, D.D., Ph.D., S.T.D., a member of the NCCB Committee on Education, and Francis J. Stafford, Chairman of the NCCB/USCC National Commission on Marriage and Family Life.

The remaining 23-member task force was composed of an assortment of "helping professionals," family life directors, and sex educators, including Nancy Hennessy Cooney, author of the notorious *Sex, Sexuality and You,*[145] and Richard Reichert, author of *Self-Awareness Through Group Dynamics.*

It should be noted, at this point, that both Kosnik and Dolesh chaired "committees" which were structured deliberately to exclude, from the beginning, any serious opposition to the "new directions" the respective "studies" would take. This point, however, does make for an interesting observation, that is, both the Kosnik "Study" and the USCC Sex Education "Guidelines" contain, as appendices to the body of their reports, The Declaration on Certain Questions Concerning Sexual Ethics promulgated by the Sacred Congregation for the Doctrine of the Faith on December 29, 1975.

According to Dolesh, the Vatican document was added as a last-minute addition to the final draft of the "Guidelines" by *non-committee* members who felt that "even though the Guidelines are pedagogical in intent, they needed a fuller exposition of Catholic moral teaching."[146] A second addition was a "footnote" on Original Sin.[147]

Kosnik, on the other hand, does not indicate why the Vatican Declaration appears as an appendix in the CTSA-commissioned and financed "Study," although one would suspect it might have also been a last-ditch effort by a CTSA non-committee member who felt compelled to give some semblance of respectability to an otherwise intellectually sterile and morally bankrupt document.

Both Kosnik and Dolesh express their gratitude to the 1976 (liberal "Catholic") Call to Action Conference, which highlighted the "need" for the CTSA "Study"[148] and which "mandated" classroom sex education.[149]

In the introduction to the "Guidelines," Dolesh presents arguments for mandated classroom sex education which are virtually identical to those given in the Kosnik "Study," that is, alarming statistics on teenage pregnancies, the prevalence of prostitution, abortion and pornography in our culture and "the debasing and dehumanizing values often propagated by the media."[150]

Despite the fact that there is nothing "Catholic" about the "Guidelines," Dolesh, like Kosnik, insists that "These guidelines are meant to support the teachings of the Church on sexuality and sexual morality. Specifically, the teaching contained in. . .*The Declaration of Sexual Ethics*. . .is assumed throughout." "Nevertheless," he continues, "the work is not an exercise in ethics or moral theology," but "pedagogical" in intent.[151]

Like Kosnik, Dolesh makes a perfunctory nod to God in the *Foreword,* mentioning the traditional role models of Jesus, Mary, the Saints, and "the importance of an interior life of prayer" and "ascetical discipline"–and then he is off and running, in "New Directions."[152]

The Measure of All Things— "The New Creation"

Whereas for Kosnik and company, the principal measure of the morality of an act is whether it contributes to or detracts from "creative growth toward integration,"[153] for Dolesh and company, the measure is "the paradigm or general concept of the 'New Creation,' "[154] which forms the foundation for the "seven theologically-based principles"[155] upon which the Guidelines are based. "The goal of Christian catechesis in sexuality," the Guidelines state, is "to communicate effectively that the person is unique, good, loved and loving, sexual, responsible, committed, and if married, exclusively faithful and procreative."[156]

After redefining the virtue of chastity to mean ". . .the living out of one's sexual life in a free and creative, yet balanced and Christian way," the Guidelines state that "This entire book could be called 'education in chastity,' if the term were correctly understood."[157]

This habit of radicalizing traditional terminology, so rampant in the Kosnik Study, likewise permeates the entire text of the USCC's Guidelines.

Drinking from the Same Poisoned Well

In any comparison of the Kosnik Study with the Dolesh Guidelines, one would be inclined to favor the former over the latter, the reason being quite simple: For whereas in Kosnik, the authors attempt to deceive their readership as to the truths of Catholic teachings on sexual morality, in Dolesh, there is not even the virtue of admitting that such truths exist. Whereas Kosnik abuses Scripture, skims the empirical sciences, and distorts the Magisterium and the existence of moral absolutes in an attempt to challenge the authenticity of Church teachings on the Natural Law, the USCC Guidelines are devoid of even a single reference to either Natural Law or to the existence of moral absolutes.

At this point, the obvious question is, if the Guidelines make no reference to these fundamental theological concepts, upon what theological truths are the Guidelines based? The answer is, "None," for like with Kosnik, the issue here is not theology at all, but a philosophical exercise, designed—in the words of Monsignor Kevane—"to introduce existentialist phenomenology into the *Doctrina Sacra* of the Catholic Church."[158] More simply put, the main architects of the USCC Guidelines, that is, Dolesh, van der Poel and Thomas, were drinking from the same poisoned well as Kosnik and his companions.

Sex in the Land of Oz

(Note: In my 1981 *Critique of the "Guidelines,"* I chose to evaluate the text on a chapter-by-chapter basis, beginning with an exposition of its "Christian Foundations," theological principles and goals and objectives, concluding with a summary of overall objections to the Guidelines.[159] The following comparative analysis of the Kosnik Study and the USCC Guidelines should bring these stated objections into even sharper focus, while at the same time shed additional light on the nature of the new sexual catechesis which has been infecting Catholic education for more than two decades.)

In a sense, reading the Kosnik Study and the USCC Guidelines is like taking a trip with Dorothy to the Land of Oz or falling down the rabbit hole with Alice in Wonderland; they emit a sense of unreality. One somehow gets the feeling that he is being suffocated by a torrential gush of "creative," "free," "interpersonal," "life-enriching," "mature," "responsible," "relational," "dynamic" sex and feels the need to reach out for sharp relief and the healthy catharsis of the lightly suggestive bawdy of Shakespeare or Chaucer.[160]

It appears that the authors of these two Studies have created a sexual fantasyland where the dark side of human sexuality—that is, the daimonic[161] nature of the sexual function—has been summarily wished away and all that the Christian need to do is to "revel in God's creation."[162]

How else can one explain Dolesh's categorization of "...rape, incest, and sexual abuse of children" as merely "inappropriate expressions of sexuality"?[163]

How else can we explain the absence in both the Kosnik Study and the Guidelines to any reference with regard to the existence of "the latency period," that is, "the period or stage...which coincides more or less with middle childhood..." during which time the child exhibits "an apparent quiescence or control of sexual drives,"[164] thus releasing his energies for Christian character development and academic pursuits, and more importantly, opening up the window of his soul to the showering of God's graces, which the Author of Nature sends little children in their innocence.

Seeing Children as "Sexual Beings"

Like his mentor, Dr. Herbert Otto, author of *The New Sex Education,* which was reviewed earlier in this book, Dolesh considers the development of the sexual person to be "clearly a life-long endeavor, encompassing the multiple dimensions of human existence."[165] Children must be given "all the biological and scientific information regarding human sexuality,"[166] Dolesh states. "Knowledge, in itself, is not harmful," he says; therefore, "every major facet of knowledge and values in relation to sexuality should be covered at some point in developing the curriculum."[167]

Thus, under "Goals and Objectives for Formal Instruction—Ages 15-18" (Chapter 4 of "Formal Instruction and the School"), we read, "The learner will...(3) know about all major aberrations of sexual development and expression and venereal disease."[168] Again, the student will "learn how to deal with psycho-sexual changes, such as menstruation, wet dreams, sexual impulses, without guilt";[169] the learner will *"understand psycho-sexual deviations, such as homosexuality, transvestism, pedophilia, incest, etc..."*[170] (emphasis added); the learner will "understand the means of and reasons for family-planning, both natural and artificial...";[171] the learner will be "introduced to scientific data regarding all methods of family-planning and the

Church's teaching on the subject";[172] the learner will "understand the possible harmful effects of sexual stereotyping. . .";[173] the learner will "explore in a Christian context some of the causes, effects and myths about masturbation";[174] the learner will "understand and evaluate the biological and psycho-sexual processes of different sexual lifestyles, commitments or noncommitments and evaluate them accordingly";[175] the learner will "understand the Church's tradition of regarding Mary as a model for responsible sexual development";[176] the learner will "understand the interrelationship of physical with psycho-sexual growth and events (e.g. attraction/seduction, physical and emotional responses in intercourse, menopause, effect of drugs, etc.)";[177] the learner will "appreciate Christ as a role model—a being sexual and relating to others, although in a way which does not involve genital activities."[178]

The message of the Guidelines is the same as that of the Kosnik Study, which Reverend Robert Bradley described thusly: ". . .the real meaning in the murk of this Study [Kosnik] is not that 'sex is for Christ' but that 'Christ is for sex.' And this inversion—this blasphemous perversion—is its real summary; it's a 'sign of the times.' "[179]

The Sexual Catechist as a Degenerative Influence

From these examples of the kind of knowledge to be acquired from Catholic school curricula and programs based on the USCC Guidelines, one realizes that *it is both the sexual catechesis and the sexual catechist that now threatens Catholic children and youth,* and that this danger is of "an entirely new dimension and kind."[180]

As Catholic Professor Germain Grisez has observed, "While posing as 'experts' in human sexuality, it has been my observation that most 'sexologists' haven't the foggiest notion of what authentic sexual behavior is all about. Rather, they appear to live for and in a world of 'pseudosex'—directed almost exclusively at 'genital arousal,' whether short [of] or to orgasm. . .for mere amusement, pleasure, distraction or release of tension."[181]

Or, as Fr. Henry Sattler, Ph.D. puts it in his book *Sex Is Alive and Well and Flourishing Among Christians,* "When their jaded appetite recovers, the endless pursuit of the cosmic orgasm resumes, with frantic efforts to add kicks by introducing ever-new varieties of technique, pattern, orifice, and/or partner."[182]

These two quotations explain in part why the architects of the USCC Guidelines insist that Catholic children need to receive K through 12 classroom instruction in sex, not only on the intimate details of heterosexual intercourse but on homosexual intercourse and the full range of sexual perversions as well, while at the same time, they deliberately withhold from these children the doctrinal teachings of the Church on matters of sexual morality and knowledge of those moral pathways which constitute part of the Catholic way of life.

Under the guise of education, the advocates of the new sexual catechesis conspire toward the early seduction of the child. Having been robbed of the natural protection to his tender psyche normally accorded to children during the latency period, the child is systematically exposed to a barrage of sexual stimuli and images. These images are impressed into the memory and imagination of the child. They can return—both voluntarily and involuntarily—to stimulate the child's libido. The child finds it more and more difficult, it not impossible, to remain chaste and to practice the virtues.[183] Base sexual instincts are released, and a pattern of sexual aggressiveness emerges. Because of the nature of sexual knowing, which—unlike other types of learning, such as math or history—involves the passions, damage done to the child by this type of explicit sex education is often irreparable. (Additional information on the harmful consequences associated with destruction of the latency period will be provided in the next chapter on sex education as a form of psycho-therapy.) In retrospect, as French writer Claude Tresmontant implies in his treatise on bad catechesis, it might be more merciful simply to drop a bomb on the children, since the latter results in mere physical destruction or physical death, whereas the former (i.e., bad catechetics) results in "interior and spiritual destruction" and annihilation.[184]

As Tresmontant states, "One can massacre children by a bombardment, but one can also slowly depress them, demean them, degrade them, turn them from their finality, and that under the influence of the ambivalent milieu, of the teaching one gives them, of the vision of the world one proposes to them. Along these lines one can degenerate children."[185]

Is it any wonder that parents, Catholic and non-Catholic, instinctively aroused to the dangers posed by the new sexual catechesis and the new sexual catechists, have sought to protect their children from the corruptive influences of both? Catholic parents especially, still inspired—some 30 years later—by the ringing exhortation to action against sex education of Pius XII, have fought together "without human timidity or respect, to stop and curtail these movements under whatever name or under whatever patronage they conceal themselves or are patronized."[186]

And what have the American bishops or the Vatican contributed to this struggle? For an illustrative answer to this question, let us once again return to the comparative analysis between the Kosnik Study and the USCC Guidelines and examine the reaction of the National Conference of Catholic Bishops and the Vatican to both documents.

The Holy See and NCCB Condemn the Kosnik Study

To its credit, the Committee on Doctrine of the National Conference of Catholic Bishops (NCCB) in its "Statement Concerning Human Sexuality"[187] issued on November 15, 1977, officially condemned the Kosnik Study, as did other individual bishops and dioceses.

Five months earlier, on July 13, 1977, the Sacred Congregation for the Doctrine of the Faith, acting with the approval of the Holy See, had already openly condemned the Kosnik Study and ordered Paulist Press to cease publication and distribution of *Human Sexuality: New Directions in American Catholic Thought.*[188]

While the much-publicized Study received mixed reviews in the secular press,[189] published scholarly reaction, including collective criticisms by other members of the Catholic Theological

Society of America (CTSA), including William May, Fr. William Smith and Fr. Henry Sattler, were overwhelmingly against the Kosnik Study.[190]

USCC Guidelines Remain in Circulation

In contrast to the prompt ecclesiastical retribution and the criticism by fellow CTSA members heaped upon the heads of the authors of *Human Sexuality: New Directions in American Catholic Thought,* the USCC Guidelines, upon release in the summer of 1981, were met with great enthusiasm by USCC officials and with reactions ranging from ecstasy to mild indifference from the American bishops as a whole. It is a matter of public record that neither the NCCB nor any individual bishop or diocese has issued a critical evaluation or written condemnation of the Guidelines, i.e., *Education in Human Sexuality for Christians.* Nor did the NCCB order that the document—which had never been presented to the entire NCCB membership for examination or vote—be removed from circulation or that distribution be halted by the USCC Office of Publications. Instead, the Administrative Committee of the NCCB said the guidelines could be circulated as a Department of Education document.

Official USCC press statements announcing the release of and virtues of the Guidelines were carried in almost every diocesan paper and national Catholic weekly in the United States. Actually, for almost a year prior to the official release of the Guidelines, the National Committee for Human Sexuality Education was already softening up the Catholic press for the uncritical acceptance and promotion of the Guidelines by committee chairman Dolesh, who in 1980 had embarked on a national roadshow to various Catholic dioceses and college campuses to promote himself as a "sexpert" and the Guidelines as "an officially approved resource to give solid direction in the area of sex education."[191]

Among the members of the hierarchy who came to the defense of the Guidelines was Auxiliary Bishop Daniel Pilarczyk, chairman of the USCC Education Committee and a member of the Task Force which had drawn up the Guidelines.

In an interview with *Our Sunday Visitor,* Bishop Pilarczyk cited Vatican II's *Declaration on Christian Education* as being the source of the mandate for "prudent sexual education" in the context of "formal schooling."[192] However, as is documented in Addendum I of this book (pp. 78-79), Bishop Pilarczyk's statement on Vatican II is not based on fact.

Guidelines Please Homosexual Groups

On August 14, 1981, shortly after the Guidelines were released, the *National Catholic Reporter* ran a lengthy article by Father Robert Nugent entitled "Sex Education Guidelines: New Gay Insights." According to Nugent, a leader of the homosexual movement in the U.S., "The fact that the 'Guidelines' are officially sanctioned will help many educators introduce and develop the topic of homosexuality with more confidence and less risk than before."[193] After citing the Guidelines' emphasis on relational sex and its "hesitant openness" to "alternative lifestyles," Nugent praised those goals enunciated in the text of the document which promote "a sense of tolerance" for diversity in "different modes of expressing human love."[194]

Curiously, in his introduction, Nugent remarks that, "To date, there has been little reaction from the Catholic right, but we can probably expect to hear much more from Catholics United for the Faith and *The Wanderer* crowd whose anticipated criticisms seem to have had something to do with the long delay in the first place."[195] And he was right!

Defenders of the Faith Blast the Guidelines

Throughout the late summer and fall of 1981, the Guidelines suffered a number of serious but not fatal setbacks.

Following the serialization of this author's lengthy critique of the Guidelines in *The Wanderer,* Catholics United for the Faith and a number of other orthodox lay organizations issued position papers and statements condemning the document.

The Fellowship of Catholic Scholars, an orthodox association composed of lay, religious and clerical members, petitioned the

NCCB and every bishop in the country to "reexamine" the Guidelines, which it described as being "timid," "harmful" and "inadequate."[196]

In the end, these groups achieved a partial, although somewhat illusory victory, based not so much on the validity of their criticisms as on a violation of ecclesiastical etiquette. As was the case with *The Many Faces of AIDS,* the architects of the Guidelines had hoped to present the American bishops with a *fait accompli* by promoting the document as "an officially approved resource"[197] and publishing and distributing copies of the Guidelines *without* prior approval by the NCCB. The strategy proved partially successful because while the Guidelines were eventually sent back to the USCC/DOE for revision, copies of the original, unapproved document have been advertised and promoted in every USCC publication catalogue to date.

The continuing influence of the Guidelines can be seen in the noxious William C. Brown sex education program series, *New Creation,* designed for children in grades 1-8. When the series underwent revisions in the late 1980's, the publishers insisted that the revised edition would continue to be "developed around the seven principles embodied in USCC's *Education in Human Sexuality for Christians Guidelines.*"[198] This assurance explains in part why the Most Reverend Stanislaus J. Brzana, Bishop of Ogdensburg, found the revised text of the "New Creation" to be seriously flawed but still worthy of sanction. He states, "There seems to be too much emphasis on certain things, like accurate information about sex, and not on other things, like the traditional means proposed by the Church to fight temptation and preserve purity."[199]

New USCC Task Force to Revise Current Guidelines

In the intervening years from the time of publication in 1981 to 1989, the process of revising the Guidelines proceeded at a snail's pace. According to a recent communication on the status of the Guidelines from Bishop William C. Newman, the new chairman of the task force on the revision of the Guidelines on human sexuality, to the U.S. Coalition for Life—under whose auspices this writer produced the 1981 *Critique*—there will probably be some modifications in both the content and methodology of the program, since only two of the original 1981 committee members were retained by the Task Force.

The number of Task Force members has been reduced from twenty-three to fifteen. There are five Episcopal members. The ultimate goal of the present Task Force, according to Bishop Newman, is to provide a proposed draft of the revised Guidelines for adoption by the NCCB.

Rome Silent on the Guidelines

In sharp contrast to its swift action taken against the Kosnik Study, the Vatican to date has never issued any public statement on the USCC Guidelines, perhaps because the Holy See mistakenly understood that the Guidelines would be removed from circulation while undergoing revision.

This obviously was not the case. In any event, however, should Rome decide to take action against the Guidelines, it is most *unlikely* that she would do so prior to the NCCB review of the revised text.

Realistically, too, the Guidelines have been in circulation for more than eight years. The damage to countless Catholic school children resulting from exposure to the Guidelines, or to programs based on the Guidelines, has already been done and cannot be undone, no matter what the bishops or the Holy See do or say about the Guidelines in the future.* Nor have children been its only victims, as the following postscript on Daniel Dolesh illustrates.

*The revised draft was approved as an NCCB-USCC departmental document in November, 1991 at the bishops' annual meeting in Washington, D.C. To date there has been no publicly voiced objection to the document from Vatican sources.

Postscript on Daniel Dolesh

Although I had compiled an extensive dossier on Dolesh for the U.S. Coalition for Life and was familiar with his anti-life associations prior to my work on the USCC Guidelines, it was not until I had actually confronted the man, face to face, that I truly came to understand the meaning of the assertion that the sexual catechist is both victim and victimizer.

The meeting took place on September 27, 1980, at St. Vincent's College in the Diocese of Greensburg, Pennsylvania, under decidedly unpleasant circumstances. Attempts by local pro-life organizations to have Dolesh removed as the keynote speaker for a Religious Education Congress had failed. The Diocesan Office of Education was extremely upset—not with Dolesh, of course, but with the pro-lifers who had attempted to make an issue out of Dolesh's membership in pro-abortion groups.

Following his morning address to the Congress on "Changing Families in a Changing World," Dolesh gave a series of workshops on human sexuality for a predominantly female audience of Catholic educators and religious. I attended Workshop No. 1.

The air was filled with a sense of anticipation as Dolesh began his opening remarks, which included a titillating reference to the female clitoris. I interpreted the remark to be a desensitizing technique, and in a subsequent article entitled "Sexology and the USCC,"[200] which appeared in *The Wanderer* on June 4, 1981, I stated as much.

Dolesh, in a letter to the editor[201] dated June 10, 1981, with a carbon to attorney Dennis Ahearn, challenged my interpretation of the incident by explaining that he had used the term "clitoris" in a description of a research project conducted by the Carnegie Foundation in Cleveland and that it was not used as a "desensitizing technique." Right, Dan! After all, what could be more germane to a religious conference dedicated to the family than research related to the erectile tissue of the female reproductive organ!

Responding to my second charge that he used the lecture to push Herbert Otto's *The New Sex Education*,[202] Dolesh responded that he only recommended the book when a member of the audience asked him where she could find information on *The New Sex Education.* Again he insisted that my interpretation of the incident was a "complete fabrication," and that my continued interruption of his presentation was resented by the audience. The latter unfortunately was true, but not the former.

I did not bring up the subject of *The New Sex Education,* Dolesh did. Further, it was clear that Dolesh did not anticipate that anyone in the audience would know what the book, *The New Sex Education,* was all about when he suggested Otto's text as a possible resource.

Until that time I had intended merely to play the role of recorder. But when I observed my colleagues dutifully jotting down the name of this anti-life book, I broke the silence, raised my hand, held up a copy of the Otto book, and without waiting to be recognized, asked Dolesh to explain why he had just recommended a text that was pro-abortion, pro-homosexual, pro-pedophilia, etc.? Dolesh was visibly shaken, but managed to blurt out something about "pedagogical intent" and continued on with his lecture. The audience, sensing the confrontational nature of the question, initially appeared bewildered, then annoyed at the intervention. But Dolesh never did give a specific answer to my question. How could he—without revealing the truth about the nature of *The New Sex Education* catechesis, and in the process without revealing a great deal about his own personal transformation from a religious educator to a sexual catechist?

The extent of that transformation was revealed almost eight months later, when I recognized Dolesh's name and that of a Sister Mariella Frye* (who had played an important role in the development of the American Church's National Catechetical Directory, NCD, which mandated formal classroom instruction on Human Sexuality—see above, p. 73) on a brochure from American University that advertised a series of Summer Institutes on Sex Education and Sex Therapy.

*Sr. Mariella Frye was a spokeswoman and staff consultant for the U.S. Catholic Bishops on their Pastoral Letter on Women.

Both Dolesh and Frye were listed as U.S. interdisciplinary representatives serving on the governing board of the U.S. International Council, which was co-sponsoring the symposia with the university. Dolesh was identified as "Dean, Continuing Education, Biscayne College, Miami"; whereas, Frye was listed as a representative of the U.S. Catholic Conference.

At the May 21-24 Sex Education Institute held at Martha's Vineyard, a number of prominent anti-life celebrities made their appearances, including abortionist Kenneth Edelin (alias "The Boston Strangler"), who delivered a talk on "Controversies in Obstetrics and Gynecology" (i.e., the problem of live babies born of late abortions); homosexual advocate Alan Bell, whose topics included "heterosexual development in children and homosexual lifestyles"; and Patricia Schiller, founder of AASEC(T).

Two months later, another series of Institutes was held on Sex Education—*Finding Innovative Pathways and Advanced Sex Therapy Skills.* Listed among the faculty for these presentations were Dan Dolesh, S.T.D., Celam Bell, Albert Ellis and Patricia Schiller.

After the controversy over the USCC Guidelines peaked in the Fall of 1981, I lost track of Dolesh's activities, although I learned that he had received a federal grant of $79,842 under Title X of the Public Health Service Act (Family Planning Services and Population Research) for continuing the work of something called the National Committee on Values and Human Sexuality (not to be confused with the USCC National Committee on Human Sexuality Education). The contractual grant period went from March, 1981 (while Dolesh was still employed by the USCC as chairman of the Guidelines Task Force) to August of 1983.[203] At the time, I could obtain no address or phone listing for the NCVHS in the greater Washington, D.C. area nor obtain any data on the Dolesh grant in detail.

However, in February of 1986, I reviewed in the USCL mailbag an issue of *The Plain Dealer* magazine of February 6, 1986, featuring an article by Diane Carmen entitled, "The Love Doctors—Sex Therapy in Cleveland."

According to Carmen, the sex therapy business in Cleveland

was "booming" thanks to the "outrageous success" of people like Dr. Ruth Westheimer, talk show host of "Good Sex."[204] Among those sex therapists interviewed by Carmen were Sherelynn Lehman, whom the reporter described as "Jewish, divorced and has two children" and as "Cleveland's Version of Dr. Ruth,"[205] plus, her partner, Daniel J. Dolesh, described as "Catholic, divorced and has five children."[206]

Carmen noted that both Lehman and Dolesh were AASEC(T) accredited sex therapists[207] and that both had appeared on "Good Sex" with Dr. Ruth during a national tour to promote their book, *Love Me, Love Me Not—How to Survive Infidelity.*[208] She and Dolesh were a weekly feature on a radio call-in show called "Sexline," said Carmen, "But the show was discontinued last fall. . ."[209] On the subject of childhood influences in human sexuality, Lehman said, "Many adults feel tremendous guilt over enjoying sex," and that "there are a lot of difficulties when people are brought up with certain religions that prescribe rigid guidelines and then nature takes its course. When the only message to a girl or boy is don't, that doesn't teach much about responsible sexual behavior."[210]

According to Carmen, Lehman and Dolesh have worked so closely over the past six years that they complement each other almost as if they were married. (They are not.)[211]

In listing his credentials, *The Plain Dealer* reporter cites Dolesh's former association with the U.S. Catholic Conference. "He helped in the development of guidelines for sex education programs in Catholic schools across the country," she says.[212]

If anyone can come up with a more convincing argument than that as to why the American bishops should not grant an immediate reprieve to Catholic children on the matter of sex education and unceremoniously dump Dolesh's Guidelines into the nearest USCC circular file, I would like to hear it!

Chapter 6
The Production of Perverts

Introduction

Thus far in our examination of the new sexual catechetics, our attention has been centered on the nature and curriculum content of sex education programs. But there is another aspect of the deadly phenomenon which needs to be examined more closely—specifically, the reason for and the nature of the pedagogical approaches used by the sex "educator" or sexual "catechist" to reconstruct the child's basic attitudes related to human sexuality and to communicate new patterns of sexual thought and behavior.

Sex Education as Reconstructive Psychotherapy

Much of the material used in this chapter is taken from "Education in Sex," an original contribution to *The Encyclopedia of Sexual Behavior,* edited by Ellis and Abarbanel.[213]

The authors of the essay are *Robert A. Harper, Ph.D.*, past-president of the American Academy of Psychotherapists, past-president of the American Association of Marriage Counselors and a member of the Advisory Committee of the American Association of Sex Educators, Counselors and Therapists, or AASEC(T); and his wife, *Frances R. Harper, Ed.D.*, of the Department of Guidance, Arlington, Virginia public schools.[214] The frankness of the Harper presentation on "new directions" in sex education affords one of the clearest views to date into the mind of the sex educator.

Sex Education as a Form of Sexual Conditioning

The Harper essay begins with a differential explanation of three terms employed throughout, namely,

- *Sexual conditioning,* which is defined as "all acquisitions (by whatever methods) of covert or overt patterns of sexual behavior."[215]
- *Sex education,* defined as "an organized program designed to instruct the individual regarding sex attitudes or actions," which is to be considered "a special, organized form of sexual conditioning."[216]
- *Sex therapy,* which is defined as a "reconstructive learning process" and a "special type of sex education, quite in contrast to the information-dispensing programs generally developed. . . Designed to make possible the changing of basic attitudes, the reconstruction of the individual's fundamental beliefs, feelings and actions."[217]

The Goal of Sex Education

According to the Harpers, "So long as discussions on the goals of sex education move at a high level of abstraction, peace reigns among parents, educators, and other concerned citizens." "All will agree," they continue, "that a goal of sex education is the instilling of "wholesome attitudes toward sex," and that "children should be led to understand the spiritual as well as the gross biological functions of sex."[218] But problems arise, the authors suggest, when one gets down to the nitty-gritty of what is meant by "wholesome" in sex attitudes and "spirituality" in sex functioning.[219]

People are afraid to adopt new "rational and realistic goals" in sex education, the Harpers state, because they are resistant to "the change of customs, especially those that are morally and religiously sanctified."[220] Once this hurdle is overcome, "parents and other adults," armed with "data from psychological, psychiatric, biological, and ethnological studies," will be "eager to guide their children toward full appreciation of sex and the wise use of it in and out of marriage."[221] This in turn will lead to a greater "sexual freedom and appreciation" for young people and adults, and in turn will "release warmth and affection in other types of interpersonal relations,"[222] they state.

The Harpers applaud the Swedish program of compulsory sex education, which is not diluted and concealed as "family-life education,"[223] and which "probably takes the least moralistic attitude toward pre-marital sex relations of any of the Euro-American civilizations."[224]

They also praise the "thoughtful and spirited discussion and investigatory efforts" of *The Report of the Committee on Homosexual Offenses and Prostitution,* chaired by Sir John Wolfenden, directed at rescinding English statutes related to sodomy, gross indecency and prostitution.[225]

Keeping in mind that the Harper essay was written in the early 1960's, the authors note that "sex education in the United States today has little separate existence" because it has been "absorbed and largely emasculated by family-life education."[226] This is their way of describing the "latency period" of the sex education movement detailed earlier in this book.

Further, "No support is forthcoming. . . for educators to examine existing cultural confessions, hypocrisies, prejudices, and myths about the role of sex in human relationships—let alone communicate the fruits of such examinations to their students."[227]

The Harpers lament the "pedantic treatment of the anatomical and physiological aspects of sex," "the rehash of the conventional morality" and the eagerness to move to "safer topics" which typify the standard fare of American sex education curriculums.[228]

The problems are not limited to educational institutions, however, because "there would be much destructive work to be undone before constructive work could in most instances begin," since "by the time the average child reaches the *first* grade of school, many of his basic attitudes toward sex have been negatively conditioned," hence the need for early childhood intervention.[229]

The Need for Classroom Sex Therapy

Because of previous negative home conditioning, the Harpers state, "there is not much hope of reaching children in a basic attitudinal way with any kind of sex education program other than one that is essentially *reconstructive psychotherapy.*" The basis of this argument is that "By the time many children reach school age, anxiety has usurped emotional security, deep-seated guilt and hostility have displaced love, and sex attitudes have become tenacious, perverted dynamisms that cannot be altered by casual superficial sex education that is linked with 'other interesting things to be learned about life.' "[230]

The main culprits in this matter, according to the authors, are parents who communicate their "anti-sexual attitudes" to their children. "Parents, and other associates," the Harpers state, fill young children with "fear, guilt, anxiety and shame regarding sex/love feelings," and deliver them "in a closely sealed and difficult-to-sexually-re-educate form at the school's door."[231]

"Correcting" Home Influences Related to Sex

The Harpers do not favor an integrated approach to sex education and state that it is not advisable "to weave in sex information and attitude formation with other aspects of life." The latter approach is not realistic, according to the Harpers, because it does not take into consideration the fact that, by the time the child enters school, he has already acquired "a set of fundamental sex attitudes" which are "reflective of a confused culture (most particularly confused on sex/love feelings)" and therefore the child is "bound to need some special remedial work."[232]

The "perverted dynamism" referred to by the Harpers earlier, of course, means in plain language that, by the time the young child reaches elementary school, he already mentally links sex with marriage, families and babies. This "perversion" can only be overcome by drastic measures—halfway measures will not do it, the Harpers protest.

Although the article does not mention *specific* "remedial techniques" which are used on children, adolescents or adults for the purpose of reconstructing their attitudes and beliefs related to human sexuality, the authors do point out that "group psychotherapy" has been particularly effective because "it encourages people with essentially the same sex/love difficulties to gain encouragement and support. . ."[233]

The Harpers note, however, that therapy groups connected with institutions and public-supported programs tend to be "contaminated" by "conventional" sex attitudes. Alas, they contend, "Contamination by the current mores is, of course, never completely overcome in the most advantageous of therapeutic circumstances."[234]

Sexual Attitudinal Restructuring (SAR) of Educators

Obviously the sex "educator" cannot effectively "restructure" his students' attitudes or values on human sexuality without having undergone the reassessment procedure himself.

Therefore, according to the Harpers, the "leaders of sexual therapy groups" must first work out their "interpersonal problems in psychotherapy" before they can put themselves in "an emotional position to provide freedom and safety for members of his group" (sic) and begin "to engage in the painful process of working through their attitudinal distortions."[235] "This, along with the special needs for remedial work in sexual beliefs and practices in the average product of our confused society, is another reason why we must think in terms of sex therapy and not merely sex education,"[236] the authors state.

Writing as they were in the early to mid-60's, the Harpers bemoaned the fact that sex therapy was, at that time, "a luxury" for the few. "Thus far, at least, we have developed no more effective, or less expensive way to reconstruct sexual attitudes and practices to a point where the average individual can function in a happy, loving, outgoing manner," they stated. "And even *if* money or popular support were suddenly available, there are no specific centers for the training of sex therapists and educators."[237]

"Sooner or later, if we are to make advancement as a civilization, we shall need to turn a great deal of our attention to a therapeutic form of sex education,"[238] the Harpers concluded.

The type of sex education programs envisioned by the Harpers came to fruition, as we know, with the creation of SIECUS in 1964 and AASEC(T) in 1967. In fact, most if not all of the concepts put forth by Dr. Harper and his wife have been fully incorporated into both the ideology and the methodology of contemporary sex education and training programs.

In addition to his AASEC(T) associations, Dr. Robert Harper also sits on the Boards of the Albert Ellis Institute for Advanced Study in Rational Psychotherapy as well as the Institute for Rational Living, founded on the principles of Ellisonian sex.[239]

The fact that Dr. Harper is on record as supporting *compulsory* population control, that is, taking away "the right to reproduce," without "the individual's approval or consent,"[240] may account for his apparent lack of concern regarding the personal, religious, civil and constitutional implications inherent in the transformation of the classroom into a laboratory, students into patients and teachers into therapists—all without the individuals' or parents' consent.

A Perfect Recipe for Producing Polymorphous Perverts

The arguments put forth by the Harpers to justify the introduction of remedial and reconstructive sexual psychotherapy into the classroom are extremely valuable to anyone seeking to understand why it is that the new catechetics offer an almost perfect recipe for producing polymorphous perverts.

Few persons have spoken as eloquently on this subject as Dr. Melvin Anchell, M.D., A.S.P.P., the author of *Killers of Children: A Psychoanalytic Look at Sex Education*[241] and an internationally known physician and psychiatrist specializing in the treatment of children and adults who have been damaged by sex education and pornography.

According to Dr. Anchell, sex education is anathema to

1) normal psychosexual development in young people, 2) fundamental psychological principles regarding human sexuality and 3) the advancement of civilization, which depends on "the curtailment of raw sexual and aggressive energies."[242]

The harm done to young children and adolescents by the new sexual catechesis can be described in both general and personalized terms.

In general, sex education courses "act to desensitize students to the intimate nature of sexual relationships" by relegating sex "to an automatic bodily function in the same category as eating, breathing, and sleeping,"[243] Anchell states.

According to these new sex education courses, he continues, the achievement of orgasm "by any means" is a primary measure of sexual health.[244] Hence sex courses condone and promote masturbation and "various techniques for achieving orgasm through self-excitement."[245] "Mature emotional growth, character development and a sense of responsibility for one's acts are retarded by repeated masturbatory acts and casual carnal relationships."[246]

Young women, perceived by their sexual partners as mere receptacles for seminal emission, acquire the "attitudes of prostitutes" and forswear any knowledge of the "ultimate affectionate and monogamous nature of human sexuality."[247] "The sexuality of young boys is equally warped and manifests itself in the desire to discharge sexual products while stimulated with sadistic pleasures which linger long after the orgasm. . ."[248]

An important theme repeated throughout Anchell's works is that this new style of "sex *education*" is in reality an *anti-educational* phenomenon.

Latency, or the latency period, that is, "that period of a child's life between the ages of six and twelve, when the child is asexual, is not a hypothetical matter,"[249] Anchell states. "No one need doubt its reality."[250]

Normally, "the child in his latency is educationally ideal," the psychiatrist notes.[251] "Curiosity and the instinct for knowledge are derived from the redirection of childhood sexual energies."[252] Likewise, the child begins to feel "affectionate love," which is initially felt for parents and which later in life will be directed toward others, including one's spouse.[253]

In sharp contrast, the young child who is the benighted "beneficiary" of sex education during middle childhood is rendered "uneducable,"[254] charges Anchell. His "curiosity" and "desire to learn" are destroyed.[255] With the artificially induced arousal of his erotogenic zones, the child experiences a "decreased capability" for academic pursuits.[256] He also exhibits an emotional retardation in connection with the development of "compassionate feelings,"[257] which pave the way for patterns of sexual behavior dominated by "sadism and masochism"[258] and drug use.[259]

According to Dr. Anchell, failure to move fluidly through the normal stages of sexual development becomes manifest in the child's fixation on "infantile libidinal pleasures"[260] and in "a marked tendency toward "exhibitionism and voyeurism"[261] (i.e., taking sexual delight in looking at indecent pictures and/or objects). A state of "psychiatric emergency" is thereby created![262]

This situation is further complicated by the fact that contemporary sex educators promote a tolerance for perversions, normally under the guise of "compassion."

According to Dr. Anchell, "the first natural reaction of the normal person toward perversion is one of shame and disgust. To shun the abnormal is a subconscious mental defense against contamination. When disgust turns to sympathy, the normal individual becomes defenseless."[263]

The implications of these observations in connection with classroom AIDS education programs—that portray homosexual behavior as a variation of the norm and encourage toleration of the perversion—is obvious.

The use of sensitivity-training techniques as an integral part of classroom-training programs and as an integral part of classroom sex education, requiring "the child to sit or mill around touching others' anatomy,"[264] is another "complication" mentioned by Anchell. He summarizes the problem of sensitivity training thusly: "Just as encouraging sexually immature persons to linger over sensual pleasures from seeing and showing produces voyeurs and exhibitionists, so [too the] encouraging of children to engage in the preparatory stage of touching causes impotence for the sex act."[265]

Altogether, Dr. Anchell concludes, "the emphasis placed on preliminary sexual pleasures, the unrestrained acceptance of perverts, the removal of shame and disgust," cause children, with their immature minds, to be "more likely to become polymorphous perverts capable of all kinds of perversions."[266]

The Modus Operandi of the Sex Educator

As the Harper essay, "Education in Sex," so radically illustrates, the sex educator is convinced that all children have a universal "right" to be "treated by schoolroom analysis";[267] and they are relentless in the pursuit of their mission.

Dr. Anchell states, "By means of denial or social blackmail. . .they evade any psychological or sociological facts standing in their way."[268] Recalcitrant parents are accused of neglecting their children because of "sexual embarrassment or ignorance," and "fatal terms of abuse, such as, 'old-fashioned' and 'sexual hangups' are heaped up on them."[269]

"They spread the belief," he continues, "that parents or guardians are responsible. . .for driving the child into an excess of sexual repression and from there into mental illness."[270]

The "sacred conviction" held by the sex educator, "that sexual knowledge and experience will eliminate. . .suffering," continues Dr. Anchell, is based on that educator's "own personal neurotic suffering."[271]

When the damage is done and the sex educator comes face to face with "violent psychopathic behavior," Dr. Anchell states, the sex educator puts the blame on "family-religious political systems inherent in our civilization," rather than on the emotional disturbances resulting from his own interference.[272]

The Triumph of the Horde Culture

The undermining and discrediting of parental and religious influences—which play a key role in the modus operandi of the sex educator—have fatal societal consequences also, explains Dr. Anchell.[273]

"The human conscience develops under the parental leadership" and is normally reinforced by "civilized ideals" which stress the restraining of the "instinctual life" and which direct "base sexual impulses to ethical and intellectual development," argues Dr. Anchell.[274]

"Without a conscience, the individual becomes a barbarian,"[275] he states.

When sex educators devalue parental influence, states Anchell, they in effect devalue the student's conscience.[276] At the *same* time, they are instrumental in "removing societal inhibitions," they intensify their efforts for "sexual openness" and they teach the students "to rely entirely on their own inexperienced and immature judgments and those of their peers."[277]

One of the results of this indoctrination process, charges Dr. Anchell, is the formation of a "horde culture,"[278] which is characterized by "sexual indulgences. . .devoid of love."[279] "The indoctrinated show no guilt, nor do they display concern for morality." They are in effect the new barbarians![280]

If civilization is to survive, if moral and civil order are to be restored, if familial and religious influences are to be safeguarded from attack, if the damage done to young psyches is to be healed and the youthful conscience restored to sanity and enlightened by authentic love and compassion, then the sex educators "must be stopped from filling the minds of our forthcoming generations with perverted sexual ideas,"[281] concludes Dr. Anchell—to which this writer replies: *Amen!*

Chapter 7
Sex Education in Catholic Drag—An Analysis of *Love and Life*

Introduction

Love and Life—A Christian Sexual Morality Guide for Teens,[282] written and designed by Coleen Kelly Mast, is a sex education program for Catholic youth which has received considerable publicity and accolade since its publication by Ignatius Press in 1986.

Within the context of the sex education controversy, the Mast program is of particular significance because it represents a "prototype" approach to the teaching of human sexuality which currently goes under the umbrella of "chastity education," rather than "sex education."

Such programs, however, which attempt to combine sexual morality or prudence with explicit sexual information within the traditional classroom setting, are undertaking the impossible. Classroom sex education is intrinsically evil. Adding a layer of "morality" does not alter the nature of the beast. Rather, it obfuscates and compounds the problems already inherent in *all* classroom sex education programs and, in addition, creates *new* problems, since such programs introduce an aura of respectability not associated with Planned Parenthood-type sex education courses.

All sex education programs are inherently flawed—Mast's included—because, as Dr. Herbert Ratner observes, "they must necessarily project into the sex life of the individual, which is an abnormal thing to do publicly," and because "sex education courses can't teach affection."[283]

Further, such programs legitimize as an authentic course of study that which does not belong in the school curriculum in the first place.

Dr. Ratner continues, "Eliminating sex education from education curriculum may be compared to a situation where a physician removes a diseased, abscessed appendix from a child, only to have the parents ask the physician what he will put back into the child's abdomen to replace the diseased appendix."[284]

In a recent interview on sex education in *All About Issues* magazine, Dr. Anchell, whose scholarly works on the latency period have already been cited in this book, was asked for his opinion of sex education programs which seek to combine sexual "openness" with "prudence." *While not mentioning the MAST program by name, Dr. Anchell's reply was nevertheless extremely relevant to the discussion at hand:*

"It is true that privately promoted sex programs striving to teach sexual openness along with prudence are preferable to established SIECUS-Planned Parenthood programs," he states. "However, arsenic also is less injurious than cyanide, but neither should be given to students."[285]

The purpose of this in-depth analysis of *Love and Life,* then, is *not* to debate the merits of modified sex education programs, but rather, to provide the reader with further argumentation and support for a total ban on classroom sex education.

Background on the Author

Coleen Kelly Mast first came into the public limelight with her public health manual *Sex Respect—The Option of True Sexual Freedom,*[286] developed under a federal grant issued by the Office of Adolescent Pregnancy Programs of the Department of Health and Human Services. The O.A.P.P. is funded under Title XX of the Public Health Service Act and has as its primary objective "the support of family-centered demonstration projects that help prevent pre-marital teen sex relations and pregnancy."[287] Mast's booklet, *AIDS—A Risky Business for Everyone,*[288] is a supplement to the *Sex Respect Program.* While the *Love and Life* curriculum is the main focus of this analysis, this writer shall, on occasion, refer to *Sex Respect* (SR) and the AIDS supplement for comparative purposes.

Mast holds a Master of Science degree in Health Education from Western Illinois University and has been involved in Family Life Education since 1975.

Love and Life's biographical data states that Mrs. Mast was a lecturer for the Pro-Life Education Fund, a consultant for the Diocesan Life Office of the Joliet Diocese, and an instructor of Christian Sexual Morality at Bishop McNamara High School in Kankakee, Illinois, where she founded the M.A.S.T. Team, a group of high school students who assist in promoting the MAST program for teens and their parents around the United States. Her biography appeared in the 1978 volume of *Outstanding Young Women in America.*

General Format of the *Love and Life* Program

The complete *Love and Life* curriculum "package" includes a *Parent's Guide* (P), a Teacher's Manual (T), and a Guide for Teens (S). Since each text presents the Mast program from a different perspective, all *three* must be carefully examined, both individually and collectively, in order to carry out a complete analysis of the author's catechetical philosophy and pedagogical approaches to the teaching of human sexuality and sexual morality, as well as the program's specific goals, objectives and content.

Although the full curriculum is designed to be used primarily as a six to eight-week parochial school program for junior high or early high school students, usually *within* the religious curriculum, it can also, states Mrs. Mast, be used as a four or five-part unit in parish programs for parents and teens, a twenty-two chapter CCD instruction program, as retreat material, or as a home/family supplement for parents and teens. (T9).

When used as a course of formal instruction in the parochial school, Mast indicates that Church leaders can encourage parental involvement through meetings before and after the course, evening speaker sessions, the use of questionnaires and "hints" for home discussion, and the promotion of family activities listed in the Parents' Guide. (T9).

Teacher Qualification

Mast notes that "personally" as well as "professionally" prepared catechists are needed to teach the program "effectively" (T9) and quotes *Educational Guidance in Human Love* (Art. 71) on the attributes of the sex educator, including "outstanding sensitivity in initiating the child and adolescent in the problems of love and life without disturbing their psychological development." However, no details are provided as to the nature of the agents or institutions responsible for the "professional" preparation of the sex educator, nor the process by which the morals and religious character of the sex educator might be determined by administrators or parents.

In terms of doctrinal allegiance, Mast indicates that teachers should be well acquainted with official Church teachings on human sexuality. However, she does not indicate that *adherence* to Church doctrine in the matter of human sexuality is a requirement for the individual teacher. (P7).

In presenting the *Love and Life* program, Mrs. Mast asserts that teachers should have a "positive and prudent" attitude toward themselves, God, their students and sexuality, and should foster an "atmosphere of peace" in the classroom, as well as "mutual respect." (T10-11).

Love and Life Pedagogy

In the *Love and Life* Teacher's Manual, Mast states her preference for the "Sesame Street" mode of transmitting the Church's message on sexuality, which, she states, should be "positive and interesting." (T11).

"Few teenagers would appreciate classroom oral reading of *The Vatican Declaration on Sexual Ethics.* We can't expect them to. They are in the Sesame Street generation. . .we reach them best with something *short, sweet, rhyming* and *colorful*. . ." (T11) (emphasis added).

Vatican Documents Cited by Mast

Mast states that *Love and Life* is based on teachings from these official Church documents:

- *Educational Guidance in Human Love*
- *Familiaris Consortio*
- *Humanae Vitae*
- *Vatican Declaration on Sexual Ethics (T9)*

In actuality, the only document quoted with any frequency, and then principally in the Teacher's Manual, with a few selective citations in the Parent's Guide, is *Educational Guidance in Human Love,* which was issued in 1983 by the Sacred Congregation for Catholic Education.

(Background on this latter document, which was very important in the development of *Love and Life,* is included in a separate chapter on *The Vatican and Sex Education,* which follows the Mast analysis.)

In the Student Text, however, we find that references to or the development of themes and teachings found in *Familiaris Consortio, Humanae Vitae,* and the *Vatican Declaration on Sexual Ethics* are either non-existent or rare. The reason for this omission of in-depth references to these fairly recent Vatican documents on marriage and family life is a very practical and simple one: It has to do with the chronological order and manner in which the Mast curriculum was developed by its author.

The Influence of *Sex Respect* on *Love and Life*

That Mast developed much of her material for *Love and Life* from its secular companion, *Sex Respect—The Option of True Sexual Freedom,* is an important factor which has to be considered in any analysis of *Love and Life.* As noted, *Sex Respect* was created in the mid-1980's with federal funds as an "alternative" sex education program in the public schools for junior high and early high school students. During this same time-frame, Mast developed *Love and Life* for Christian youth, and the program was eventually picked up by Ignatius Press. Both publications bear the same copyright date, 1986, although *Sex Respect* had already undergone several printings.

In comparing both of these curricula, *Sex Respect—The Option of True Sexual Freedom* and *Love and Life—A Christian Sexual Morality Guide for Teens,* one cannot help noticing the similarity of themes, concepts and pedagogy. Indeed, some sections are virtually identical.

There are some important differences, however, one of them being that *Sex Respect* does *not* include a specific description of the sex act nor the detailed biological material found in *Love and Life. Sex Respect* does include, however, a lengthy explanation of the stages of sexual arousal (petting, etc.), including a sexual arousal chart detailing the progression of sexual feelings and giving extensive coverage to the full range of venereal diseases.

Of special interest to prolifers is the fact that the chart on fetal development found in the Student Workbook of *Sex Respect* (SR/60) begins with "implantation" and not "conception," although, in the section on biological definitions, the latter is identified as being the point when a new life begins.

The Fatal Flaw of *Sex Respect*

Although it is not this writer's intention to include a critical evaluation of *Sex Respect* in this book, there is one important feature of this secular program which sheds considerable light on the content and pedagogy of its parochial companion, *Love and Life.*

If you look at the cover of *Sex Respect,* this feature will hit you right between the eyes: It is the description of the text as "A Public Health Workbook for Students," that is to say, *Sex Respect* intends that human sexual behavior is to be discussed within the framework of "public hygiene." This approach, Mast states, teaches "Sex Education With Confidence, Not Controversy." (SR/T5).

Mast's approach to teaching sex education is rationalized in the following manner:

"Religious freedom is highly valued in our country, and our

laws help protect this freedom by keeping the responsibility for specific religious instruction in our homes and churches. . .due to the variety of beliefs. . .It is best that deeper discussions be held in the home with moral guidelines provided by parents and church leaders." (SR/T6).[289]

While noting that "spiritual values are an important aspect of human sexuality," Mast instructs the teacher that "the public schools, however, are not the best place for religious instruction. Therefore, you may not test students on absolute moral principles, nor may you discriminate against any faith denomination." (SR/T6).

Thus, sex education can be peddled "without controversy" in what Lutheran theologian Pastor Richard John Neuhaus calls the "naked public square,"[290] provided that a price is paid, the price being that "religion and religiously grounded values" be "excluded" from the "conduct of public business,"[291] including public education. Thus, public school teachers may *teach* chastity or sexual abstinence, provided they do so under the label of public hygiene or public health.

That is, traditional morality must "disguise" itself as a form of "secular morality,"[292] or be forced to move to the back of the bus.

To defend such an "arrangement," as Mast does, by suggesting that it protects "religious freedom," of course is pure *fraud,* since the denial or exclusion of the moral, religious and spiritual character of sexual relations is a prejudiced control of the ground rules for understanding sex, which in effect *"guarantees an anti-religious presentation to students as well as facilitates an aggressive desacralization of sex."*[293] Thus "the meaning and purpose of sex are on trial in a classroom, and the religious defense is not allowed to speak or even to be present."[294] The price of "no controversy," then, is extremely high, and the result inevitable—"the secular value system is expanded at the expense of the traditional moral value system."[295]

Secular Influences of *Sex Respect* Dominate *Love and Life*

Now, of course, in the development of a "Catholic" sex education program, Mast suffered from *none* of these secular "restrictions." She was absolutely free to establish solid Catholic ground rules for moral behavior based on the Natural Law and the existence of moral absolutes, as enunciated by the universal Magisterium of the Church.

But this would have meant starting all over again, because her prototype package, i.e., *Sex Respect,* was built on a secular platform. Evidently a more practical solution to the problem of starting all over was arrived at by the author, retaining the *Sex Respect* format and basic themes and concepts, but *adding on* a Catholic "dimension." This attempt at layering Catholic values *over* secular values produces a program which appears superficially to be Catholic, but which I will demonstrate is *NOT* Catholic in heart or mind or spirit.

There is a very applicable quotation from G. K. Chesterton which illustrates perfectly the problem within the *Love and Life* curriculum:

> The real peril...is marked by one rather queer quality: which has always been the unique note of the Faith, though it is not noticed by its modern enemies, and rarely by its modern friends. It is the fact symbolized in the legend of the Antichrist, who is the double of Christ; in the profound proverbs that the devil is the ape of God. It is the fact that falsehood is never so false as when it is very nearly true. It is when the stab comes near the nerve of truth, that the Christian conscience cries out in pain.[296]

In reviewing the *Love and Life* text from a Catholic perspective, one quite frequently senses this danger: that is, the author comes *close* to stating the whole truth, but it is *not* the whole truth. It is in fact a falsehood! At other times, the statements contained in the text are simply wrong.

Early Critics Target Secular Influences

For the record, I should state that my critical evaluation of *Love and Life* is a "Johnny come lately" in the sex education controversy. In the summer of 1987, Judith Ammenheuser of the Catholic Caucus newsletter *WATCH* published an excellent critical review of the *Love and Life* curriculum.[297]

Among the criticisms leveled against the Mast program were 1) the incorporation of values clarification techniques and the use of a brand of personalism, humor and cartoons which are characteristic of a SIECUS-AASECT approach to sexuality;[298] 2) the use of "cutesy" and "with-it" slogans, exercises, activities and language, which serve to demean the true nature of human sexuality;[299] 3) the heavy emphasis of the text on sex and the use of the SIECUS term "sexual being";[300] 4) the avoidance in the student text of a discussion of the Church's opposition to masturbation and homosexuality;[301] and 5) the emphasis on the "emotional," "personal," "social," and "physical" consequences of sins against chastity, at the expense of "the effects of mortal sin upon our eternal life."[302]

The Ammenheuser critique was one of the first to identify the fundamental danger of Mast's new parochial school sex education curriculum that is mirrored in the Chesterton quote, namely, that *Love and Life* gives the *illusion* of Catholic doctrine but *not* the substance. Its philosophical underpinnings, like those of the USCC's *Education in Human Sexuality for Christians (1981),* are not rooted in Christian tradition, but stem from an alien and hostile secular humanist philosophy.

First Impressions of *Love and Life*

Overall impressions given by a book or text are extremely important, especially to naive students. The first impression I got from my initial reading of the *Love and Life* text some years ago was a very negative one, based primarily on its *lack of reverence.*

Sex is sacred, that is, of God, holy and worthy of reverence. This truth comes to us from these sources: the Natural Law, authored by God the Creator, Sacred Scripture, inspired by God the Holy Ghost, and the Tradition of the Church as reflected in the teaching Magisterium of the Church. However, the sacredness of sex is in direct conflict with one of the primary goals of sex education, which is the desecration, that is, the desacralization of sex.

It seems obvious, therefore, that any text on sexual morality which calls itself Catholic, or even "Christian," would take special care to treat the subject matter in such a manner as to reflect its sacred and reverential nature, and that this elementary precaution would extend to both the manner of presentation as well as to the actual text itself. Unfortunately, this sense of reverence finds little expression in the Mast presentation.

The use of nerdish comic book characterizations bears an uncomfortable resemblance to Planned Parenthood-promoted adolescent comics, such as Sol Gordon's vomitive *The Ten Heavy Facts About Sex* and *Protect Yourself From Becoming an Unwanted Parent.*[303]

Equally offensive is Mast's use of inappropriate and trite phrases and titles, which verbally desecrate Christian beliefs. For example, the author refers to the Redemption of the human race by the bloody suffering and death of Our Lord on Calvary as "The Main Event." (S51).

As noted earlier, Mast's perception of catechetical instruction on sexual morality is based on the concept of education as a form of entertainment, sort of a ''Sesame Street'' a la mode. The fact that doctrinal truths do not lend themselves to this format appears sadly to have escaped the author's sense of the sacred.

Mast's preoccupation with slogans and jingles is as unsuitable to a Catholic book on human sexuality as is her use of inappropriate graphics and titles. As Dietrich von Hildebrand once remarked, ''Slogans have the ability to vilify even very good things.''[304]

Cutesy slogans, such as, ''Pet your cat, not your date,'' and ''Sex is God's wedding gift to you—No fair peeking!'' are utterly demeaning. Others, like ''Love is not a feeling. Love is a commitment'' are simply silly. Whoever heard of a person in love who did not "feel" a passion, a longing to be united with the beloved? No doubt the author meant to convey the idea that authentic conjugal love goes *beyond* our emotions and encompasses a will to commit oneself to the exclusive and permanent union of marriage. True love *is* more than a feeling, but it can never be *less* than that and still be human.

Again, under the category of first impressions, I noted immediately upon reading *Love and Life* that the text contained some incomplete and therefore inaccurate statements of Catholic teachings on marriage and family.

For example, in her discussion of the "two purposes for sexual intercourse," Mast states that one of those purposes is "to bring children into the world." (S32). As it stands, the statement is untrue. Rather, the Catholic Church has always taught that the primary purpose of conjugal love is the procreation *and the education* of offspring. This Church teaching stands as a direct *refutation* of the humanist principle that procreation is merely a process of physical gestation.

Another specific citation, one which borders on the bizarre, is found in Chapter 10, inappropriately titled "The Greatest Show on Earth," in which Mast recalls St. Paul's description of the Catholic Church as the Mystical Body of Christ and then goes on to state:

> The Holy Spirit holds this Mystical Body together. The bones of this Body are the Pope and Bishops in union with Him. Their authority comes from Christ and gives shape to the Church. It will never be destroyed, just as Christ's bones were never destroyed. (57).

Traditionally speaking, in Scripture the parts of the Mystical Body of Christ are referred to as "members," *not* "bones." Why would Mast give this peculiar interpretation?

Love and Life Has Subtle Anti-Parent Bias

Mast's attitude toward parents, as reflected in the Teacher's Manual and Parent's Guide, is condescending and offensive. She seems to lack a sense of humility with regard to her own limitations and biases and an abysmal lack of appreciation for the accumulated wisdom of mothers and fathers who are practiced in the art of child-rearing, which includes the inculcation and development of character and virtue in the young.

The introductory sentence of Section I to the Parent's Guide is indicative of the indefatigable "parent-baiting" that runs subtly through the Mast text: "My parents never talked to me about sex, and I did just fine. Why can't we do just the same?" (P9).

In unit two of the Teacher's Manual, which deals with one of the most controversial sections of the *Love and Life* program (i.e., Chapter 6), Mast tells the teachers, "Try to arrange for parents to educate their children about sexuality." (T47). "Parents today," Mast asserts, must be "positive and convincing in showing that sexuality is sacred and good when used in accord with God's plan." (T47).[305]

With regard to parental direction and responsibility, Mast seems to have missed some important points. First, whereas it is true that in the past, many parents did not give what Mast refers to as "formal instruction or counseling" on sex to their children (P9), they nevertheless did fulfill their responsibilities in this delicate area by 1) offering their children a good example (i.e., marital chastity and fidelity); 2) by the proper formation of conscience and practical guidance and instruction on moral virtues; and 3) by their emphasis on the "affective" nature of conjugal love.

Secondly, a given child's specific questions regarding sex would have usually been managed on an informal and individual basis with regard to instruction on sexual matters; that is, it would have been given in *proper time,* in *proper measure* and with *proper precautions.* With regard to the sex act itself, parents have always innately understood that *no description* of the mere biological aspects of sex can ever fully explain the great mystery that sex is, which each person must discover for himself or herself, and in his or her own unique way.

Now for its part, the Catholic Church has always held that parents are both the *natural* and *competent* teachers of their offspring, particularly with regard to sexual matters. Yet, when reading Mast, one is left with an impression that Christians have had to wait for almost 2000 years—until the advent of current classroom sex education—to appreciate fully all the implications of youthful formation in the area of sexual behavior and morality.

Of course, it is true that the early Christians didn't have R- and X-rated home videos, but they *did* live in a pagan culture, saturated by every form of sexual degradation and perversion.

Youth struggled then as now with open temptations to chastity and purity, many resisting to death. Then and now, young people fell into the habit of sexual sin, not so much from "ignorance of intellect as weakness of a will exposed to dangerous occasions and deprived of the means of grace."[306]

Christian parents likewise have had to struggle and defend themselves and their children against the assaults on marriage and family life. Then as now they strove to form in their children a correct and upright conscience and strength of character, both by instruction and personal example, and to provide their offspring with individual and familial instruction and knowledge related to sexual development and sexual morality during suitable, teachable moments that make up the course of daily living.

Holy Mother Church did its part, by catechizing the Faithful, including the young, in the Way of Life—as opposed to the way of death—which included instruction in sexual morality.

However, as one might suspect, this traditional, time-honored approach to moral development and the transmission of sexual wisdom to youth by the family—reinforced by Church teachings (and inevitably supplemented by peers)—is at *direct odds* with the interests of the professional "sex educator," whose career is dependent on the transformation of sex into an object of "free" and "open" discussion outside familial parameters. After all, if parents proved to be "too competent," the sex educator would find himself looking for honest employment.

Love and Life Examined From a Catholic Perspective

Concerning the nature of the Mast curriculum, a number of basic questions remain which need to be posed and answered before attempting to evaluate its authenticity as a Catholic guide on sexual morality. Oddly enough, one of those questions is whether or not Mast actually claims to have written a text which is *specifically* Catholic.

As noted earlier, the initial model for the *Love and Life* curriculum was the secular-based *Sex Respect.* Both programs share a common methodology and similarity, though they are not identical in content. A careful examination of the text's subtitle, "A Christian Sexual Morality Guide for Teens," would indicate that the author does not specifically identify *Love and Life* as a "Catholic" text. The word "Catholic" makes only a rare appearance in the Student Guide—twice, to be exact—in the one hundred eighteen pages of the text.

▪ Under the chapter title "The Greatest Show on Earth," the author says, "Christ's teachings are freely given through the Catholic Church to protect and guide us." (S38).

▪ Under the subtitle "The Sacrament of Penance," she states, "The Catholic Church offers a unique opportunity to experience God's mercy." (S86).

In the Parent's Guide of 48 pages there are *three* mentions of the word "Catholic":

▪ "The Catholic Church, as the Universal Church, is large and diverse." (P15).

▪ In a description of family activities we read, "These activities. . .will help to reinforce the 'liveable, lovable, and good' Catholic teachings in *Love and Life*." (P22).

▪ Under the unit title, "The Call to Serve Christ in Love," Mrs. Mast says, "Why should young Catholics develop a devotion to Mary and the Holy Rosary?" (P25).

The Teacher's Manual of 153 pages, containing the student guide *plus* additional lesson-plan materials, has three additional references:

▪ "The background information in confidence and Catholic values is helpful. . ." (T7). ". . .and gifts of the Catholic faith." (T9). ". . .the special qualities and attitudes of Catholic sexual morality, teachers are. . ." (T9).

Love and Life as a "Confidence Builder"

It is also important to note that in her introduction to the various texts, Mast does *not* indicate that the primary purpose of *Love and Life* is to educate and guide the student toward an understanding and acceptance of the Catholic Church's teachings on sexual morality, as revealed in Sacred Scripture and Sacred Tradition and enunciated by the Vicars of Jesus Christ. Instead, the introductory statement to the Parent's Guide reads like a deodorant commercial:

"*Love and Life* is a *positive, confidence-building* program designed to meet the spiritual and educational needs of teenagers who are maturing physically, emotionally and psychologically into young men and women..." (P7).

The Student handbook opens with "Adolescence is a wonderful, adventurous time of life. However, it is filled with many difficult questions...and confusing feelings...This book is designed to help you answer some of those questions and understand your *feelings.* It will give you goals which will help you to *maintain order* in your life." (S9).

The opening text of the Teacher's Manual states, "*Love and Life* is a program in chastity formation for adolescents...*The background information in confidence and Catholic values is helpful*..." (T7). (All emphasis is added).

Vatican Documents Play No Prominent Role

In my introduction to the Mast program, I indicated that although the author claims her text is based on teachings from several recent Vatican documents on sexual morality, marriage and the family, references to these documents are either non-existent or minimal in the Student Guide.

For example, *Familiaris Consortio (The Role of the Christian Family in the Modern World,* 1981) is *never* mentioned in the Student Guide and reference to it appears only once in the Teacher's Manual, as cited in the preceding section. The Parent's Guide cites No. 37 of the document, which refers to the education of children in the essential values of human life (P8) and states that *Familiaris Consortio* is "a beautiful teaching on the family in the modern world." (P16). Yet this "beautiful teaching" is nowhere to be found in the Student Text. As a matter of fact, the *Love and Life* curriculum contains *no thematic development of family life or concepts specifically associated with the family as enunciated in "Familiaris Consortio,"* concepts such as "fatherhood," "motherhood," "filiation and fraternity," the natural bonds of "flesh and blood" and "the evangelization mission of the family."[307] All are conspicuously missing, although the format of the curriculum could easily have accommodated an in-depth discussion of the importance and value of family life.

In reality, Mast's treatment of the meaning and important value of family life is extremely superficial. Absent is any wholesome exposition on the family which would present to young people "who are beginning their journey towards marriage and family life..." "new horizons to help them discover the beauty and grandeur of the vocation to love and the service of life."[308] (From the Introduction to *Familiaris Consortio*).

It is interesting to note that in Chapter 4, devoted to the theme of friendship, no mention is made of siblings or other members of the extended family, such as grandparents, or the wonderful world of friendship that develops with parents as adolescents grow into young adults and begin having children of their own. (S26-S30).

Vatican *Declaration on Sexual Ethics* Ignored

It seems strange that a text which purports to teach sexual morality should fail to mention the Vatican's important 1975 *Declaration on Certain Questions Concerning Sexual Ethics.* There are *no* references to this *Declaration* in the Student Guide, although the document is mentioned once in the Teacher's Manual (T9), and twice in the Parent's Guide (P16, P19).

This unfortunate omission in the Student Guide is rationalized by Mast on the basis that young people cannot be expected to "appreciate" such a presentation (T11) and that young teens find "subjects such as masturbation, homosexuality, and birth control embarrassing, especially in mixed classes." (T46). Let us examine the validity of her statements.

First, the *Declaration on Certain Questions Concerning Sexual Ethics* is not only well written, it is also highly readable and interesting. I do not think young teens would have any difficulty in understanding the essentials of the document—especially Sections 3 and 4, which deal with the existence of the Natural Law and moral absolutes, and Section 5 on objective standards of morality. Of importance also is the Declaration's condemnation of premarital sex, masturbation and homosexuality, which is accompanied by a reaffirmation of the Church's teaching that "mortal sin, which is opposed to God, does not consist only in formal and direct resistance to the commandment of charity. It is equally to be found in this opposition to authentic love which is included in every deliberate transgression, in serious matter, of each of the moral laws." (10).

Throughout the history of the Church, clearcut but modest references to illicit sexual conduct have been made from the pulpit and in catechetical instruction programs to young people and adults without "embarrassment" and without explicit and graphic details, which might arouse the passions and become an occasion of sin.

Keeping in mind that Mast wrote an entire supplement on AIDS as an addendum to her *Sex Respect* manual that is designed for young teens, one has difficulty in believing that a brief statement on the Catholic Church's condemnation of masturbation and homosexuality was eliminated from *Love and Life* to avoid "embarrassment."

More than likely, the decision to exclude the issues of masturbation and homosexuality was made for more pragmatic reasons.

Mast's failure to incorporate into the text of *Love and Life* the fundamental concepts of Catholic sexual morality presented in Pope Paul VI's *Declaration on Certain Questions Concerning Sexual Ethics* is doubly unfortunate for the students because the document could have served as a perfect springboard for a discussion of some very important questions, such as, "What are the norms or criteria by which the morality of acts is known?" In an age when young people are bombarded by "situation ethics," such a discussion of the nature and determinates of morality would have been particularly helpful and enlightening.[309]

Humanae Vitae in an Historic Vacuum

Pope Paul VI's encyclical *Humanae Vitae* is mentioned briefly in the Student Guide in Chapter 19 with reference to four specific qualities of married love (i.e., "human," "total," "faithful," and "fertile"), and the document is cited as the "Official Church teaching on human life, love and marriage." (S117). Mast does a good job in terms of stating the unitive and procreative aspects of marriage. (S106).

The unfortunate feature of Mast's presentation of *Humanae Vitae* is that the document is presented in an historical vacuum. With the exception of Scriptural references, all Church documents cited in *Love and Life* are post-Vatican II. How can a young Catholic begin to appreciate the marvelous continuity of the Church's traditional teaching on sex, marriage and the family, which spans almost 2000 years, when documents are presented outside of an historical context?

Certainly, specific references to the teachings of the Council of Trent and Pope Leo XIII's encyclical *Arcanum Divinae Sapientiae* (1880)—which "affirmed the sacramentality, unity and indissolubility of Christian marriage"[310]—or to Pius XI's incomparable *Casti Connubii*—which Fr. Robert Bradley, S.J. calls "the most comprehensive and eloquent statement on marriage in the entire history of the Church"[311]—would have given the young reader a broader perspective on marriage and the family than that afforded him by the brief and singular citation to *Humanae Vitae* found in *Love and Life.*

Educational Guidance in Human Love— Outlines for Sex Education

It is interesting to note that the one Vatican document which is highlighted no less than *thirty* times in the Teacher's Manual—with *four* references in the Parent's Guide and one in the Student Guide—is *Educational Guidance in Human Love,* the only one (of the four Church documents cited by Mast) which does *not* carry an official or express approval by a Pope. Rather, at the time of its release on December 1, 1983, by the Sacred Congregation for Catholic Education, the Congregation statement simply described the document "as an educational message, and centres (sic) on educators' sense of responsibility."

Since I have chosen to evaluate *Educational Guidance in Human Love* as a separate entity, following my analysis of Mast, I shall simply note that a goodly portion of the difficulties found in the Mast presentation can be traced to both the *use* and *misuse* of statements made in EGHL on the issue of sex education.

What the Catholic Church Teaches About Sex

Before examining the authenticity of the *Love and Life* curriculum in terms of its adherence to traditional Catholic teachings on sexual morality, marriage and family, it might be helpful to provide a brief summary of just *what* the Church does teach and *how* the Church has traditionally catechized the faithful in these matters.

I believe it is fair to state that any genuine effort at conscience formation and education of Catholic youth with regard to the authentic position of the Church in matters related to sexual morality, marriage and the family would include the following precepts:

- The Roman Catholic Church teaches with *absolute authority* in matters of faith and morals.
- These moral absolutes are *knowable, objective, immutable,* and *universal.*
- The moral teachings of the Catholic Church are not matters of sectarian discipline, but are rooted in the laws of nature, that is, they have a meaning beyond theology in that they are linked to the "constitutive elements of human nature,"[312] as designed by God, the Author of nature, and implanted in man as part of his being. They are therefore binding on all men, for all time, in all places and in all circumstances.
- There exists a Divine Plan for human sexuality which is articulated both in the "Book" of Nature and the Book of Sacred

Scripture, and the truths of this Divine Plan are transmitted to the Faithful, from generation to generation, through the ordinary and universal Magisterium of the Church.

■ Sex is "Nature's deepest secret" and "only the most degenerate of people dare to expose it by open, public exhibitionism."[313]

■ The authentic Christian tradition recognizes the sex act not as an end in itself but as a means of sanctification within the Sacrament of marriage whereby the procreative and unitive dimensions of human sexuality are inextricably bound.

■ The Catholic understanding of chastity, one of the forms of the cardinal virtue of temperance, by which we restrain our passions, is *incomprehensible* apart from the doctrines of Original Sin and Redemption, and chastity is a moral virtue for everyone in every state in life.[314]

■ The practice of sexual self-control requires more than ordinary human effort: It is "The Difficult Commandment" because it involves the passions as well as the will and intellect, and as such it is "not only pleasing to God, but extraordinarily sanctifying."[315]

■ In the pursuit of this lifelong task, recourse to the Sacrament of Penance and the reception of Holy Communion, as well as the inspiration of the Saints, especially the Virgin Mary and St. Joseph—who are our chief models of purity—are the primary sources of strength in resisting temptation and advancing in the spiritual life.

■ And finally, "The Family holds directly from the Creator the mission, and hence the right, to educate the offspring, a right anterior to any right whatever of civil society and the state, and therefore [this right is] inviolable on the part of any power on earth. This mission cannot be wrested from parents without grave violation of their rights."[316] With specific regard to the delicate matter of education of children and youth in matters related to sexuality, this "basic right and duty of parents must always be carried out under their attentive guidance, whether at home or in educational centers chosen and controlled by them. In this regard, the Church affirms the law of subsidiarity, which the school is bound to observe when it cooperates in sex education, by entering into the same spirit that animates the parents."[317]

The Pattern and Gravity of Sexual Sins

In *Morality and Sexuality: What the Church Teaches,* Monsignor William B. Smith points out that with regard to the pattern of sexual sins "Catholic moral tradition is a greater respecter of realism. Insofar as anything has something real about it, it has something good about it. But, insofar as the real lacks something that should be there—like a real dimension—a constitutive dimension of human sexuality—it has something bad about it (*Summa Theologica,* I-II, q.18, a. 1)."[318] This is to say that human sexuality is a two-edged sword:

"Human sexuality is a good. It is a God-created and therefore a God-given good. . .Both Sacred Scripture. . .and Sacred Tradition attest to this fact. . ."[319] states Msgr. Smith.

But he suggests also that we must recognize the "daimonic" quality of the sexual function, that is, the power of the sexual instinct to take over the whole person and its ability to resist integration into the total person. "[Msgr. Phillipe] Delhaye is correct in seeing the disorder of sexual desire [as] a consequence of disobedience to God in fundamental guilt [i.e. Original Sin], personal sins, lack of self-mastery and even contempt for the virtue of chastity," he states.[320]

With regard to the gravity of sexual sins, there is no question that "Christian tradition and the Church's teachings, and a right reason also, recognizes the moral order of sexuality involves such high values of human life that every direct violation of this order is objectively serious [i.e., a mortal sin]" (*Persona humana,* 1975),[321] Smith concludes.

With regard to the special nature of sexual sins, the Apostle Paul makes the point in a manner somewhat more personal and practical when he says, "Flee fornication! Every sin that a man committeth, is outside the body; but he that committeth fornication, sinneth against his own body." (*1 Cor.* 6:18).

Every boy or girl, man or woman who has experienced the natural sense of shame, guilt and humiliation that accompanies sins of impurity—in thought, word or deed—knows exactly what St. Paul is talking about. Sex is not only nature's deepest secret, it is *man's* deepest secret because it touches the very essence of his being. Despite the fact that "...in the catalogues of sins...sexual sins do not occupy the first place on that list nor are they morally the most deadly,"[322] mankind appears to be peculiarly affected by sins of a sexual nature because of the knowledge of having violated the sanctity of one's own body.

How the Church Instructs the Faithful On Sexual Matters

Not only is it important to know *what* the Church professes about the nature and purpose of sex, marriage and family, but it is equally important to know *how* these truths have been traditionally passed on to the faithful.

The Role of the Ordinary And Universal Magisterium

In her splendid exposé of the real meaning behind the Post Vatican II Modernist attack on *Humanae Vitae,* entitled *The Desolate City—Revolution in the Catholic Church,* Anne Muggeridge gives an excellent summary of the role of the hierarchical Magisterium in the life of the Church.

"In contrast to the anti-dogmatic and anti-hierarchical principles" loosed by the Reformation, the Catholic Church has "always believed, and still professes in the documents of Vatican II, that the teaching vested in the successors of the Apostles is competent to interpret authoritatively, not only the Scriptures, but also the natural moral law, and that this infallibility in matters of Faith and morals is vested in a special way in the primacy of the successor of Peter,"[323] Muggeridge explains.

"In the Catholic Church, the Magisterium—the teaching authority of the Pope alone, and of the bishops united with the Pope—makes claim to be the guardian and interpreter of the revelation of God to man," she states, and "The Church's authority derives from this claim to authoritative interpretation."[324]

More simply put, "all moral authority derives from God,"[325] "the supreme and eternal principle of power"[326] and is "exercised in the Church by direct commission from Christ and through the Apostolic succession."[327] That is, in matters of Faith and morals, the Catholic Church has the final word.

In a world of continuously shifting values, the Church proclaims the reality of moral absolutes which exist for all times, for all people and in all places and circumstances.

In *Sexuality and Marriage in the Teachings of the Church,* Reverend Robert I. Bradley makes two interesting observations about sex, which he defines as "the physical use, in thought or deed, of the power and instinct called sexuality."[328]

His first observation, which has been voiced elsewhere in this book, is that "sex has always and everywhere been regarded as something 'special' to man, in the literal sense of being specific to him,"[329] and that "in all historic cultures, sex has been surrounded by limitations, which have invariably been connected with a sense of the sacred."[330]

"Now, among all the historic limitations and sacred sanctionings regarding sex, and as it were fulfilling them, stands the teaching of the Catholic Church,"[331] he continues.

In his second observation, Fr. Bradley notes that the Catholic Church's teaching on sex was never codified in solemn Canons, as was the case, for example, with the Church's teachings on Original Sin, especially as enunciated in the great Tridentine Canons.[332] Instead, the Church proceeded "as though this matter of sex were so immediate and pervasive in the lives of her children that the more appropriate form of her teaching concerning it would itself be the immediate and pervasive form we call the Ordinary and Universal Magisterium."[333]

This traditional approach of the Church to its teachings on sexual matters is quite evident in the reading of such documents as the *Declaration on Certain Questions Concerning Sexual Ethics,* where the immediate appeal is directed at the necessity of man's internalization of the divine law: "In the depths of his conscience, man detects a law which holds him to obedience. . . For man has in his heart a law written by God. To obey it is the very dignity of man; according to it he will be judged." (No. 3).[334]

This reasoning explains in part why, for example, in the debate over contraception, "where a traditional teaching has become so internalized through long assenting practice. . .when attack suddenly comes, there are no compelling arguments, other than the fact of the tradition, ready for articulation."[335] It is a truism that the obvious defies explanation.

Instruction at the Individual and Family Level

At the pastoral level, particularly through the *Catechism of the Council of Trent,* the Catholic Church has taught that instruction with regard to sexual matters requires "great caution and prudence"[336] and should be carried out in a manner which stresses "brevity rather than copiousness of exposition,"[337] lest, even unintentionally, such instruction may "instead of extinguishing. . .serve rather to inflame corrupt passion."[338] The faithful are to be taught and earnestly exhorted to cultivate continence and chastity with all care, to cleanse themselves *from all defilement of the flesh and of the spirit, perfecting sanctification in the fear of God.*[339] (Cf. 2 *Cor.* 7:1). In accord with Sacred Scripture, pastors and spiritual directors have traditionally preached as the principal means of practicing purity, 1) avoidance of idleness, 2) avoidance of immodesty of the eyes, 3) avoidance of immodest dress, 4) avoidance of impure conversation, reading and pictures, 5) frequent reception of the Sacraments and 6) mortification of the body and sensual appetites.[340]

At the familial level, the Church has enjoined Christian parents—mothers to daughters and fathers to sons—to impart ". . .*at the proper time, in the proper measure and with the proper precautions,* the revelation of the mysterious and marvelous laws of life," so that these truths will be received "with reverence and gratitude" and will "enlighten their minds with far less danger than if they learned them haphazard, from some unpleasant shock, from secret conversations, through information received from over-sophisticated companions, or from clandestine reading."[341] On the specific question concerning the licitness of "sex education" or even "sex initiation," a Decree of the Holy Office delivered on March 21, 1931 clearly replies in the negative. "Answer: No. . .*no approbation whatever* can be given to the advocacy of the new method, even as taken up recently by some Catholic authors and set before the public in printed publications." (Emphasis added).

It bears repeating, over and over, that Pope Pius XII's prescription of *PROPER TIME, PROPER MEASURE,* and *PROPER PRECAUTIONS* can *never* be carried out in *any* classroom setting or with *any* group program, including Mast's! The classroom structure is by nature open, public and de-personalized; the teacher is, for all practical purposes, a stranger who cannot possibly even begin to fulfill the requirements cited above, considering the wide range of levels of understanding and maturity of any student group at any particular level. One has to wonder at the remarkable degree to which parents have been brainwashed and browbeaten by so-called "experts" or "professionals" to have them turn over their children to perfect strangers in a matter which is so intimate and personal—the "secret-self" of each child.

Briefly, then, I have outlined for the reader those fundamental principles and teachings of the Catholic Church related to the content and method of instruction traditionally associated with sexual morality. The extent to which these truths are embraced and incorporated, without timidity or ambiguity, into a particular text would be fair measure, I believe, of the validity of the claim that the text authentically reflects the Catholic Church's teachings in this area. The *Love and Life* program evaluated in this text, for the reasons given above, fails to measure up to the Church's criteria for school instruction of the young.

Mast Ignores the Importance of Natural Law

The doctrine of the Natural Law has been called "the central citadel of Catholic morality,"[342] Natural Law being defined by St. Thomas Aquinas as "the communication of the eternal law to rational creatures. . .,"[343] "the specifically rational, moral way in which rational beings conform to the eternal law."[344]

Or more simply, the Natural Law is the unwritten moral law which is inscribed in the very nature of man.

In any discussion of Catholic sexual morality, Natural Law morality, which Bishop Cahal B. Daly, M.D., D.D. of Ireland identifies as being "rational, personalistic morality," is of great importance because it stands in opposition to and in stark contrast to "the inhuman and anti-personalist morality of liberal agnosticism or scientific humanism."[345]

It appears strange, therefore, that the author of *Love and Life* should devote an entire chapter of the Student Guide to what she calls the "immature" astronomical theories of Ptolemy in order to demonstrate the "immature" theory that the world revolves around sex; whereas, she fails to even spell out—much less explain—the existence and meaning of the Natural Law.

Indeed, there appears to be some confusion in Mast's mind as to the distinction between Natural Law and positive law, including Divine Law. For example, in Chapter 11, under the subtitle, "The Law," Mast states, "God wrote His own Law on our hearts. . .the Ten Commandments spell out God's Will, which all people can recognize by using their minds. . ."[346]

Not only is there no clearly defined statement in *Love and Life* regarding Natural Law, there is also no reference to the claim of the Catholic Church to teach with *infallibility in matters of faith and morals* and to the role of the *Ordinary and Universal Magisterium of the Church* in the instruction of the Faithful, especially in matters related to human sexuality, marriage and the family. (Note: discussion of the term "Magisterium" is cited only as an option in the Teacher's Guide.) (T73).

Mast on the Theme of Sexual Maturity

While Mast falls short on doctrine, she rides high on popular psychological themes normally associated with secular-based sex education programs. One of these dominant themes is that of "sexual maturity," which Mast defines as "the ability to express ourselves as men or women in a manner which will glorify God and serve His people."

According to Mast,

- "Sexual maturity results from knowing what true human sexuality really is. . ." (S14)

- "The mature notion of human sexuality helps us to understand many ways by which we can show our love for God and demonstrate His love to the world..." (S17).
- "...So a more mature view of our sexuality allows us to see where sex belongs..." (S18).
- "...When we begin to see the system in this order, we can grow in sexual maturity." (S18).
- "...Sexuality is a basic part of our personality, the way we communicate with others, the way we feel, the way we express our human love and the way we progress toward maturity as a male or female person." (S39).
- "...If you are healthy, you will most likely become physically, sexually mature without exerting any conscious effort...But...will you become sexually mature in all the other ways...Save sex for marriage and you'll have a good chance of becoming sexually mature as God planned for you." (S42).

From the above one would suppose that sexual sins are simply the result of "immaturity," and that the cure lies in striving for "maturity"—not in grace and virtue. The mind of the Church, however, is decidedly otherwise.

In a 1983 article on the identical theme of sin as a "deviation" from "maturity," the Canadian publication *Challenge* makes the following observation:

"St. Jerome had an interesting point of view when he wrote in 384:

> The Apostle Paul, who was a chosen vessel set apart for the Gospel of Christ, because of the spur of the flesh and the allurements of sin, keeps his body down and subjects it to slavery, lest in preaching to others, he himself be found reprobate. But still he sees that there is another law in his members fighting against the law of his will and that he is still led captive to the law of sin. After nakedness, fasting, hunger, prison, scourging and torture, he turns back upon himself and cries, 'Oh wretched man that I am, who shall deliver me from the body of this death.'

But then St. Paul and St. Jerome had not heard that all that was troubling them was due to immaturity."[347]

Mast on the "Virtue" of Self-Esteem

> In order to construct the edifice of virtue and solid sanctity, we must lay the foundation of a profound and sincere humility. This is effected primarily by the destruction of pernicious self-love, which corrodes and vitiates everything and deceives and blinds us in all things, *making us think that we are something, when actually we are nothing.* (*Gal.* 6:3).[348]
>
> From *The Mystical Evolution*
> by Fr. John G. Arintero, O.P., S.T.M.

All masters of the spiritual life down through the ages, including Fr. Arintero, have taught that humility is the fountainhead of sanctity.

Christ Himself did not only preach humility: "Learn from me, for I am meek and humble of heart" (*Matt.* 11:29), but He lived it. In the words of St. Paul, "He emptied himself, taking the nature of a slave. . .humbling himself, becoming obedient to death, even to death on a cross." (*Phil.* 2:7-8).

It should be remembered that humility is a virtue which is "uniquely Christian, something quite unknown among the pagans, for whom the term connotes something weak, vile and abject."[349] For Christians, however, it is "indispensable for advancement in the spiritual life, particularly with regard to the mortification of the senses and passions. . ."[350]

It should then come as a considerable surprise to readers of *Love and Life* that *"Self-Esteem,"* which Mast defines as "favorable opinion of oneself; confidence" (T26), is the *first* foundation of mature human sexuality, *followed* by *"Love of God."* (P7). Mast makes more than a dozen references to "self-esteem," including an entire chapter in the Student's Guide on the importance of self-esteem and how students can get more self-esteem. Catholic students are advised:

- "By practicing Christ's command. . .we grow in maturity and self-esteem." (S20).
- "Our families. . .are only human; they will sometimes fail. So our most reliable source of self-esteem is always God and His love." (S21).
- "God. . .is the only *true source of self-esteem.*" (S22).

- "Friendship can help you grow in self-esteem." (S26).

In contrast, the Catholic student gets *zero* instruction on the virtue of humility. As a matter of fact, the word never even appears in the Student text.

In the Teacher's Manual, humility appears once, in a list of virtues and again in a brief statement under Teaching Notes: ". . .Obedience and humility are essential for teenagers and all too often neglected or overlooked." (T26).

In contrast, the Unit Three Background section devotes an entire half-page to "Keys to Esteem," which include the use of regular Confession. Teachers are instructed that "One of the greatest divine gifts you can get your students to accept is the freedom and self-esteem that come with a regular confession." (T81).

Mast as a Victim of Pop Psychology

There can be no doubt that Mast has been strongly influenced by humanist selfist theories which abound in contemporary sex education programs.

For those who are unfamiliar with this phenomenon, a reading of Paul Vitz's book, *Psychology as Religion—the Cult of Self-Worship,* will be exceptionally helpful.[351]

I would like to quote a few sections from this classic text to illustrate how far removed Mast is from traditional Catholic teachings on the subject of "the self" and the acquisition of "self-esteem."

"Christianity, with its injunction to *lose* the self," Vitz states, is obviously at direct cross-purposes with "the relentless and single-minded search for and glorification of the self. . ."[352] "For the Christian, the self is the problem, not the potential paradise.

"Understanding this problem involves an awareness of sin. . .Correcting this condition requires the practice of such un-self-actualized states as contrition and penitence, humility, obedience and trust in God," he continues.[353]

Reflecting on the Christian conception of love, as summarized in the two Great Commandments: "Thou shalt love the Lord thy God with all thy heart, with all thy soul and with all thy strength" and "Thou shalt love thy neighbor as thyself," Vitz notes that "there is no direct command to love thy self—an adequate degree of self-love being assumed as natural."[354]

"Self-theorists like Carl Rogers," charges Vitz, transform "the devout believer's conviction of God's unconditional love for him...into a full-fledged self-devotion."[355]

Citing the particular teachings of Carl Rogers, Vitz notes, "His (Rogers') self-love theories," are "completely at odds with the Christian doctrine of sin" and "still more critically in conflict with the doctrine of God's judgment."[356]

Vitz makes the important observation that, "like all popular heresy, selfism has some positive and appealing properties. That you should look out for yourself is nice (and useful) to hear; that you should love and care for others is a familiar and great moral position."[357]

The problem, however, according to Vitz, is that "the essentially vertical dimension of Christianity," i.e., the relation to God—the spiritual life of prayer, meditation and worship—is sacrificed to the essentially "horizontal heresy" of selfism, "with its emphasis on the present, and on self-centered ethics..."[358]

Selfist theories have, according to Vitz, a great appeal to young people because they "appeal to narcissism, with its undue stress of attachment to self and the acquisition of more and more self-esteem."[359] The situation is further complicated by the fact that such behavior involves "an increased instability in people's self-evaluation."

According to Heinz Kohut and Otto Kersberg, whose views Vitz summarizes in his text, "...today's externally controlled evaluations often lead to intense self-love and self-esteem followed by self-hate and then a general mood of meaninglessness...Such people are potentially very open to authorization social movements like EST, the cult of Reverend Sun Myung Moon, and the like."[360]

Mast critic Judith Ammenheuser sums up the arguments against self-esteem courses in her latest *Watch* alert entitled "Self-Esteem Programs of Deception in Disguise":

"Self-esteem programs are the least understood but are being increasingly used and talked about and almost without question. At the mention of the words 'self-esteem' no red flags go up. Yet as one begins looking into the programs and materials, it is easy to see that self-esteem programs are the perfect companion to values clarification...Values clarification programs direct a child's conscious thoughts toward his own self; whereas, self-esteem programs reach for the child's subconscious mind and direct the child to become even more deeply involved in himself. If in a values clarification exercise one is prompted to question whether he may believe in God; in self-esteem programs, one is prompted to get in touch with the God within themselves. [sic]"[361]

Values Clarification as a Form of Psychotherapy

In connection with Mast's promotion of the "virtue" of self-esteem, it is important to point out that the author employs a number of values clarification techniques in *Love and Life,* including role-playing and the use of personal questionnaires and journals. These techniques have been promoted in educational circles as innovative pedagogical advances. This is a deception of the first degree.

Values clarification techniques are a form of psychotherapy, and as such are normally reserved for clinical relationships between a patient and the doctor or therapist. However, the classroom is not a clinic, the teacher is not a therapist, and the student is not a patient.

Thus, serious violations of personal liberties are at stake when these techniques are used in the classroom, especially when parents lack the necessary knowledge regarding the true nature of values clarification techniques.

Love and Life's Controversial Chapter Six

There is no doubt that Chapter Six of the Mast program is the most controversial segment of the *Love and Life* curriculum. Whatever public criticism has been leveled at Mast to date centers upon this particular chapter of the Student Guide entitled, "God Says That It Is Good" (S39-46), which deals specifically with the act of sexual intercourse.

In this writer's mind, far from being "positive" and "prudent," Chapter Six is inherently *"negative"* and *"imprudent"*! It not only violates the student's sense of modesty and his right to privacy, as well as the rights of parents under the law of subsidiarity, but more profoundly, it violates the laws of nature and of nature's Author.

To understand the exact nature of the violation, however, it is necessary to have some knowledge of the content and pedagogy of Chapter Six.

Explicit Physiological Description

As the subtitle of the Mast program indicates, *Love and Life* is marketed as a *Christian Sexual Morality Guide for Teens* and is usually presented as part of a religious or Confraternity of Christian Doctrine (CCD) program in parochial schools (T9) within this specific religious context. Therefore, it borders on the bizarre to have included in the text of the Student Guide a detailed biological description of physiological changes associated with puberty, including a lengthy explanation of the development of primary and secondary sex characteristics and a detailed description of male and female genital organs. The female menstrual cycle is also discussed, as is the male nocturnal emission. (S40-41). Following the biological exposition, Mast gives some Scriptural background concerning the nature of married love.

Then she goes back to biology, giving an explicit description of "the holy act of sexual intercourse." She explains that "the erect penis is inserted into the vagina, climaxing with the release of semen." Mast then goes on to explain fertilization and fetal development and the birth process. (S44).

It surely appears that Mast intended that the mechanics of the sex act be communicated to the student *with or without parental consent.* Chapter Six is stapled into the general text and cannot be removed without physically destroying the manual.

How does Mast rationalize this gross violation of the student's sense of modesty and rightful sense of privacy, as well as the usurpation of parental rights in this delicate area?

Well, if we examine the Parent's Guide, we note that Mast recommends that Chapter Six be taught at home and not in the school or group setting. (P28). But if Mast really intended the material to be used at home, why then is Chapter Six included in the Student Text, which is designed specifically for classroom use? Mast tells parents that they may want to read the student text before going over it with their child, the assumption being that Mast knows best as to when and how the facts of life should be presented and that the duty of parents is to begin where *she* leaves off. It doesn't even seem to occur to Mast that the inclusion of the description of the sex act in the Student Text may rob the parent of his or her right to handle this delicate matter on an individual and private basis with his or her own child, or that the parent may object to her interference in the matter.

In the Teacher's Manual, Mast repeats the statement that her biology chapter "should be taught at home with the parents" (T46), but then she goes on to suggest that "if the school curriculum requires teaching the reproductive system, it is suggested that the student *read the chapter silently during class time*." (T46).

The Harm of Mast's Clinical Reference

The harm done by Mast's sexology reference can only be understood within the context of the psychosexual development of the young adolescent—the target audience of the *Love and Life* curriculum. Once again, the works of Dr. Melvin Anchell provide insight into this phase of post-latency development.[362]

In describing the different patterns of psychosexual development in the young male and female who are just emerging from the latency period, Anchell notes that when latency comes to an end, direct sexual feelings are once again awakened.

In the case of the young adolescent boy, Anchell states, the matter is fairly simple because these "reawakened" sexual urges are "straight-forward and are centered in the genitalia."[363]

But for the young girl emerging from her latency cocoon, so to speak, the situation is much different and more complex.[364]

Her immature biological structures and incomplete feminine psychological development make her experience a "natural aversion to sexual intercourse,"[365] Anchell argues.

Unlike her male counterpart, the erotic feelings of the young teenage female are not strictly compartmentalized in the generative area, but rather, are "entwined" with the concepts of love, romance and affection.[366] This, states Anchell, is the normal psychosexual pattern for the young female adolescent.[367]

On the other hand, the portrait of the eager young man is slightly different. As Christopher Derrick, the indomitable defender of *Humanae Vitae,* states quite plainly, "A young man, in the heat of his energies, can pursue the girls endlessly for years, and never once admit to himself the nature of the happening that he so ardently desires and sometimes achieves. Physically, he is a male animal in rut; his body intends the pregnancy of the girl who attracts him. . .Objectively the whole performance is ordered to the making of a baby."[368]

Those of us privileged to have participated in this great mystery of married love smile inwardly when we view the first signs of youthful interplay between the sexes that normally marks early adolescence—the giggles and glances, the hand-holding, the endless phone chatter with girlfriends and boyfriends, the first date, the first school dance. We smile because we know where Nature is leading them, and because we understand that in the end, as it was in the beginning, sex *is* about marriage, family and babies.

There is no doubt that, particularly in the case of the young boy, Mast's gynecological description of the sex act is an attack upon the mind and soul of the young adolescent. The fact that the author precedes the description with "God words" does not automatically insure mental, clinical disinterest or a subdued libido on the part of the student. Sex involves not merely the intellect and will—it also involves the passions.

The Greeks have a word, "phantasmagoria," which describes images and fantasies which make their impression on the mind and imagination. Those images which are associated with sexual matters often come and go automatically, it would seem, or as if they had their own will, and, increasing or decreasing in vividness, they can pass into each other and fade away. These sensual images do not disappear completely, however, but return again and again—sometimes by specific invitation, but at other times without an act of the will.

While serving as a source of sexual stimulation for the young male, Mast's "open" and "mechanical" description of the physical act of sex is likely to be emotionally disturbing to the young teenage girl, whose immature emotional, mental and physical make-up prevents her from embracing the reality of the true meaning and nature of the spousal union. The knowledge of this reality will come with time—barring interference from the "sexperts"—and with normal psychosexual maturation, whereby the "affectionate" and the "spiritual" aspects of sex are integrated into the physical act of sex. But for now, the junior high or early high school girl is more attracted to the romantic as opposed to the biological aspects of sex. She should be left to enjoy these love fantasies, as long as they are chaste, without adult interference, however well-meaning it may be.

In summary then, the incorporation of the sexology reference in *Love and Life* is both imprudent and irreverent. It represents a clear threat to chastity. Lastly, it has no single redeeming feature, except to illustrate the degree to which Mast has been seduced by secular influences promoting sex education.[369]

Role Models in Short Supply

Any text for Catholic youth on sexual morality which fails to highlight *up front* the role of our Blessed Mother, St. Joseph and all the Saints in the development of moral virtue is seriously deficient.

Sadly, Mast's single reference to Our Lady and St. Joseph on pages 101 and 102 of the Student Guide and her superficial treatment of saints and martyrs notable for chastity are placed toward the *end* of the text (pages 90-92). It is but another indication that the author did not intend *Love and Life* to be a true Catholic exposition of Catholic teaching on sexual morality.

From a more practical point of view, the deletion and/or minimizing of Catholic doctrine and devotion does make it more marketable to other Christian denominations, who do not share traditional Catholic views on such fundamental concepts as Natural Law, papal authority or the sacramental life, or on the special role of Mary as perfect model of purity and powerful intercessor in time of temptation.

Mast on the Nature of Sex

Repeatedly throughout Mast, this writer is reminded of the Chesterton quote: "...Falsehood is never so false as when it is very nearly true." This is particularly true when Mast discusses the nature of human sexuality.

In the Student Guide, the sexual drive is referred to as a "naturally good gift." (S33). Young Catholics are told that "...the sexuality advertised on our 'arousing' culture is way out of bounds with what God established as natural and good." (S31). Conspicuously absent from the student text are any descriptive terms such as "intimate," "private," or "sacred," which would reveal to the young person the *whole* truth about the mystery of that which we call sex.

For when Mast describes sex as "natural," she is speaking a portion of truth; but it is not the whole truth, and where it stands alone, it is in fact a falsehood. Human sexuality embraces *both* the natural and the supernatural.[370]

As Bishop Daly explains in his remarkable exposition on the nature of human sexuality in *Morals, Law and Life,* "The scientific humanist regards sex in man as being essentially, originally, like sex in animals, an uncomplicated, animal instinct."[371]

"But it is a gross error to think of human sexuality in animal terms," he continues, "because there is nothing in man that is properly to be called animal..."[372] "He is one being, complicated of flesh and spirit at every level of his nature, in every part of his experience," states Daly. "His sexual nature is not an animal part of him. It is informed and infused with his spiritual nature."[373]

Daly argues that in man, "because sex is permeated by the human spirit and shares in the sacred value of the human person, whatever touches the biological nature of sex immediately touches the person and value of man and the destiny of humanity."[374]

"Sex has never been found in history without associations with religion and morality,"[375] Daly reminds his readers. "Small wonder that men could explain sex only by religion, accept sex only as from God and should demand that the sex union be consecrated by divine blessing through religious rites."[376]

For this reason, "Sex. . .cannot be treated in a perfectly 'natural' manner because it is more than a purely 'natural' phenomenon. For human sexuality is shrouded in mystery. . .the essential mystery which surrounds our origin; the Unknown from whence we came, and the Unknown to which we go," Daly concludes.[377]

Mast on the "Virtue" of "Family Planning"[378]

That a text ostensibly devoted to Catholic views on love, marriage and family for junior high and early high school students should preoccupy itself with the theory and practice of "family planning" is a sad commentary on the degree to which Catholics, including Mast, have been influenced by contemporary anti-child propaganda.

Before examining the philosophical underpinnings of *Love and Life's* chapter on the virtue of "family planning" and the "planned child," however, I should like to state for the record that any classroom discussion of the concept of birth control, by whatever means, natural or artificial, is *entirely inappropriate* for the young teen. In matters of love and life, the education of youth "should be oriented toward an understanding of the meaning of marriage and family and the value of children,"[379] not concepts of child prevention.[380, 381, 382]

As Dr. Herbert Ratner has stated, "One of the most important missions the Church can undertake with regard to the education of the young in matters related to marriage and family life is to inculcate in them the gift, the pleasures and the values of children."[383] This is all the more important because we live in a society dominated by a "secularized prudence," which is "overly concerned with the price to be paid, not the value received, and it is over cautious in regard to dangers or risks."[384] The remedy is to be found by encouraging "true prudence," which approaches judgment-making "with a trust in Divine Providence and includes hope in the final decision,"[385] Ratner states. He concludes with the pearl of wisdom that with regard to calculating the value of children, young people should be instructed in the ideal of the large family, which has always found merit in the eyes of the Church.

Having made these preliminary remarks, let us examine the content and concepts of Mast's chapter on "family planning," entitled "Love and Life: A Heavenly Bond." (S106-109).

"Family Planning" as a Norm of Conjugal Love

Although the subject is handled slightly differently in each of the three texts of *Love and Life,* there is no question that Mast views "family planning" as a given, that is, a norm of the conjugal relationship. The only issue for Mast is the manner in which the "planning" is carried out—that is, the method to be employed.

In the Student Guide, Mast opens the discussion of Natural Family Planning thusly:

> God *has a fulfilling plan for chaste living in marriage,* which keeps life and love together, glorifies God and helps married people grow in:
>
> —cooperation
> —communication
> —trust and
> —generosity.
>
> *It's called Natural Family Planning or Fertility Awareness.* (S106). (Emphasis added).

Mast tells the students that "true sexual maturity can be reached more easily when we practice natural family planning" and that "when used unselfishly, N.F.P. is a way of working with God and nature, respecting the love/life bond." (T108).

The statement on natural family planning is followed by a rather lengthy section on birth control and the sin of contraception. (S108).

In the Parent's Guide, the matter is discussed in a section on Love/Life distortions, under the subtitle "Birth Control," which also includes topics not handled in the Student Guide, such as masturbation, sterilization, homosexuality and artificial insemination. (P31-32).

Humanae Vitae is quoted with reference to the "inseparable connection, willed by God" between the unitive and procreative aspects of the marriage act. (P31). "In a world filled with contraceptives, it is important that we help our children understand God's plan in a positive light," Mast begins. (P31).

After noting that "to interfere with God's gift of fertility is a serious violation. . ." Mast makes the following statement:

> *The Church's teaching against contraception does not mean that the Church is opposed to family planning. The Church encourages couples to plan children with fertility knowledge and self-control, and to make responsible, prayerful decisions.* (P31). (Emphasis added).

Mast continues by stating that there is "a big difference" between "natural family planning" and "artificial family planning."

> Some people have taken on the contraceptive mentality in fear that they couldn't practice the self-control necessary *to plan the right size family* or that God would not provide for them as He has promised. (Emphasis added).

After briefly describing various family planning methods and common forms of contraception and early abortifacients, Mast concludes:

> *With today's scientifically accurate and reliable methods of natural family planning, there is no need to suffer the side effects, inconveniences or sinfulness of birth control devices.* Through the enlightenment of our Church, we can truly experience God's love and life in our families. (P31). (Emphasis added).

In the Teacher's Manual, Mast presents key concepts related to married love, including the role of natural family planning "to protect the love/life bond" in marriage. (T135).

Under Teaching Notes we read, "Fertility awareness, or natural family planning, is another gift from God, revealing further the beauty and order He has designed in His plan for human sexuality."

Under Class Activities, Mast suggests that a speaker from the local natural family planning organization be brought into the classroom to talk on the benefits of N.F.P. (T135).

In the Teacher's lesson plan for Chapter 21, on Pro-Life Issues, there are two sentences which are particularly helpful in discerning the author's mindset on the matter of "family planning."

Question 5 for classroom discussion is, "What are some peaceful and just solutions to an *unplanned pregnancy?*" (T140). (Emphasis added).

Under *Teaching Notes,* Mast instructs teachers to emphasize that in any discussions of abortion, students should be told:

> Even a young life *that may not have been "planned" by its parents* has been given God's love and life at conception.

Note that in Question 5 the "unplanned pregnancy" is *equated* with an "unwanted" or "problem" pregnancy, for which one must seek "peaceful and just solutions."

In the Teaching Notes, the single word "even" referring to the unplanned child reveals a similar line of thought. The inference is clear.

To Mast's way of thinking, the "planned" child holds the favored place, *"even"* though a young life that may not have been "planned by its parents" still retains its right to exist.

The question this writer wishes to raise at this point is not related to Mast's views on family planning; those are quite clear. Instead the question is this: Are these views as expressed in *Love and Life* representative of authentic Catholic thought?

Injecting the Poison of "Family Planning" Into the Youthful Conscience

St. Thomas Aquinas, in his *Commentary on the "De Caelo"* of Aristotle, makes the observation that "A small error in the beginning becomes a big error in the end."

The "small error" in Mast is the assumption that because the Church supports programs of "natural family planning" (to be used only when a couple has an objectively *serious reason* for doing so), it therefore endorses the norm of "family planning." This assumption, however, is *completely at odds* with the traditional Catholic position on "family planning," which has been one of *opposition, not endorsement.*

As Reverend Sean Donnelly, an Associate Member of the Fellowship of Catholic Scholars, has pointed out, "There is no conciliar or papal document which encourages couples—in principle—to limit family size."[386] Quite the contrary. "...*Humanae Vitae* (#10), also *Gaudium et spes* (#50), commend couples who prudently and courageously undertake to raise a large number of children."[387]

As Father Donnelly suggests, "The attitude expressed by, 'Yes, Father, we want to have children...but not right away,' does not reflect the spirit of the Church's teaching...As one priest put it, 'The first decision of the responsible couple is to have a child (without delay).' "[388]

"Even the Church's teaching on natural family planning is not an unconditional endorsement," he reminds us.[389]

> If then, there are serious motives for spacing births, motives derived from the physical or psychological condition of husband or wife, or from external circumstances, the Church teaches that it is then permissible to take into account the natural rhythms immanent in the generative functions and to make use of marriage during infertile times only... (*Humanae Vitae,* #16).[390]

Family Planning Terminology as Newspeak

There is also an additional rationale for the Church's rejection of the "family planning" ethic. This ethic is rooted in the antilife Sangerite philosophy and, like its handmaiden "sex education," has its origins *also* in the Malthusian-Eugenics Sexual-Reform Movements of the late 1800's. As IPPF chronicler Beryl Suitters states, "Today's Family Planning Association is yesterday's Malthusian League..."[391]

The term "family planning," a universal euphemism for the practice of "birth control" (i.e., no births and no control), is what Bishop Daly refers to as "guilt-assuaging and moral-satisfaction-suggesting stimuli."[392]

The development of this anti-life newspeak requires that common language be "persuasively re-defined," that is to say, "the usual *meaning* of the phrases is being subtly changed so that the moral and emotional approval elicited by the *words* may be attached to a new form of behavior which it is desired to recommend.[393]

By way of illustration, Bishop Daly examines the phrase "family planning," that is, where "contraceptive intercourse is the rule and natural intercourse the calculated exception."[394]

"Practitioners of the former are said to be 'continent,' while practitioners of the latter are labeled 'incontinent,' " Daly says. "Whereas *in fact* it is precisely the contraceptionist who finds continence impossible and is therefore 'incontinent.' "[395]

Under the current rate of Sangerite exchange, Daly continues, "Only habitual contraceptive-users are permitted to be called 'voluntary parents' and only the babies and families of habitual contraceptive-users are permitted to be referred to as 'wanted babies' or 'planned families.' "[396]

Following this line of thinking, Bishop Daly concludes, "All the pregnancies of non-contraceptive-using parents are by definition 'accidental pregnancies,' and all their babies are by definition 'unwanted babies.' "[397] "In other words, 'wanted babies' are babies of those who throughout their married lives habitually do not want babies and who ensure, by regular use of contraceptives, that they do not have them; but who, on a carefully restricted number of occasions, cease to 'unwant' babies and suspend temporarily the use of contraceptives."[398]

A Baby Is a Gift, Not a Product

At a deeper theological level, the Catholic Church has always taught that a baby is a gift from God, not a "product" to be planned. Not only are children a blessing theologically speaking, they are also a blessing biologically, because, as Dr. Ratner points out in his classic work, *The Natural Institution of the Family (Marriage: An Office of Nature)*, "Man is a relatively sterile animal."[399]

These teachings unfortunately go unacknowledged in the *Love and Life* curriculum, because Mast focuses almost exclusively on methodology, that is, "natural" family planning versus "artificial" contraception. That one might possibly object to the "planning" feature of both completely escapes the author.[400]

Lest this writer be accused of trying to be "holier than the Pope," it should be noted that Pope John Paul II himself has warned against both the abuse of natural family planning and the philosophy that promotes the limitation, even the exclusion, of children in the conjugal relationship.

The warning was issued on September 5, 1984 during a series of papal lectures on the prophetic vision of *Humanae Vitae,* in which the Pope repeated the traditional Church teaching in opposition to contraception.

On the matter of natural family planning, the Holy Father stated that even methods which are based on sexual abstinence during a woman's fertile period can become "the source of abuses if couples seek in such a way to avoid, without just reasons, procreation..."[401]

Pope John Paul said *Humanae Vitae,* which was addressed to all men of good will, urges couples to act according to the "objective moral order established by God," and *"In no way is it exclusively directed to limiting, much less excluding children."*[402] (Emphasis added).

Love and Life Lacks the Christian Ideal of Family

Because of Mast's secular orientation, there is little attention paid in the Student Guide to the Christian ideal of family life.

Rather than introducing the poison of "family planning" into the *Love and Life* curriculum, the author could have made a positive contribution to the understanding of love, marriage and the family by incorporating Christian ideals on family life into the format text, including the special contribution of large families, the value of children and perhaps one of the most important things that life teaches us, *that the best things in life are unplanned—falling in love, family, friends and children.*

Mast on "Voluntary Permanent Sterilization"

As noted earlier, the subject of sterilization is only listed in the Student Guide (S109), but it is covered in the Parent's Guide. (P31-32).

Under the title *Voluntary Permanent Sterilization* (P31-32), Mast describes the birth control procedure as "a permanent surgical destruction of one's healthy fertility, usually through vasectomy or tubal ligation." By "sterilizing ourselves," she states, "we reject the gift of fertility, which is one of the most sacred gifts God has given us. If we really think about it, sterilization is a form of despair," she continues. When one is sterilized, he or she is saying, "I will never be able to control my sex drives to plan the size family I should have..." (P31). (Note again Mast's reference to "planning" of family size.)

Given the growing popularity of permanent sterilization by married couples, including Catholics, and the rising menace of eugenic sterilization imposed by the state, one might have expected something more from Mast than this perfunctory treatment of a "family planning" practice which has always found great favor among the Sangerites, as evidenced by the following quote taken from the *IPPF Chronicles:*

> Persuading people to accept contraception was not the end of the battle...many did not sustain their efforts to use devices...sterilization gained ground...because once accepted there was little chance of turning back, and no further action on the part of the patient was called for.[403]
>
> "Sterilization" like abortion is a "subsidiary" means of family planning and eugenic and population control. Abortion...is a costly and wasteful form of birth control...some women will not accept abortion...Sterilization settles the problem once and for all.[404]

In sharp contrast to the birth controllers, the position of the Catholic Church on direct sterilization, temporary or permanent, for eugenic, social or contraceptive purposes, has been one of consistent *condemnation*.[405]

Natural Law, articulated in the Magisterium of the Church, makes claim to the truth expressed in *Casti Connubii,* "that private individuals have no power over the members of their bodies than that which pertains to their natural ends, and they are not free to destroy or mutilate their members, or in any other way render themselves unfit for their natural functions."[406]

Seven years later, in response to the use of eugenic sterilization, Pius XI issued another encyclical, *Mit brennender Sorge* (1937), which was a condemnation of sterilization and was in defense of not only the individual human person but all humanity; a defense "of man's rights and dignity and freedom against totalitarian tyranny."[407]

One wonders why Mast appears unwilling clearly and forthrightly to articulate to Catholic parents the authentic position of the Catholic Church with regard to direct sterilization, *both* temporary and permanent.

Mast on Artificial Insemination

Likewise, in treating the topic of artificial insemination, covered under the heading "Technological Human Reproduction," Mast again makes no mention of the absolute condemnation of this practice by the Catholic Church without appeal, as a violation of the Natural Law and the Divine Law.

According to Mast, "artificial insemination...*may seem desirable for childless couples...however, it raises serious moral questions*...newly conceived lives are destroyed...[it] takes away the unitive dimension of the sex act and distorts the procreative dimension...The Catholic Church cares deeply for the integrity of love and life..." (P32). (Emphasis added).

Again, what is missing is any sense of moral outrage. Artificial insemination is in *direct* and *open contradiction to EVERYTHING the Church teaches about the nature and purpose of human love and human life*—supposedly the very theme of the Mast program.

As Daly states with his usual clarity, "Artificial insemination is not merely a technique to be pronounced morally wrong: it is anti-moral, anti-man, and anti-God."[408]

"Artificial insemination is evil because procreation is never merely a biological process. A man cannot morally be a father in a 'merely materialistic sense' because a child is not a material thing,"[409] Daly states. "Fatherhood or motherhood, in particular, is a spiritual relationship incarnated in a physical relationship and these are inseparable, as body is from soul."[410] "Artificial insemination sunders flesh from spirit, and turns, like Manicheism, into contempt of both."[411] This act of severing the physical from the spiritual "is not animal but perverse spirit," he continues, "that is to say, diabolic."[412]

"The consequences of artificial insemination within the conjugal circle are no less grave,"[413] Daly states. "The A.I.D. [*artificial insemination* with *donor's* seed] child in the home will be a permanent reminder to the sterile husband of his inferiority and impotence."[414] "The child, which should be a bond and pledge of union...has instead become a barrier of division, a proof of inequality, a threat to the stability of the marriage."[415]

"The legal gymnastics of artificial insemination are as indefensible as the moral gymnastics utilized to defend the practice," states Daly, because "in their insistence on the need for secrecy, the parents, the attending physician and sometimes the law collaborate in fraud and deception."[416]

When birth certificates are altered to confer on a child the name of a putative father, the medical practitioner is "the instigator of and accessory to the crime" of "making a false and fraudulent record."[417] The alternative, as suggested by the Reverend Mr. Joseph Fletcher, is that parents should frankly tell the child that it has been "co-opted"![418]

With regard to the child himself, Daly states, "It is surely one of the most cruel frauds one could perpetrate on a human being—a lie about his name and identity. *For those responsible, it is very close to the 'lie of the soul'; not a lie one tells, but a lie one lives and is.*"[419] (Emphasis added).

Tied in with this reality, that the child conceived through artificial insemination "shall never be able to call any *person* 'my father,' " is still another reality, that the "artificial insemination ideology" not only makes "redundant" one parent, but abolishes "the very meaning of human parenthood as such. It is the sacred name of Father that is being subverted."[420]

"Nor is it only human fatherhood that is marked down for destruction; it is also, and indeed primarily, the Fatherhood of God, the very notion of God, which is being eliminated,"[421] Daly concludes.

Some Final Thoughts on Mast

Since the Mast program is considered by many of its promoters to be a prototype text of what has become known as "chastity education," I should like to comment on the latter as it pertains to a separate course of formal instruction in Catholic schools.

My first observation is that such courses which attempt to isolate and teach "chastity" apart from other virtues are unwise and almost always harmful for the young person. As we all know, both the theological and cardinal virtues are interdependent and build one upon the other. It is impossible to understand the real meaning of chastity without some understanding of prudence, justice and fortitude—the cardinal virtues which precede temperance, of which chastity is a part. Further, and most importantly, remaining chaste is principally a matter of true Catholic formation and of God's grace, and not of information, per se.

My second observation, which is akin to the first, is that the isolation of chastity as a specific course of study in Catholic elementary and secondary schools is foreign to the traditional manner by which the Church instructs the faithful, particularly the young, in matters of sexual morality.

If Catholic schools were teaching traditional doctrinal catechetics in elementary and secondary schools, there would be no need for a separate course on chastity. Generally speaking, references to sexual morality, covered by the 6th and 9th Commandments, should, in a regular course of religious study, neither be emphasized nor under-played, but rather treated within the total context of traditional Church teaching, which includes the Commandments, the theological and moral virtues, the fruits of the Holy Spirit, the Beatitudes and Sacred Scripture.

A sense of humility and honesty should move us to admit that the development of "chastity education" courses came about as a knee-jerk reaction to finding an alternative to "sex education" programs. However, as evidenced by the *Love and Life* curriculum, the cure may be worse than the disease.

In conclusion, I should like to point out that this critical analysis of the Mast program is not so much a condemnation of one particular program. Rather, it is an indictment of the generally sad state of affairs of doctrinal catechetics in the Catholic Church in America today.

That the *Love and Life* curriculum has been praised by many traditional-minded Catholics is but a confirmation of the fact that authentic Church teachings on sex, marriage and family have been so desecrated that almost anything that poses as "Catholic" is eagerly embraced. And this is the *real* tragedy of Mast's sex education program.

Chapter 8
The Vatican and Sex Education

Introduction—A Sorry State of Affairs

In early June of 1989, all the bishops of the United States received a memorandum mailed from the Office of the General Secretary of the National Conference of Catholic Bishops (NCCB) concerning the status of the thrice-revised, controversial *New Creation* sex education program for elementary grades 1-8, published by the Religious Education Division of The William C. Brown Co. of Dubuque, Iowa. (Original edition, 1984; revised 14-Lesson Edition, 1987; and Revised 7-Lesson Edition, 1988.)

The six-page communication, initiated at the behest of Archbishop Daniel Kucera of Dubuque, contained recent correspondence between the Archbishop and the Holy See—specifically, Joseph Cardinal Ratzinger, Prefect of the Sacred Congregation for the Doctrine of the Faith, and William Cardinal Baum, Prefect of the Sacred Congregation for Catholic Institutions (Education)—on the matter of classroom sex education in general and the *New Creation Series* in particular.

Archbishop Kucera Seeks Clarification from Rome

In his introductory cover letter to the American bishops, dated May 17, 1989, Archbishop Kucera detailed his involvement with the *New Creation Series,* which bore the *Imprimatur* of retired Archbishop James J. Byrne for the first half of the series and that of Kucera for the second half.

Kucera explained that in 1987 a revised text of *New Creation* was undertaken at his request and embodied suggestions received from the Pope John XXIII Center, Braintree, Massachusetts.

The Archbishop maintained that despite long-standing criticism of the sex education series by groups and individuals throughout the United States and demands that he withdraw his *Imprimatur,* his "contact with the Holy See in person and through our Pro-Nuncio, Archbishop Pio Laghi," had assured him that he had followed proper procedures in procuring the *Imprimatur* and that it was "canonically correct."

Kucera defended his consistent refusal to "engage in theological discussion with groups or individuals in person or by mail," stating that his responsibility in the matter was "directly to the Holy See, through the usual channels of the established Congregations of the Roman Curia."

He noted that some of his fellow bishops "have been receiving letters critical of the series and even suggesting that it was in disfavor at the Holy See." But he expressed confidence that the resultant "confusion and uncertainty" would be allayed by the Ratzinger and Baum letters, which he hoped would help the hierarchy fulfill their "canonical and pastoral responsibilities in what is certainly a delicate area of religious education" and at the same time "ease the consciences of many well-meaning people who are naturally concerned about the whole area of sex education, given the permissive nature of American society with its rampant disregard for moral values."

Ratzinger Defers Pedagogical Decisions to Baum

In his letter of February 23, 1989 to Archbishop Kucera concerning the doctrinal status of *New Creation,* Cardinal Ratzinger acknowledged his Congregation's receipt of Kucera's correspondence of December 21, 1988, which brought the Holy See's attention to "certain difficulties and concerns" relating to the sex education series and the subsequent revision of the program "according to the recommendations of a number of experts from the John XXIII Center who had studied it at your request..." As Prefect of the Congregation for the Doctrine of the Faith,

Ratzinger clarified this dicastery's position on the program in question by stating that the recently revised text of *New Creation* "has resulted in a clearer presentation of the Church's moral teaching" and that "the program does not appear, then, to be problematic from the doctrinal point of view." However, the Congregation recognized that "overall pedagogy" and "the maintenance of prudence" remained.

Further, Ratzinger stated that the Congregation was also aware "that there are parents who judge their rights and interests to have been ignored by local Church authorities when this program, designed for classroom use, is implemented and their real ability to affect the extent of their children's *exposure to this kind of material* is thereby checked." (Emphasis added).

Regarding the resolution of these issues, Ratzinger said his office would remand the question and its further examination "to the competence of the Congregation for Catholic Education" and "the opportune judgment of His Eminence, William Cardinal Baum" and that "inquiries concerning this review or its possible results ought to be directed then to the Congregation for Catholic Education."

Baum Remands Final Judgment To Local Ordinary

Two months later, Cardinal Baum responded to the Ratzinger invitation to take up additional questions related to the implementation of the *New Creation Series* in Catholic classrooms by issuing a formal statement on behalf of his Congregation, dated May 8, 1989.

In his opening comments to Archbishop Kucera, Cardinal Baum expressed "the deep concern felt by this Congregation with regard to the very delicate and important matter of education in human sexuality for children and young people."

As to the question of doctrinal integrity, Baum reassured Kucera that the Ratzinger letters to him (Kucera) and the Congregation for Catholic Institutions (Education) had closed the matter—that is, "anxiety about doctrinal aspects of the program. . .would seem to be without foundation." "However," he continued, "the question of what is appropriate in a classroom setting in the light of child psychology and religious formation must be taken into account." Baum cites his Congregation's 1983 document *Educational Guidance in Human Love,* which "gives preference to education in human sexuality on a one-to-one basis, precisely because of the delicate nature of the subject matter." (Cf. nn. 58 and 71).

The remainder of the Baum text returns specifically to the conduct of sex education instruction in a formal group setting, which the American-born primate claims is "welcomed" by "the majority" of parents. Following a reference to the necessity of "proper safeguards," "especially to clear presentation of the moral and spiritual values which preserve the sacredness of the human personality in all its aspects," Baum states that *"responsibility for determining proper teaching aids and texts. . .whether the subject be human sexuality or some other sphere of religious education. . .is within the competence of the diocesan bishop"* (cf. c.i.c. n. 775, #1 and EGHL, n. 55), as noted in "the Code of Canon Law, in articles 775 and 804," which "wisely places responsibility on the one charged with the spiritual formation of the local church, the bishop." (Emphasis added).

"This Congregation, therefore, deems it best to deal with parental and other concerns for the *New Creation Series, or indeed for any texts,* through the spiritual shepherd of the diocese, the bishop. In this way, the spiritual development of young people can best be assured and the wishes and needs of parents best be fulfilled," Baum reiterates. (Emphasis added).

The Baum letter continues with an expression that Kucera will find the foregoing reflections "helpful" as he (Kucera) endeavors "to promote 'a positive and prudent sex education' as deemed necessary by Vatican Council II. . .encouraging the development of a full and proper partnership between parents and teachers in this extremely important and sensitive sphere of child and youth formation." Baum ends his "reflections" with assurances of "profound gratitude" for Bishop Kucera's "tireless and devoted efforts and of the continued support of this Congregation for Catholic Education."

Raw Moral Sewage

The following shocking, but representative, quotes were taken from the 7-Lesson Edition of the *New Creation Series* (1988) for Catholic schools, grades 1-8. There were scores of others to choose from, but these, I believe, are sufficient to illustrate the absolute obscenity of the Kucera-Ratzinger-Baum correspondence.

> ...Remember how you came to be. Sperm from your dad joined with an egg from your mom. You were conceived. This happened when your father deposited sperm from his penis in your mother's vagina. [From "Sharing Love," *The New Creation Series,* Grade 3.]
>
> ...A boy's body begins to change quickly about the age of twelve or later...Hair appears under his arms and around his penis (PEE niss). The testicles (TESS ti kels) and the scrotum (SKROH tum) containing them drop down from the body a little bit...His penis gets larger..." "At times the boy's penis may become erect. It becomes hard and stands out from his body. This erection (e REC shun) just happens...The penis does not stay erect for more than a few minutes at one time..." [From "How Boys Change," *The New Creation Series,* Grade 5].
>
> ...We can experience new, often pleasurable feelings, especially in our genital organs. Boys sometimes experience an erection of the penis along with these feelings. Girls sometimes will experience more moisture at the opening of the vagina. Sexual feelings in girls and women center around the clitoris (KLI to ris), a small organ in front of the vaginal opening. [From "Programmed for Puberty," *The New Creation Series,* Grade 5.]
>
> ...The tiny, bud-like organ located in the front of the opening of the passage leading to the uterus and which is the primary source of sexual pleasure in women is called the (circle one) clitoris, urethra, ovum, menses. [From "More than Facts," *The New Creation Series,* Grade 7.]
>
> ...for the parents, being pro-life is not just having babies...*Each couple will have to decide for themselves at what point deciding to have more children becomes a contra-*

> *life,* rather than a pro-life choice. Even if the couple can "afford" it, it could be contra-life to risk having more children, for example, if the mother is in poor health...
>
> ...For married couples this decision about having and not having children is one of the most serious they have to make. They have to be honest with themselves. *This is called family planning.* [From "Marriage is Pro-Life," *The New Creation Series,* Grade 8. Emphasis added].
>
> ...Even though the "test tube baby" technique has helped many couples become parents, the Church is cautious and continues its traditional teaching that reproduction of a human life should come only from natural sexual contact or intercourse by married couples...Discussions of the moral problems related to this technique will continue as the technique is further developed.[422] [From "Test Tube Babies," *The New Creation Series,* Grade 8. Emphasis added].

Here we have children as young as seven or eight years of age, who during their latency—which the Holy Father describes in *Familiaris Consortio* (N37) as the "years of innocence"—*ought* to be the beneficiaries of sound doctrinal catechetics, which will lead them to the knowledge and love of the adorable Trinity and the Blessed Mother, St. Joseph and all the Saints. *Instead,* these children are being systematically desensitized, seduced and violated—under the very shadow of the cross—by this raw moral sewage. And these prelates have the gall to try to pawn off this scatology as "religious education," while at the same time attempting to disarm and anesthetize the consciences of concerned parents and critics of classroom sex education by proclaiming the revised *New Creation Series* to be "doctrinally non-problematic"!

The "pass the buck" strategies explicit in the Ratzinger and Baum letters will have the effect of putting the remnant of Faithful Catholics in America, most particularly children and youth, at the mercy of the "New American Church" which controls the direction and content of Catholic education through its administrative bureaucracies in the NCCB/USCC. Further, their actions can be construed so as to minimize and/or discredit the opinions of those Curia members who have been critical of *The New*

Creation Series, specifically Cardinal Edouard Gagnon, President of the Pontifical Council for the Family, who in the Fall of 1988 issued a well-publicized condemnation of *The New Creation Series* and warned that the program was so pedagogically and psychologically riddled with errors that *any* future attempts to "revise" the series would prove "unsatisfactory."[423]

This chapter on the Vatican and sex education is designed to bring readers up-to-date on the current status of the issue of the licitness of formal classroom instruction on explicit sexual matters in Catholic elementary and secondary schools. It will reexamine some of the suppositions and statements found in the Kucera-Ratzinger-Baum correspondence in light of other recent Vatican documents issued by Pope John Paul II and the various congregations, councils and offices which make up the Roman Curia. Since my chronology of key Church documents and events related to teachings on human sexuality, marriage and the family presented in Chaper IV ends with the publication of the USCC-Dolesh Sex Education Guidelines in the Fall of 1981, this would appear to be a likely point to pick up the matter once again.

Vatican Criticism of USCC "Guidelines" Silenced

During the U.S.-Vatican summit with Pope John Paul II, the Curia and the American Archbishops held from March 8-11, 1989, Edouard Cardinal Gagnon, President of the Pontifical Council for the Family, addressed the topic of "The Family."

In the portion of his text on "Education for Chastity," Gagnon made this extraordinary revelation concerning the 1981 USCC-Dolesh Sex Education "Guidelines":

> The Pontifical Council for the Family, then under the direction of Cardinal Knox, received as one of its first missions that of studying the implications [which] the document *Education in Human Sexuality for Christians: Guidelines for Discussion and Planning* could have on preparing young people to a successful married life and helping them preserve chastity before marriage.[424]

In 1981 this writer completed a 78-page *Critique of the USCC Sex Education Guidelines*,[425] which documented the sorry history, pedagogy and content of the new sexual catechetical movement in Catholic elementary and secondary schools. In Chapter V of this text, the USCC-Dolesh "Guidelines" are compared to the "adult" version of the document, i.e., the 1977 Kosnik "Study," *Human Sexuality: New Directions in American Catholic Thought.* In my dual analysis, I indicated that whereas Rome took rapid and decisive action against the Kosnik "Study," no public criticism of the USCC "Guidelines" was forthcoming from the Vatican. In light of Gagnon's March, 1989 statement to the American bishops, however, my earlier comment appears to be in need of some modification.

Subsequent research confirmed the fact that under the presidency of the late Australian-born Cardinal Knox, a critique of the USCC "Guidelines" was prepared by the Pontifical Council and circulated for comment to a number of Curia offices, including Cardinal Baum's Congregation for Catholic Education, where the report was promptly sandbagged—to use an American colloquialism—and with impeccable timing!

As noted earlier, by the late Fall of 1981, the USCC "Guidelines" were under heavy fire from a number of prestigious Catholic groups demanding the retraction of the document, which had *never* been approved by the U.S. bishops in the first place. A thumbs down vote on the "Guidelines" by the Vatican at this critical junction would no doubt have signaled death for this particular program and slowed the progress of the new sexual catechetical movement in the United States.

To forestall such a setback for the modernist apparatus, it would be necessary to wrest the matter from the jurisdiction of the Pontifical Council for the Family. As Prefect of the Congregation for Catholic Education, Baum argued, with apparent success, that as a catechetical matter, the sex education "Guidelines" fell within the purview of his office. The Knox report—still in an "in-house" draft stage—was promptly set aside and its content never made public. In its stead, the Congregation agreed to conduct a more inclusive "study" of the sex education matter, which subsequently was released some two years later under the title *Educational Guidance In Human Love.*

As for the USCC-Dolesh "Guidelines," thanks to the Baum intervention, they have remained in active circulation for more than eight years, inspiring such programs as the *New Creation Series,* the object of the Kucera-Ratzinger-Baum correspondence in the Spring of 1989.

The Congregation for Catholic Education Issues "Educational Message" For Bishops and Educators

In October of 1983, at the world Synod of Bishops, Cardinal Baum announced that his congregation would soon be issuing guidelines on sex education,[426] "as an educational message, and centres on educators' sense of responsibility."[427] (sic).

The final document, *Orientamenti educativi sull'amore umano*[428]—"Educational Orientations on Human Love," poorly translated into English as *Educational Guidance in Human Love*[429] (EGHL)—is dated November 1, Feast of All Saints, but was released by the Sacred Congregation for Catholic Education on December 1, 1983.

In his press statement Cardinal Baum said that for a long time his congregation "had been receiving requests for advice and also protests on the delicate problem of sexual education in Catholic schools."[430] According to Baum, the document was issued "after long and well considered consultations."[431]

"The document will be of pedagogical and pastoral character. Pastors will be asked to make use of it as a means of reflecting [sic] for those responsible for the education of youth,"[432] the American-born prelate concluded.

Father Michael Sharkey, a staff member of the Congregation, also told members of the press that it would be a mistake to see the Guidelines "as a mandate just for schools and to forget about parents."[433] He stated that all school programs should be "marked by parental cooperation, especially in the area of private consultation with a student by a teacher,"[434] and that

"Parents should be consulted as to whom they wish their children to speak with if their children want to speak with someone privately."[435] Sharkey concludes with the admonition that the new guidelines state that "individual sex education always retains prior value" and "that the person who speaks with children on sex should be one who is a person of faith. . ."[436]

The Catholic Press in America Uniformly Applauds the Document

Both the National Catholic News Service (NC) and the Religious News Service (RNS) carried extensive and favorable coverage of *Educational Guidance in Human Love* (EGHL) upon its release in December of 1983.

Diocesan papers across the country carried front page NC articles on various aspects of the new document, including the rights and duties of the family, the role of parochial schools and other ecclesial institutions in the collaboration with the family, the necessity of integrating Christian values into sex instruction of youth, the specific problems of premarital relations, masturbation and homosexuality, and the importance of civil authority in the protection of public morality and of the State in safeguarding citizens against the abuse of minors, sexual violence, permissiveness and pornography.[437]

The RNS release—carrying a Vatican City dateline—placed more emphasis on the Holy See's strong condemnation of illicit sexual *acts* tempered by solicitous pastoral care for the *individuals* involved, the importance of sports as a healthy outlet for young people, the grave harm caused by sexually explicit textbooks, and the importance of the family in preparing young people for their vocation in life, including indissoluble marriage, the priesthood or a religious order.[438]

Secular Press Gives Document Mixed Reviews

Reviews of *EGHL* in the secular media varied in objectivity from the *New York Post's* forthright front page article, "*Vatican*

Rips Sex Without Marriage''[439] (12/1/83), to the blatantly anti-Catholic editorializing of *Newsweek's* Religious Editor, Kenneth Woodward, who denounced the "sterile moralisms of many past Church pronouncements" on the question of sexual morality,[440] and took a verbal swipe at opponents of classroom sex education by claiming, "Parents who oppose sex education in Roman Catholic schools can no longer look to Rome for support."[441]

New York Tribune columnist and educational commentator Howard Hurwitz used the issuance of the Congregation's guidelines as an occasion to compare them with the new sex syllabus for New York City's public schools, which was also released in early December.

Hurwitz's comparison between the two reports is summed up thusly: "The Vatican's views have gestated for 2,000 years and are planted in traditional morality. The Board of Education labored for five years and its issue is stamped with the new morality—'If you can't be good, be careful.' "[442]

With a haunting refrain, Hurwitz notes that, whereas the New York City Board attempted "in limp, and left-handed effort to deflect flak from the church"[443] by including the June, 1968 "Interfaith Statement on Sex Education" (which the reader will recall was signed by Monsignor James T. McHugh for the United States Catholic Conference),[444] ". . .morals and ethics are as foreign to sex education, New York City style, as human rights to the Gulag Archipelago."[445] The unfortunate, but predictable effect on children who manage to survive this assault on their psyche, Hurwitz concludes, will be that "they will be titillated, not educated, to the point of exhaustion. . .and Rule Genitalia will become the national anthem if the New York City lyrics reverberate in the rest of the country."[446, 447]

The NCCB-USCC Issues an Official Response to *EGHL*

Shortly after the release of *EGHL,* Father Thomas Lynch, Family Life Director of the NCCB-USCC—who had previously distinguished himself in the sex education field by his public condemnation of Catholic parents who have "not dealt with their own sexuality, so they can't teach their kids"[448] —praised the Congregation's document, saying it gives "a green light to promote creative sex education."[449]

A separate statement issued by the NCCB-USCC Committee for Pro-Life Affairs took the position that the new guidelines would end the Catholic debate over classroom sex education:

> For more than a decade, there has been considerable controversy about sex education in the schools. This document [*EGHL*] addresses the issue in terms of the Catholic school, and it provides the opportunity to move from debate to dialogue, and ultimately to cooperation and unity of effort. It dispels the notion that there is no role for the school, but also provides a theological foundation and moral principles which guide the development of such programs. It is not addressed to such programs in the public schools.[450]

Catholic Lay Groups Offer Words of Caution

On December 8, 1983, one week after the release of *EGHL*, a National Coalition of sex education opponents sponsored a joint press conference in Newark, N.J. to warn Catholics that attempts would be made by the neo-Modernists to undermine and twist language of the document to suit their own ends.[451]

Lay and clerical representatives of the National Coalition Interstate Committee of Clergy and Laity, now known as the National Coalition of Clergy and Laity (NCCL), used the occasion to stress the gravity of the sex education scandal in parochial and public schools throughout the United States and singled out for specific condemnation those programs which would fall immediately under the ax if *EGHL* were authentically promulgated—including the Benziger, Sadlier and Forliti "family life" programs and the sexology texts of Hugo Hurst, Nancy Hennessy Cooney, Michele McCarthy, Ronald J. Wilkins and Richard Reichart.[452]

In what turned out to be a flash of prophetic insight, the pro-faith, pro-chastity Coalition refocused attention on the pivotal role played by Monsignor McHugh in bringing the Planned

Parenthood-SIECUS-AASEC(T) trojan horse into Catholic schools across the nation during the mid-1960's and '70's and called upon McHugh to repudiate both the controversial *Education in Human Sexuality Guidelines* of the Archdiocese of Newark and the USCC-Dolesh "Guidelines," *Education in Human Sexuality for Christians,* in light of the condemnation of "pagan and naturalistic" sexology found in *EGHL.*[453]

In February of 1984, Catholics United for the Faith published a generally favorable critique of *Educational Guidance in Human Love,* written by E. William Sockey III, CUF Executive Director. While praising the document for giving "full support to Catholic parents who have been opposing false, immoral and imprudent sex education in Catholic classrooms"[454] and for the guidelines' emphasis on individual education in sexual matters by parents or someone appointed by them,[455] Sockey laments the fact that with regard to the "particularly serious problem" of co-ed sex education classes, "in the present, permissive environment in the English-speaking world, it is unfortunate that sex education in mixed groups is not prohibited altogether by the Church."[456]

Sockey makes an interesting observation concerning the document's use of the term "trauma" to describe the degree of harm done to youth who are exposed to sexually graphic sex education materials,[457] and he concludes his remarks with an expression of outrage "that any child should be subjected to this danger (i.e., mental and emotional injury) through those teachers or those materials being used in the school—far more than if the child were subjected to *physical* abuse at the hand of his or her teacher."[458]

Anti-Life Organizations Hail Church "Sanction" of Classroom Sex Education

It must appear somewhat incredible that a document on a subject as controversial as sex education should draw the praise of groups which are diametrically opposed to one another in *every* way, that is, traditional Catholic, Jewish and Protestant pro-life and pro-family forces on the one hand, and Planned Parenthood and company, which includes a wide assortment of special interest groups with anti-life predilections (homosexuals, feminists, abortionists, eugenicists and the sort), on the other. Although this apparent contradiction will resolve itself later in the chapter, the reader may want to keep this seemingly paradoxical situation in mind when he reads the following commentary, which is quoted almost in its entirety as it appeared in the Winter, 1984 quarterly newsletter *Issues and Action Update,* published by the Center for Population Options, an anti-life offshoot of Planned Parenthood.

Titled "Vatican Issues Statement on Sex Education," the CPO statement reads as follows:

> *In a shift from its previous stance,* the Vatican recently issued a 36-page document supporting "positive" sexuality education in parochial schools. The statement, which stresses the primary role of parents in sex education, *represents the Church's first official support for sex education in schools, although many parochial schools in the United States have offered programs for years.* While upholding the Church's traditional condemnation of pre- and extra-marital sex, homosexuality, and masturbation, the statement suggests that teachers employ an understanding approach to these issues. . .[459] [Emphasis added].

Commenting on the mixed response to the document, which ranged "from unrestrained enthusiasm to hesitant support and serious concern,"[460] the Center for Population Options article goes on to quote Father Tom Lynch, "a representative of the National Conference of Catholic Bishops," as stating that the newly released Vatican document is "a positive step forward. . .we believe [that] education in human sexuality. . .should take place in the home, but that the home needs help."[461]

Barbara Whitney, the Executive Director of SIECUS, was quoted as agreeing with Lynch on the importance of family involvement, but went on to explain, "*The Vatican supports most sexuality educators in the U.S. today who would make the same claim.* However, we must also acknowledge that most parents are unable or unwilling to assume this responsibility without the significant support from other community agencies."[462] (Emphasis added).

According to the CPO article, Whitney also expressed concern about the emphasis on Catholic doctrine in *EGHL* at the possible expense of cooperation with other denominations and the secular community. "The Vatican claim that sexual education should never be separated from the morality of the Roman Catholic faith may be appropriate for Roman Catholics in parochial school settings," she said, *"but it contradicts the U.S. Catholic Conference, which urges the Catholic community to be aware of public schools' sex education programs and to cooperate with and supplement them, rather than establish alternatives, which might lead to polarization or isolation."*[463] (Emphasis added).

Overall, the CPO editorial statement concluded that *Educational Guidance in Human Love* would be a bonus for the anti-life forces:

"Despite differing reactions, there was widespread agreement that the effects of the Vatican statement will be felt both within and outside the Catholic community. *Not only does the document sanction parochial school sex education programs, it may also ease pressure from Catholic organizations to curtail sex education programs in the public schools. Already, it has opened up a new dialogue between sex education advocates and the Catholic Church.*"[464] (Emphasis added).

The Foreign Press Offers Variety of Commentaries on *EGHL*

Unlike the Catholic press in the United States, whose reactions to *Educational Guidance in Human Love* were as a whole non-questioning and standardized in favor of the document, the European press displayed a broader diversity of opinions on the document, with some negative commentaries coming from both "liberal" and "conservative" elements within the Church.

All of the following selections from various European dailies and news journals were taken from a commentary on international press responses to *Educational Guidance in Human Love* which appeared in the January-June 1984 issues of *Seminarium,* published by Cardinal Baum's Sacred Congregation for Catholic Institutions (Education). The author of the article is Fr. Gianfranco Grieco, O.F.M., editor of the "Vatican News Service" for *L'Osservatore Romano.* In addition to reviewing Italian and foreign press comments, Fr. Grieco also takes up a strident defense of the document against critics whose convictions are rooted in an anti-Christian concept and philosophies.[465]

From England, *The Universe: The Catholic Newspaper of London* (12/9/83) editorialized, "If one wants a message to attain its goal, it must be intelligible. . .On the contrary, *the recent document on sexual education has a lot which is obfuscated, although it is admittedly directed at educators and bishops.*"[466] (Emphasis added).

The Catholic Herald took a brighter view of the document, although it also made mention of the problem of "vagueness," especially with regard to the practical principles to be applied to the classroom setting, the difficulty for parents in reading the "Vatican-styled" document, which was prepared for bishops and educators, and the fact that *"the important issue of teacher preparation must still be resolved by individual bishops."*[467] (Emphasis added).

The Paris daily, *La Croix* (12/2/83), under the title "Sexual Education is Education to Love," reported favorably on the document, which it credited as "a great pedagogical and pastoral contribution."[468]

Ja (12/2/83), the Madrid daily, praised the document's emphasis on "the duty of the State to defend citizens against moral disorder" and commented that "the Church is opposed to a system of sexual information separated from moral principles."[469]

La Libre Belgique, Corriere della Sera and *Il Giorno* of Milan voiced similar favorable opinions on the Church's attempt to restore modesty, chastity, and love in sexual relations and its reaffirmation of the Church's condemnation of homosexuality, premarital or extramarital relations, contraception, masturbation and the pressure on even the youngest of children to engage in sex play.[470]

Educational Guidance in Human Love received extensive

coverage in the Italian press and special emphasis in the Grieco commentary.

Under the headline, "Sexual Education Is Not Only Information," in *Il Populo* (12/21/83), Vatican Journalist Narducci declared that "the concept of a naturalist sexual education, which would like to reduce all to fashionable, premature, and detailed information. . . in terms of human anatomy and physiology, as well as fashionable psychological notions, was clearly refuted by *Educational Guidance in Human Love.*"[471]

"Sex Education: Duty of the Family" was the headline in the December 2, 1983 edition of Rome's *Il Tempo.* The article stressed the need of the Church and the school to "collaborate with parents."[472]

In the December 7th edition of *Avvenire,* the national Italian Catholic daily newspaper, writer Giorgio Basadonna, who *incorrectly* identifies *Educational Guidance in Human Love* as a "pontifical document," praises the orientation of the document toward love—an orientation which is carried out without inhibiting the personality and without disturbing the latency period, which Basadonna identifies very accurately as "the peaceful awareness of youth."[473]

Perhaps the most important press comments found in the Grieco review, however, are those which oddly enough confirm the statement made by the anti-life "voice box," Center for Population Options, which is quoted earlier in this chapter, that is, the statement that the document represents the Vatican's "first official support for sex education in schools."[474]

In his introduction, Grieco himself notes that "Many colleagues in the press. . fled from a very original aspect of the document, which treats sexual education in the school."[475]

More to the point, the Roman newspaper *Il Messaggero* (12/2/83) writes that *Educational Guidance in Human Love* "*. . . in 37 pages contains the summa (whole) of papal thought on the merits of sexual education,*" and that this "*is the most complete document on this subject ever to have been circulated by the Vatican, and doubtlessly its directives will influence the attitude of many Catholic groups in Italy and abroad which are discussing the eventuality or practical mode of sexual edu-*

cation, within the environment of public instruction.''[476] (Emphasis added).

From a number of perspectives, the *Il Messaggero* commentary is quite incredible, and for the following reasons:

First, because the formal text of *Educational Guidance in Human Love* contains not a single specific reference to previous papal statements made prior to 1981 on the matter of public sex education—all of which expressed an absolute condemnation of the practice.

Secondly, whereas the Italian daily suggests that the document will "eventually" pave the way for "public instruction," Catholic elementary and secondary schools in the United States have been groaning under the weight of the "new sexual catechetics" imposed by the American church for more than two decades.

Lifting the Veil of Mystery from *Educational Guidance in Human Love*

Considering the wide press coverage given to *Educational Guidance in Human Love* in the Americas and in Europe, it is more than passing strange that there were two critical factors pertaining to *EGHL* which were almost completely ignored by the international press corps at the time of its release—the first pertaining to the document's "status" and the second pertaining to the identity of one of its key drafters.

Given all the international headlines announcing the release of the document by "the Vatican," "the Holy See" and the "Sacred Congregation for Catholic Education," one could hardly escape the impression that *Educational Guidance in Human Love* was officially sanctioned by the Holy Father. In fact, *every* source this writer contacted in the United States and in Rome concerning the exact juridical status of the document expressed the belief that it carried the express approval of the Holy Father. As noted above, even the influential *Avvenire* identified it as a "pontifical document,"[477] and one member of the Curia went so far as to tell this writer that the document was "binding on the conscience" of all Catholics. What then is the truth of the matter?

First, it can be stated—unequivocally—that *Educational Guidance in Human Love* carries *no express approval from the Pope.* Unlike such documents as the *Declaration on Certain Questions Concerning Sexual Ethics,* which was issued by the Sacred Congregation for the Doctrine of the Faith and presented to Pope Paul VI by Prefect Franjo Cardinal Seper for his approval and confirmation at an audience granted on November 7, 1975, or the more recent *Instruction on Respect for Human Life in its Origin and on the Dignity of Procreation—Replies to Certain Questions of the Day,* which was presented to Pope John Paul II for approval by Prefect Cardinal Ratzinger for the Sacred Congregation for the Doctrine of the Faith on February 22, 1987, there is no indication that *EGHL* was ever presented to the Pope for an official approbation. But more certain than that, *none was ever given,* although the text of the document, as is the case with any Congregation statement to be publicly circulated, would have been routinely examined by the Holy Father prior to circulation.

Second, the *Acta Apostolicae Sedis (The Acts of the Apostolic See),* which is the bound volumes of all official documents of the Church—including those issued by the Sacred Congregations—contains no reference to the document. Also, whereas the document was issued in Italian under the title *''Orientamenti educativi sull' amore umano''* (Note: the original text as printed in *Seminarium* contains no subtitle) and subsequently translated into several other languages, there was no official Latin translation intended for the universal Church.

To his credit, Cardinal Baum never stated in his Congregation's press release on *EGHL* that the document *was* anything more than "an educational message" for "Episcopal Conferences"[478]—although on the debit side of the ledger, his congregation never corrected the popular impression given in the secular and Catholic press that the document carried the full weight of a papal document or was an expressly approved papal document, whereas it was not. Had the faithful known this, there might have been a more objective scrutiny and a more aggressive evaluation of the document by fighters for orthodoxy, who, as Dietrich von Hildebrand has observed, ". . .because of their submission to ecclesiastical authority. . .will never be as aggressive as the so-called progressives."[479]

Certainly, except for the moral norms and doctrinal principles in *EGHL* that had already been enunciated in the traditional teachings of the Church, there is no question of the document's binding Catholics in conscience. This is particularly true with regard to the "original" element contained in the document, that is, *the approval of classroom sex education, which has heretofore always been consistently condemned by the Church.*

The Reappearance of Monsignor McHugh

The second critical factor pertaining to the document, which despite its special significance was entirely overlooked by the Catholic press in the United States, was the reappearance on the sex education scene of Monsignor James T. McHugh and his role in the drafting of *Educational Guidance in Human Love.* Once again, had this knowledge been made public when the document was released on December 1, 1983, it is more than likely that organizations fighting classroom sex education would have evaluated *EGHL* with a more critical eye.

As it turned out, it was Monsignor McHugh himself who first publicized his association with *EGHL* in a full-page interview in *Our Sunday Visitor,* entitled, "Sex Education—The Right of the Family, the Duty of the School,"[480] some two months after Cardinal Baum's Congregation released the document.

According to *Our Sunday Visitor,* Monsignor McHugh, identified as the new Director for Natural Family Planning for the NCCB, "assisted in the drafting" of *Educational Guidance in Human Love,* as well as the Charter of the Rights of the Family, a separate work, based on Pope John Paul's *Familiaris Consortio.*[481]

Confirmation that McHugh did indeed play an important role in the development of *EGHL* was given to this writer by a staff member of the Congregation for Catholic Institutions (Education) in a phone conversation to Rome in the Summer of 1989, in which McHugh was described as a "leading expert" from the United States on the sex education document.

In the *Our Sunday Visitor* interview, in response to the opening question, "What is the main point of the document?" McHugh replies:

> The document stresses that parents not only have the right but the serious duty to provide sex education for their children. It insists that parents cannot remain silent in dealing with the responsibility, and therefore have a right to look to Catholic schools, educators, pastors and catechists for help in providing sound sex education for the young.[482]

Asked: "Isn't that what the Church has been saying for a long time?" McHugh answered:

> There has been a controversy for some time in the Catholic community about sex education in Catholic schools. Some oppose it. They point to a prohibition issued by Pope Pius XI in the 1930's. Others, concerned by the present day sexual permissiveness, want to bypass Catholic parents and turn over sex education to teachers and schools. *This new document provides for a reconciliation between these two conflicting groups.* It is telling parents that their responsibility for proper sex education can and should find an ally in other areas of the Catholic community and most particularly in the work of Catholic teachers and pastors.[483] [Emphasis added].

Later in the *Our Sunday Visitor* interview, McHugh was questioned about the goals of "Catholic" sex education, and he replied:

> We must teach more than just biology and behavior. Catholic sex education is not seen simply as supplying sexual information and scientific background. The moral component of Christian values is part of our education. But the approach cannot be just, "Do this and don't do that." We must provide an education that leads the young to appreciate the moral values involved. Where there are sexual excesses or disorders, teachers must look more to the cause than to direct repression of the phenomena. By teaching the young to respect people of every age and condition, to respect life in all its variations, the young can come to see sexuality and sexual behavior in a positive way.[484]

In light of the fact that the Holy Father *never* gave his express approval to *EGHL*, McHugh's response to the final question of the *Our Sunday Visitor* interview as to whether or not the sex education document and the Charter "reflect the thinking of Pope John Paul II" is of special interest:

> Unquestionably, they reflect the commitment of the Holy Father to support the family and to urge the bishops of the world to develop pastoral approaches to benefit family life. . .these two documents are very much in line with the Pope's desire to give families the tools they need to defend, to live and enjoy the Christian life.[485]

Readers will want to keep in mind that after the USCC sex education debacle in late 1981, Dolesh had fled the NCCB/USCC department of sexology, leaving a serious vacuum in the leadership of the "Catholic" Sex Education Movement in the United States, until the return in early 1984 of Monsignor McHugh from Rome, where he had completed his doctoral studies in medical ethics and served as a visiting lecturer at the Pontifical Lateran University.

By the time of his appointment as auxiliary bishop of Newark, New Jersey in January of 1988, McHugh had regained that position of leadership.

In addition to holding the Directorship of the Bishops' national program for Natural Family Planning, McHugh has secured a seat on the NCCB's Commission on Marriage and Family and on the NCCB/USCC Task Force on the Revision of the Guidelines on Human Sexuality (i.e., the USCC/Dolesh 1981 Sex Education Guidelines). As part of his "extra-curricular" activities, McHugh has served as a consultant to the new and noxious Benziger *Family Life Program* for Catholic grades K-8, which was recently the subject of an excellent sixty-eight page critique by Robert Marshall.

The conclusion reached by Mr. Marshall, one of the nation's top pro-life research analysts for the American Life League, was that the Benziger series is "not in accord with the mission and purpose of the Catholic school," and its emphasis on a "naturalistic" approach to human sexuality makes it unfit for consumption by Catholic school children.[486]

At the international level, McHugh continues to serve as an Advisor on Population Affairs to the Mission of the Holy See at the United Nations and recently was appointed to membership on the Vatican's Pontifical Council for the Family.

To all this add the fact that, as of December 31, 1992, he continued to serve as a member of the Bioethics Advisory Committee of the March of Dimes—the nation's number one promoter of eugenic abortion—and one can plainly see that McHugh's power to influence United States and Vatican policies in the areas of marriage, family, natural family planning, population control, abortion, euthanasia and sex education has expanded, not diminished, over the last ten years.

A Second Look at *Educational Guidance in Human Love*

Having reviewed some of these lesser-known historical footnotes to *Educational Guidance in Human Love,* let us now reexamine this 1983 document, this time from Monsignor McHugh's perspective, that is, the Vatican document as a "compromise" between two opposing groups, that is, Catholics who believe the Church's universal ban on public sex instruction for children and youth (as enunciated by Pope Pius XI) is still in effect and those who argue, on behest of the American Church, for formal classroom sex education as a feature of evolutionary doctrinal advancement and sexual enlightenment.

The General Format of *Educational Guidance in Human Love*

The introduction to *EGHL* opens with the Vatican II *Declaration on Christian Education's* singular, shop-worn mention of "a positive and prudent sex education"[487] (Abbott translation) and a statement as to the competency of the Sacred Congregation for Catholic Education to "make its contribution for the application of the Conciliar Declaration, as some Episcopal Conferences have done already." (Par. 1).

"The precise objective" which the document sets for itself is

"To examine the pedagogic aspect of sex education, indicating appropriate guidelines for the integral formation of a Christian, according to the vocation of each." (Par. 2).

"Also, though it does not make explicit citations at every turn, it always *presupposes the doctrinal principles and moral norms pertaining to the matter as proposed by the Magisterium*." (Par. 2). (Emphasis added).

Under the subtitle "Declarations of the Magisterium" the reader is instructed that "The Magisterium's declarations on sex education mark out a course which satisfies the just requirements of history on the one hand and fidelity to tradition on the other." (Par. 14).

An obtuse statement? Quite! But there is nothing obtuse about footnote 5, which reveals more about the underlying principles of the document than does the entire formal text.

Establishing the Church's "Evolutionary Progress" Toward Classroom Sex Education

The leadoff sentence for footnote 5 reads as follows:

> Pius XI, in his Encyclical *Divini Illius Magistri*, of December 31, 1929, declared erroneous the sex education *which was presented at that time, which was information of a naturalist character, precociously and indiscriminately imparted.* (AAS 33, 1930, pp. 49-86). (Emphasis added).

Are we to assume from this bit of paraphrasing that today's sex education is different from that which was condemned by Pius XI? Is it less naturalistic? Less precociously and indiscriminately imparted? Hardly! If anything, it is more naturalistic, more explicit and more ruthlessly applied toward the destruction of childhood innocence and latency than anything Pius XI could have imagined. It is difficult to believe that whoever drafted the footnote to include the insertion of the phrase "at that time" was ignorant of this reality. Rather, the inclusion indicates an attempt to offer a defense of classroom sex education by suggesting that the nature and mode of implementation of contemporary group sex instruction in Catholic schools today differs fundamentally from that which was condemned by Pius XI in 1929.

The above-quoted line of argumentation is continued in the 200-word footnote with the notation that, like his predecessor, Pius XI prepared the way for the Conciliar Declaration *Gravissimum Educationis* (conclusion of footnote 5), which presumably expressed itself in the "approval" of classroom sex education by the NCCB/USCC in the late 1960's.

Later in the introduction, the authors of *EGHL* discuss the "difficult" situation of looking for "a suitable sex education from every source" (Par. 8); the "problem" of insufficiently prepared educators and parents (Par. 9); and ". . .the complexity of the diverse elements (physical, psychological, pedagogical, sociocultural, juridical, moral and religious) which come together in educational action." (Par. 11).

Praise is then offered to "some Catholic organizations in different parts—with the approval and encouragement of the local Episcopate" who *"have begun to carry out a positive work of sex education;* it is directed not only to helping children and adolescents on the way to psychological and spiritual maturity, but also, and above all, to protecting them from the dangers of ignorance and widespread degradation." (Par. 12).

Careful note should be made of three additional suppositions regarding sex education that have been introduced thus far into the document:

- Instead of stressing the naturalness and competency (enhanced by grace) of parents to carry out the task of educating their offspring in sexual matters, the document would virtually require a Ph.D. in sexology for individuals undertaking such a seemingly monstrously complex task.
- By referring to the "positive work of sex education" and the "difficult" task of searching out "a suitable sex education," the drafters of the document sweep away *all historical evidence* as to the anti-life origin, nature and objectives of the universal Sex Education Movement and *all knowledge* concerning the *moral rot and spiritual devastation wrought by so-called "family life" or "sex education" programs.*
- Having framed the Sex Education Movement in a most favorable light, *ipso facto,* there is no need to call for an

accountability—much less censure—of the members of the hierarchy who have taken leadership roles in the advancement of classroom sex education in both parochial and public schools.

The Body of the Text Amplifies the State of Confusion

The remainder of the body of the text includes:

- *Section I:* An exposition on the Christian concept of sexuality and on "the nature, purpose and means of sex education." (Pars. 34-47).
- *Section II:* An explanation of the role of various institutions in the implementation of sex education programs for children, youth and adults, including the family, the Church, the school and civil society (Pars. 48-75) and of the development of "appropriate teaching materials" by "specialists in moral and pastoral theology, of catechists, of educationists and Catholic psychologists." (Par. 76).
- *Section III:* A commentary on the conditions and mode of sex education, centering on teacher preparation (Pars. 79-82); the quality of teaching methods (Par. 83); the character and qualities of the sex educator (Pars. 86-89); and "education for modesty and friendship." (Pars. 90-93).
- *Section IV:* A treatment of certain problems which may confront the sex educator in the carrying out of his or her "mission," including masturbation (Pars. 98-100) and homosexuality. (Pars. 101-103).
- *Conclusion and Footnotes:* An appeal to parents not only to "repair the harm caused by inappropriate and injurious interventions, but above all to opportunely inform their own children, offering them a positive and convincing education" (Par. 106), and to cooperate with "the Christian communities" and "educators" in this important task for "the future of young people and the good of society." (Par. 111). Of the non-Scriptural footnotes found at the conclusion of the formal text, only footnotes 5 and 39 predate Vatican II. The remaining citations are taken principally from *Gravissimum Educationis, Familiaris Consortio, Gaudium et Spes, Lumen Gentium, Humanae Vitae, Inter Mirifica, Humanae Persona* and the teachings of John Paul II.

The Document Is Verbally Sabotaged

What may not have been apparent in the introductory portions of the document most assuredly becomes quite clear when one reads the entire text of the document; that is, in order to produce a rational document on "Catholic" sex education, which would appear to be in keeping with the Magisterium, the drafters of *Educational Guidance in Human Love* had to do a fundamentally dishonest thing. They had to take a known anti-chastity and anti-life entity, that is, "classroom sex education," and so radically redefine its original meaning, nature and objectives as to insure that their "new creation" would be accepted as a legitimate extension of the traditional teachings of the Church.

This nasty little practice of using the same word to cover different meanings, or redefining terms so as to accomplish a complete inversion of their commonly understood meaning, is of course a practice which is not limited to *Educational Guidance in Human Love.*[488] It has been a growing source of confusion and mischief in the Church for a number of years.[489]

As *Challenge,* the Catholic monthly of Canada, points out in its December, 1983 critical review of *EGHL,* the document "seems in places to equate sexuality with love. This concept, foreign to Catholic tradition, according to many people, seems in places to be one that is adopted by the Sacred Congregation for Catholic Education."[490]

But more importantly, the authors of *EGHL* successfully managed to juxtapose and interchange the term "sex education" with "education in chastity" and "education in love" so as to entrap the Church in a verbal snare, from which it will have great difficulty in extricating itself, and to draw the Holy See even deeper into enemy territory and the sex education maelstrom.

The understandably startling proposition that *EGHL* was deliberately designed to effect specific ends directed at undermining the ordinary and universal Magisterium of the Church will obviously not sit well with a number of Vatican offices, especially the Sacred Congregation for Catholic Institutions (Education).

Apologists for *Educational Guidance in Human Love* will undoubtedly point out that the document was generally well received by both "conservative" and "liberal" elements within the Church. Further, they will note that *EGHL* contains a number of statements upholding parental rights in education and reaffirming the Church's condemnation of fornication, homosexuality and masturbation, in order to demonstrate the document's consistency with the traditional Catholic teachings on human sexuality, marriage and family.

Elements of Truth Used to Cover Falsehood

What is overlooked is the fact that *truth,* which is meant to enlighten, may also be used to deceive, or more accurately, to camouflage *untruth.*

In *Educational Guidance in Human Love,* the truths of the Faith have been used to cover a singular falsehood—a falsehood upon which the entire document rises or falls—that is, that the Catholic Church recognizes and sanctions classroom sex education as a licit form of catechetical instruction for children and youth and that such instruction by virtue of its nature, purpose and means has as its fundamental objective the sanctification of the human person, according to the vocation of each, in accordance with Holy Scripture and the Magisterium of the Church.

This Document Neutralizes the Opposition

In addition to achieving their primary objective—the introduction of the new sexual catechetics into the *Doctrina Sacra* of the Catholic Church—the architects of *Educational Guidance in Human Love* effectively neutralized the opposition to their efforts by rendering a positive verdict for those who "have begun to carry out a positive work of sex education" (Par. 12), while at the same time radicalizing the image of Catholic opponents of school sex education by making such opposition to the aforementioned "positive work" appear unwarranted and unreasonable.

Further, the strategy of linking classroom sex education with the virtues of chastity, of self-control, of modesty and Christian love tends to diffuse parental anxiety and reduce the level of parental resistance to the very real dangers to children from exposure to classroom sex education.

True, the document contains isolated references to "bad" sex education programs, which seek to impart "sex information dissociated from moral principles" (Par. 19) or which "crudely present sexual realities for which the pupil is not prepared" (Par. 76), but the casual reader would never divine from these remarks that there was anything inherently wrong with classroom sex education per se.

Indeed, one of the ever-present dangers of *EGHL* is that it holds out the *promise* of an authentic or correct Catholic sex education program, but this is a promise which can never be realized, given *the intrinsically evil nature of open and public group sex instruction for children.*

The core issue, however, is never addressed in the document. There is no need. But having successfully turned the common definition of "sex education" on its head, the writers of *EGHL* do not have to counter the facts concerning the anti-Christian origin, objective and methodology of classroom sex instruction. Their task becomes merely one of proposing the conditions, modes and strictures under which the program can be carried out. Thus *Educational Guidance in Human Love* focuses primarily on the finding of "a suitable sex education" (Par. 8); on the development of "appropriate teaching materials" (Par. 76); on "teacher preparation" (Pars. 79-82); and the "quality of teachers and teaching methods." (Pars. 83-89).

In the subsection on teaching methods we read, "In reality, *the criticisms normally raised* [to sex education] *refer more to the enterprise itself.* These methods must have definite qualities, both in the teachers themselves and in the end to which such education is proposed." (Par. 83, emphasis added).

The document refers to "special safeguards" which are "required" for "sex education in groups," "above all in mixed groups," and turns the responsibility for establishing "guidelines for sex education in groups" over to bishops.

As to the exact nature of the "safeguards" to be employed after the Pandora's Box of sexual information and discussion has been opened in the classroom, we are left in the dark. But of one thing we can be certain: since the text assures us that "all matters can offer an opportunity to treat themes in their relation to sexuality" (Par. 71), we must presume that these "safeguards" would have to be in effect at all times, in all classes and by all teachers. And, since the Church reaffirms the law of subsidiarity, which the school is bound to observe when it cooperates (with parents) in sex education, and since sex education "must be carried out under their [the parents'] attentive guidance" (Par. 17), we can presume the necessity of round-the-clock parental monitoring.

These are but a few of the unsettling and unresolved (or more accurately, unresolvable) problems connected with the practical application of so-called "safeguards" to be applied to group sex instruction.

Some Critical Annotations on *EGHL*

Soon after I had begun my research on *Educational Guidance in Human Love,* it became apparent that a thorough analysis of the document would fill a separate book, especially if the several hundred pages and collected materials, commentaries and interviews related to the work were included in my investigation.

The following comments and notations, therefore, are based on those passages from *EGHL* which have a direct bearing on the issue of classroom sex education in parochial schools and CCD classes.

Sex as an Object of Scientific and Academic Pursuit

The point that sex is not ordinarily a subject of traditional scientific and academic pursuit can be made rather simply by gauging the natural response to the statement that a college graduate had earned his baccalaureate by majoring in history and minoring in sex (or vice versa).

With the obvious exception of those professions which require a detailed knowledge of certain aspects of human sexuality—including reproductive physiology, sexually related illnesses and psychoses, legal and moral issues related to specific sex acts, and assorted anthropological and sociological aspects of sex, especially as they relate to marriage and the family—the study of "sex" as such has never been a general subject of formal and public instruction for adults, much less for children and youth.

Even those who consider themselves "sexologists," or who are involved in "scientific" sex research and studies, have been forced to admit:

> If empirical observation in the area of sexual behavior were to be confined to visual observation, no data, at least in the Western world, would be available. Direct visual observation is difficult to achieve, except in specific experimental situations, to which sexual behavior does not readily lend itself. Visual observation of sexual responses has been used only by physicians to learn of the change in brain waves under coitus and recorded by an encephalograph or by experimenters, such as Masters, who have been interested in the physiology of orgasm. Observations of behavior of people in coital situations or in human situations preliminary to coitus or other sexual activities have been rarely reported in the scientific literature.[491]
>
> [Therefore], to gain information on or about human sexual behavior, behavioral scientists use the same methods used to gain information about. . .other human behaviors: indirect techniques [such as] interviews, questionnaires, content analyses, and scales, [all of which present] scientists with innumerable problems.[492]

The Dark Side of Sexology

In recent years there has been a number of published works which have helped focus the public spotlight on academic fraud and criminal activity within the field of "sex research."

In *Kinsey, Sex and Fraud,* co-authored by Dr. Judith A. Reisman, Dr. J. Gordon Muir and Edward W. Eichel, a long shadow is cast over the scientific validity of sexual experiments conducted by Dr. Edward C. Kinsey, whose epochal "studies" on male and female sexual behavior revolutionized American sexual morés for more than two decades.

(Note: The revolting nature of the acts described in this and the following section illustrates the predicament that writers like myself face when trying to explain to the uninitiated the perverse nature of sex education and the putrefactive character and morals of persons like Calderwood, who make up the upper echelon of the movement's leadership. If one tells the truth, then one must accept the risk that truth intended to inform may corrupt or tarnish the person so informed. If one holds back and simply refers to the perversity in non-offending general terms, then the reader is unlikely to be moved to action because his sense of outrage has not been triggered.[493]

In the end, however, I believe that this apparent dilemma must be resolved in favor of truth-telling because one must recognize that the *ultimate target of Calderwood and the SIECUS Co. is not only adults, but*[494] *primarily children,* who are held captive in a classroom and who, unlike Eichel, cannot defend themselves from those who violate their person. And if the price to be paid is a momentary turning of the stomach and sickness of the heart—symptoms of the mind's natural defense against a primordial evil—then let us offer up our pain to Him who said, "To them that love God, all things work together unto good." —*Rom.* 8:28.)

The charges against Kinsey by Reisman center on the manner in which the researcher and his colleagues at the Indiana University for Sex Research—now the Kinsey Institute for Research on Sex, Gender, Reproduction, Inc.—obtained data on "child sexuality," that is, whether Kinsey received his data on "child sexuality" from known child molesters or from personally conducted experiments in which known sex offenders were permitted criminally to abuse children in Kinsey's custody, 28 of whom were infants less than a year old. According to Reisman, many of the 317 children used as subjects for data entered into Kinsey's first report, *Sexual Behavior in the Human Male,* were subjected to "varied and repeated" sexual stimulation—three for 24 hours straight—trembled, wept, screamed, fainted, went into convulsions and fought their "partners" (Kinsey's euphemism for the criminals sexually abusing them).[495]

Pansexuality as a Cornerstone of Sex Education

Edward W. Eichel, M.A., Reisman and Muir's fellow researcher and chronicler of the SIECUS-AASEC(T)—Planned Parenthood axis, undertakes the task of exposing Kinsey's "pansexual agenda," which follows two of the researcher's basic tenets, namely, "1) that bisexuality is the norm of sexual health and 2) that pedophile relations are beneficial for children."[496]

According to Eichel, Kinsey's "grand scheme" was incorporated into his (Eichel's) training programs as an educator in the Human Sexuality Program at New York University.

Eichel has described his experiences at a summer colloquium in Maastrich, Holland in 1983, directed by well-known SIECUS personality and official, Dr. Deryck Calderwood, experiences which Eichel charges were directed at getting heterosexuals like himself "to explore homosexual experiences."[497]

According to Eichel, although Calderwood claimed that his (Calderwood's) depiction of bisexuality in his video "Kinsey Three, the Bisexual Experience" was "an unbiased point of view," the programming seemed to move people in one direction, toward same-sex experiences. Eichel also describes certain "exercises" which took place in "a nude body workshop," in which the educators took turns "looking at everyone's genitals," then "were blindfolded" and directed to "feel everybody's genitals" to see if they could guess each individual's identity.[498]

In the same workshop, Calderwood, who had recommended anal intercourse for males in order to experience "role reversal," instructed his charges "to trade prostrate examinators with a partner."[499] Later, at the Holland sexology seminars, the participants were subjected to a deluge of pro-pedophilia propaganda and were addressed by a former member of the Dutch Parliament who Eichel later learned had spent time in prison as a convicted pedophile.[500]

To add to the moral degradation already cited, Eichel notes that Calderwood's students "were asked to be photographed in compromising poses, which could later be an embarrassment."[501] In Eichel's group, Calderwood photographed "naked asses."[502]

EGHL on the Development of Sex Educators

Educational Guidance in Human Love has a great deal to say about the character, the formation and training of "Catholic" sex educators.

As the Catholic Canadian journal *Challenge* reported in its December, 1983 article entitled "Vatican Sets Extraordinary High Standards for Teachers of Sex Ed,"

> If the Vatican guidelines mean literally what they say, there are few persons who would be willing to undertake to be teachers of sex education in the schools. For the guidelines impose qualifications on sex ed teachers that few would be able to meet without yielding to the sin of pride.[503]

In Part III of *EGHL,* "The Conditions and Mode of Sex Education," which treats the matter of teacher preparation, we read:

> The mature personality of the teachers, their training and psychological balance, strongly influence their pupils. An exact and complete vision of the meaning and value of sexuality and a peaceful integration within the personality itself are indispensable for teachers in constructive education. Their training takes shape according to environment. Their ability is not so much the fruit of theoretical knowledge, but rather the result of their affective maturity. This, however, *does not dispense with the acquisition of scientific knowledge suited to their educational work, which is particularly arduous these days*... (Par. 79, emphasis added).
>
> The teacher who carries out his or her task outside the family context needs a suitable and serious psychopedagogic training, which allows the seizing of particular situations which require a special solicitude... (Par. 81).
>
> Given the importance of sex educator in the integral formation of the person, teachers, taking account of the various aspects of sexuality and of their incidence in the global personality, are urged in particular not to separate knowledge from corresponding values, which give a sense and orientation to biological, psychological and sound information. Consequently, when they present moral norms, it is necessary that they show how to find their *raison d'etre* and value. (Par. 89).

Following a section cited earlier, which praises the efforts of "some Catholic organizations" who "have begun to carry out a positive work of sex education. . .directed not only to helping children and adolescents on the way to psychological and spiritual maturity, but also, and above all, to protecting them from the dangers of ignorance and widespread degradation" (Par. 12), there is a sentence which appears to refer to sex research and investigation. It reads as follows:

> Also praiseworthy are the efforts of many who, with scientific seriousness, dedicate themselves to studying this problem, moving from the human sciences and integrating the results of such research in a project which conforms with human dignity, a project carried out in the light of the Gospel. (Par. 13).

Quis Custodiet Custodes?— "Who Watches the Watchmen?"

Just as in Huxley's *Brave New World,* where no one thinks to ask who will direct the director of the hatcheries,[504] so the authors of *Educational Guidance in Human Love* never appear to raise—much less answer—the ultimate question, "Who will teach the teachers?"

EGHL talks of "the acquisition of scientific knowledge" but does not indicate from whom such "knowledge" shall be obtained.

From the in-house testimony of people like Edward Eichel, we know that every major university-based center for the education and training of sexologists and sex educators, counselors and therapists in the United States is controlled by and carries out the pansexual agenda of the Kinsey Institute, of SIECUS (which controls sex education curriculum development) and of AASEC(T) (which awards professional certification).[505]

Where then will the catechetical candidates be trained who are, to quote *EGHL*—"to carry out the positive work of sex education" and fill the ranks of sex educators for Catholic schools in the United States or elsewhere? Who will design the curriculum for this educational enterprise? What ethical standards will be applied to sex research and experimentation, and who shall enforce these standards? Key questions, but to these *EGHL* gives no answers, not even clues.

EGHL Puts Children and Youth at Risk

In *Educational Guidance in Human Love,* there is an explicit invitation directed at Christian educators and catechists to take up the "positive work of sex education," to which, as I have already noted, the drafters of the document have already assigned a totally new definition and purpose. Yet the document contains no warning to those to whom the invitation is issued of the unbelievably corrupt and seedy world they will face when they enter the *real* world—not the *EGHL* fantasy world of sex education and sexology.

The fact that certain aspects of the sex education and sex research field are so opposed to the norms of human decency and to the natural instincts of familial and self-preservation has prompted even avowed humanists to distance themselves from such programs.

For example, as W. R. Coulson, Ph.D. and J. D. Coulson, M.S. reveal in *Confessions of an Ex-Sexologist,* Abraham Maslow, the acknowledged co-founder of humanistic psychology, who "had a period of brief but stunning success as a sex researcher,"[506] had, when approached by Kinsey for tutoring lessons, told the budding sex researcher that he (Maslow) had "changed fields," pleading, "I'm a family man."[507] According to W. R. Coulson, a former associate of Maslow, the "family man" admission—by which Maslow justified his turning away from his career in sexology—was due in part at least to the fact that "such a career...included interviewing women about the intimate details of their sex lives. It risked too much."[508]

Presumably, then, the drafters of the "Vatican" document would want to exhibit at least equal caution as, if not more than, Maslow demonstrated in protecting the moral welfare of Catholic educators, including celibate priests and religious, who engage in sexual studies or research.

I would also think that any Catholic educator, catechist or scientific researcher who possessed all the wisdom and virtues described in *EGHL* would be intuitively adverse to deliberately putting himself (and his students) in a morally hostile and seductive environment, be it a sex education workshop or a training program, a research laboratory or a formal classroom setting for sex instruction.

Contrary to the impressions given in *EGHL,* sex education is not just another form of catechetical instruction, nor does it qualify as "education" in the strict sense of the term. Sex involves the passions as well as the intellect. Anyone who forgets this truth—who perceives himself as being immune to sexual temptation and seduction by reason of age, vocation or spiritual "maturity"—is a fool, however noble his intentions.

EGHL Reflects a Myopic View Of Sex Education Damage

At the conclusion of the *EGHL* text, parents are admonished that they have a duty to "give positive and gradual affective sex education to children, adolescents and young adults," that "silence is not a valid norm of contact in this matter," particularly when one considers "the socio-cultural situation" and the existence of "hidden persuaders...," and that *"it is up to parents, therefore, to be alert, not only to repair injurious interventions,* but above all to opportunely inform their own children, offering them a positive and convincing education." (Par. 106, emphasis added).

EGHL also contains an earlier reference to "some school textbooks on sexuality" which, "by reason of their natural character, are harmful to the child and the adolescent." Most specifically condemned are those textbooks containing "graphics and audio-visual materials...[which] create traumatic impressions or raise unhealthy curiosity, which leads to evil..." (Par. 76).

I am particularly grateful for the inclusion of these two paragraphs in *Educational Guidance in Human Love* because they permit me to address certain argumentations—in support of a universal ban on sex education by the Catholic Church—which I have already presented, but which, because of their tremendous importance, need to be highlighted and repeated.

Some Damage Is Not Repairable

First, *EGHL* does not make clear that the "inappropriate and injurious interventions" of which it speaks result not only from secular influences, but also from "Catholic" sex education programs currently used in parochial schools and CCD programs in the United States and abroad. Secondly, it does not make clear that children may be "traumatized" just by the very fact of being forced to be in a classroom where explicit sexual details are openly discussed—never mind the addition of graphic visuals. Third, it does not clear up the sobering fact that *much of the damage done by classroom sex education programs can never be undone by any human being and that the damage in some instances may actually be fatal.* This damage includes:

- Destruction of innocence and latency.
- The sexual seduction of children, youth and adults.
- The increase in sins against chastity, which lead to
  - the loss of virginity,
  - the increase of out-of-wedlock pregnancies,
  - the increase of induced abortion,
  - the increase of sexual perversions,
    which leads to
    - increased drug use,
    - New-Age occultism and
    - suicide.

And all of these evils, as mentioned, lead to a loss of supernatural faith, to spiritual death and ultimately to Hell, which is the principal reason we must oppose them.

Sexual Experimentation Ends in Death

(Note: The nature of the following tragic true story may be upsetting to some readers.)

On March 23, 1989, the *Minneapolis-St. Paul Star Tribune* carried a lengthy feature on "autoerotic asphyxia" entitled "Sexual Experimentation Can End in Death."

In this very moving article, Slovut details the death of Bradley Boyum, a 14-year-old honor student, who accidentally hanged himself while attempting to "heighten the sensation of masturbating by using his belt to squeeze off the flow of oxygen to his brain."[509] Bradley's body was discovered the next morning by his father and brother, "hanging by the neck, his feet touching the floor."[510]

According to the testimony of family members and friends, Bradley was a fine young athlete and scholar who was "not depressed," nor had he ever shown any warning signs of having experimented with the dangerous practice leading to his death.

However, according to Slovut, "Two weeks before his death, Mary Boyum [Bradley's mother] and Bradley completed a sex education course called 'Valuing Values' at All Saints Catholic Church in Lakeville.

"It was a wonderful course," Mary Boyum said. "They talked about many important things, *including masturbation, in a non-judgmental way.* But they didn't discuss autoerotic asphyxiation. If only they had, then. . ."[511] (Emphasis added).

Bradley's mother states that the sex education coordinator knew about the practice, but did not include the information about it in the course. "Now," however, Mary Boyum states, she "believes the subject matter is being presented at the church in 'Valuing Values' to ninth grade Confirmation class members."

When interviewed about any possible changes in the nationally designed program of "Valuing Values," the director of religious education for the Archdiocese of St. Paul and Minneapolis stated that instructors could respond to student questions concerning the practice, but suggested the subject might not be appropriate for students in the seventh through ninth grades.[512]

Several weeks after Bradley's death, a school assembly was held at McGuire Junior High School on the subject of autoerotic asphyxia in which the principal, Jerry Pederson, is quoted as telling the youngsters, parents and community representatives that "We weren't putting values—good or bad—on this [masturbation]. . .we said that masturbation is all right, but a combination of masturbation with a very dangerous behavior of oxygen deprivation isn't."[513]

The story ends with Mary Boyum's sorrowful lament, "We spent our whole lives protecting and nurturing him. I guess we will never have that security again. I can think of millions of things mothers and fathers should warn children about. We never even heard about this before."[514]

Valuing Values: Reverence for Life and Family II is a course which is the work of Father John Forliti, whose "letters of introduction" in the field of sex education include 1) dissent from *Humanae Vitae* in 1968,[515] 2) being a "theological consultant" for the notorious Wm. C. Brown Co.'s *New Creation* program and the *Issues in Sexuality* audio-visual program,[516] and 3) being a former project director and member of the board of directors of the Search Institute, the producer of *Values and Choices*,[517] with its theme song for teens, "If you can't be good, be careful. . ."

Mrs. Boyum was perfectly correct when she said *Valuing Values* discusses masturbation "in a nonjudgmental way." Regretfully, she did not perceive this as a possible contributory factor to her son's sexual experimentation. Nor, despite her belief that her son learned the practice from fellow classmates, does she seem to make any possible association between the "open" and "non-judgmental" masturbation dialogue and the subsequent "schoolyard" exchange on techniques to increase the pleasure of masturbation. Yet, the possibility of a cause and effect does exist, particularly since the hanging occurred only two weeks after the conclusion of the sex education course.

To consider (much less resolve) some of the questions raised by the death of Bradley Boyum is to invite more pain. Certainly the Boyum family does not need this additional emotional burden. Nor is it likely the Archdiocese of Minneapolis-St. Paul will undertake to investigate the possibility of any connection between deadly sexual experimentation and the home-based Forliti sex education program.

On the other hand, considering the high stakes involved in the continued promotion of sex education in parochial schools and CCD classes by the American Church and the possibility that the Vatican will be drawn into the labyrinth of the great sex education experiment, Catholics are obliged not only to raise the issues but to search for answers—as well as to fight for the only sane and morally correct solution, which is a complete ban on classroom sex education.

The Implications of Treating Sex Education As Revealed Truth

EGHL perpetrates *two great myths* regarding sex education:

Great Myth Number 1 is that sex education is made virtuous when attached to moral norms.

Great Myth Number 2 is that sex education should be administered by parents.

Both myths are founded on the belief that sex education is sort of a "revealed truth" which *must* be implemented. Thus we witness in *EGHL* the desperate search for a "suitable sex education from every source." (Par. 8).

With specific regard to Great Myth Number 1, the argument is put forth that sex education is OK—even praiseworthy—when it is presented in a moral context. And the Neo-Modernist apparatus in the Church could not be more obliging.

Following is an illustration of how the sex education and morality game is played in the Catholic classroom: The subject under "non-judgmental" discussion is birth control, normally referred to under its more euphemistic label, "family planning."

The students are told that this practice and its attendant philosophy are sanctioned by the Church, providing moral means are used. The instructor tells the student that the Church does not approve of "artificial" means of birth control but does approve of "natural" means of birth control and proceeds to instruct the students in the use of *all* methods of birth control: the pill, the IUD, foam, etc., being sure to include Natural Family Planning in the same anti-child arsenal. Thus, the teacher *uses* the Church's teaching against contraception as a vehicle by which he or she can graphically describe, demonstrate and promote *immoral* activity.

A similar procedure is followed in so-called "AIDS education," where students are introduced to vice and homosexual perversion under the guise of "health education." It should be noted that there can be no "AIDS education" without "Sex education" since discussions of condom use, "safe-sex," etc. would presuppose that the students understood the meaning of intercourse, anal sex and similar terms.

Damian Fedoryka, President of Christendom College and a great Catholic scholar, has made a tremendous contribution in demonstrating the moral bankruptcy of classroom sex education programs, including those which seek to combine Church morality with explicit sexual details.

In a brilliant address on AIDS "Education" and "Sex Education" to the National Coalition of Clergy and Laity on June 25, 1988, Fedoryka makes the following pedagogical distinctions:

> ■ Morally neutral behavior, or behavior that is not intrinsically wrong *and* causes sickness and disease, may be described in detail in order to teach how it may be rendered safe or how it may be avoided.
>
> ■ Behavior that is intrinsically wrong *may not* and *should not* be described in detail, unless there is an overriding justification. *Thus, there is never a moral justification for describing, for the purposes of general information, or as part of a general education, the procedures for artificial contraception, or the procedures for different kinds of abortion.*
>
> ■ The detailed description of immoral behavior, because this is the only way of teaching how to render that behavior safe, is an illegitimate pedagogical procedure and is intrinsically immoral. A detailed description could be justified if the reason for it were not the intention of teaching how to render an intrinsically immoral behavior harmless.[518] [Emphasis added].

Further, Fedoryka points out that in regard to AIDS education, individual citizens:

> a) Have a right *and* an obligation not to have their children taught how to render safe behavior which they are convinced is intrinsically evil, and that they
>
> b) have a right not to be forced to participate, by way of taxation, in such teaching.[519]

With specific regard to Catholic schools, Fedoryka warns, "Under no condition may the *Catholic* school use the neutral approach in talking about the harmful consequences of intrinsically immoral behavior; *a fortiori,* it may not teach how to render such behavior 'safe.' "[520]

With regard to the practice of combining sex education with morality, Fedoryka makes the following important observation:

> *As long as such sex education includes making sexuality explicitly thematic and public, I disagree. My position is that the very nature of human sexuality demands that it be excluded from a public classroom treatment.* I do not include in this, classroom references in the most general terms, "sexual immorality," or "premarital and extramarital sex," or "adultery," "fornication" and "non-marital sex."[521] [Emphasis added].

Great Myth Number 2—Parents Should Administer Sex Education to Their Children

The Church has always taught that parents are the natural, competent and primary educators of their children.

From this truth comes the false argument that the *parents,* then, should administer a "sex education" program to their children, and schools can assist by helping parents "clarify" their values on human sexuality. Note again the assumption that formal sex education in itself is a good. In this case the issue is put within the context of "parental rights."

The major premise of this book, of course, is that any formal "sex education" is an objective evil—a moral plague—most commonly spread by classroom contact. But there can be another source of this contamination, which brings up the terrifying prospect of parents becoming transmitters of the plague to their own children—or an alternate of this, the Church's facilitating that transmission by instituting parent courses in formal "sex education."

Even without instruction in the various ways to commit sins of impurity (concerning which St. Paul says, "Let it not so much as be named among you"—*Eph.* 5:3), formal or group "sex education" is grossly immodest and a near occasion of sin—mortal sin. Moreover, to place oneself (or one's offspring) in the near occasion of mortal sin is itself a mortal sin, as the Church has always taught.

But if one examines the typical fare of so-called "Catholic" sex education courses, such as the USCC-Dolesh Sex Education "Guidelines," one will find instruction offered on *all* forms of birth control and *all* forms of sexual deviations.

But as Father William Smith, S.T.D. has bluntly stated,

> *Why in the name of God would any Christian expose a 12-year-old to the full possibilities of the chemical-industrial complex of complete contraception, sterilization and abortifacients. This has no place in a Catholic* **home**, *and it has no place in a Christian school. . .*[522] [Emphasis added].

What Parents *Should* Do

Parents themselves need to be on guard against adult or parent sex education courses offered by schools and parishes which seek to "clarify" parental values on sexual matters or to instruct parents in the new art form of "non-directive" counseling of youth on sex (as well as smoking and drugs) by which the parents "help youth decide."[523]

As the sex education battle heats up, we can expect the Neo-Modernist apparatus at the NCCB/USCC to pump more efforts into "Parenting" courses, or "Adult Sex Education" programs. To be forewarned is to be forearmed.

To say that parents should *not* give their children "Sex Education" is *not,* of course, to suggest that parents have no obligations to instruct their children in sexual morality and to offer proper instruction in conformity with the Church on sexual matters *as they arise,* taking care not to offend natural modesty and to exercise proper precaution with regard to the stimulation of the passions. As Pope Pius XI stated in his encyclical *On the Christian Education of Youth:*

> Hence it is of the highest importance that a good father, while discussing with his son a matter so delicate, be well

> on his guard and not descend to details, nor refer to the various ways in which this infernal hydra [impurity] destroys with its poison so large a portion of the world; otherwise, it may happen that instead of extinguishing this fire, he unwittingly stirs or kindles it in the simple and tender heart of the child.[524]

Falling into the Language Pit

Unfortunately, part of the problem with regard to the matter of Sex Education is the fact that we have permitted the Neo-Modernists to define the terms used to wage the war. In other words, faithful Catholics have fallen into the language pit in which we often find ourselves trapped by our own words.

In order to extricate ourselves from this verbal morass, we must abandon the ambiguous and the nuanced and return to the precise in our manner of speech and writing. This is an urgent task for all—including the Holy See. With specific reference to the term "Sex Education," one should never use the words apart from an absolute condemnation of the philosophy and the practice of classroom instruction in sexual matters.

Educational Guidance in Human Love And the American Bishops

In the concluding paragraph of *Educational Guidance in Human Love,* the Congregation for Catholic Education turns the general matter of implementation of the guidelines over to Episcopal Conferences:

> The Congregation for Catholic Education turns to Episcopal Conferences so that they will promote the union of parents, of Christian communities, and of educators for convergent action in such an important sector for the future of young people and the good of society. The Congregation makes this invitation to assume this educational commitment in reciprocal trust and with the highest regard for rights and specific competences, with a complete Christian formation in view.

From an American perspective, one would have to go to great lengths to find a statement further removed from reality that the conclusion of *Educational Guidance in Human Love,* which, for all practical purposes, puts the Sex Education problem back into the hands of the American bishops and the NCCB/USCC bureaucracy, where the "problem" began in the first place.

Pope John Paul II has continually had to reprimand many of the bishops on their various visits to Rome, particularly in the area of sexual morality and catechetical instruction. It is no secret that the promotion of the new "sexual catechesis" is at the top of the "most wanted" list of the American Church, along with liturgical "renewal," "inclusive language," eradication of "homophobia" and sundry other "reforms" to bring the Church in step with the Modern World. Over the last twenty years the new "sexual catechesis" has replaced the traditional doctrinal catechesis of the Catholic Church in most dioceses in the United States.

The Homosexual Factor and Sex Education

Most of the reasons for the American Church's forcible implementation of sex education have already been enunciated or alluded to in this book and need no further explanation.

There is one area, however, which I shall mention, in general terms, because of its importance to the issue.

The Sex Education Movement, as already stated, has, as one of its key objectives, the promotion of a "pansexuality" or "bisexuality" agenda in which homosexuality and pedophilia play a key and pivotal role.

The growing number of homosexual and pedophile priests and brothers, including homosexual bishops, as well as lesbian nuns, have formed a "Sixth Column" within the Church in the United States. Many of these individuals have played important roles in the development and promotion of the new sexual catechetics in parochial schools, which, like the USCC Sex Education "Guidelines" and the Kosnik Report, promote homosexual and bisexual activity as a "variation on the norm," not a perversion.

As the internationally known German Thomistic scholar, Josef Pieper, states in his classic work *The Four Cardinal Virtues,*

"Unchastity most effectively falsifies and corrupts the virtue of prudence. . .unchastity begets a blindness of spirit which practically excludes all understanding of the goods of the spirit; unchastity splits the power of decision; conversely, the virtue of chastity, more than any other, makes man capable and ready for contemplation."[525]

Pieper's further observation that "Unchaste abandon and the self-surrender of the soul to the world of sensuality paralyzes the primordial powers of the moral person: the ability to perceive, in silence, the call of reality, and to make, in the retreat of this silence, the decision appropriate to the concrete situation of concrete action"[526] may help explain, in part, why many American bishops, priests, and religious appear to exhibit a "lazy inertia incapable of generating anger,"[527] even when confronted by distraught parents with the most vile and pornographic sex education materials imaginable.

The Holy Duty of Bishops

Dr. Dietrich von Hildebrand, an outspoken opponent of Sex Education programs, in response to a claim that bishops who live in a state of celibacy are no experts in the field of sex and thus can take no position toward Sex Education, has forcefully argued that "This is an attitude which we cannot accept and will not accept. It is the holy duty of Bishops to forbid at least the totalitarian overruling of the sacred rights of the parents, even if they do not understand the horrible damage done to the soul of the children, from a moral and a human point of view."[528]

According to von Hildebrand, it is a great travesty of justice when the State "falls prey to totalitarianism" by mandating Sex Education programs in the public schools; but when the representatives of the Church, "who should be the great protectors of the sacred rights of the individual and of the family, act in a totalitarian way (and thereby exhibit the worst type of clericalism), it is simply treason, a denial of the spirit of Christ. It is a complete abdication in front of the spirit of the world."[529]

Sex Education Gives a New Meaning To "Rescuing"

Dr. von Hildebrand was of course one of the greatest philosophers of the twentieth century and is especially esteemed for his writings in defense of the Faith, particularly in the areas of marriage and family. He was also known to be a very humble and gentle man. It is, therefore, of the utmost significance that a man of his genius and temperament should write,

> I am no friend of picketing, and I thoroughly dislike this kind of "demonstration." But when so grave a question as the souls of our children is at stake, then demonstrations are legitimate and even necessary. We must ceaselessly inundate the Bishops with protests, so that if—which, may God forbid!—we do not succeed in opening their eyes to the abomination of sex education, they will at least yield to the pressure exerted by truly Catholic parents. I mean those parents who are the glory and strength of the Church, who believe firmly the *Credo* of Paul VI, who believe in the infallibility of the Church in matters of faith and morals, and who, unlike the small but noisy group of avant-gardists, accept obediently and lovingly the teaching of *Humanae Vitae.* It is these quiet millions whose parental rights are being usurped. It is their children whose souls are endangered.[530]
>
> . . . Let us fight relentlessly all the Catholic schools which introduce such practice [i.e. sex education]. Not one penny should be given to a pastor who tolerates or endures this abomination.[531]

Dr. von Hildebrand, in his Roman Forum tract, *Sex Education: The Basic Issues,* co-authored by Dr. William Marra of Fordham University, concludes with this stern admonition to the hierarchy,

> Let all Bishops, the timid, the retiring, the insecure with respect to things sexual, be at once confirmed and admonished by these words of the Lord:
>
> "But he that shall scandalize one of these little ones that believe in Me, it were better for him that a millstone should be hanged about his neck, and that he should be drowned in the depth of the sea."[532]

Certainly everything that Dr. von Hildebrand has written on the subject of Sex Education supports the fundamental premise of this book—that formal Sex Education is of itself intrinsically evil and that the promotion and/or tolerance of this barbaric murder of innocence and purity is objectively gravely sinful. Further, anyone—including bishops—who fully understands the nature and objectives of Sex Education and knowingly and willingly promotes or tolerates it is knowingly and willingly cooperating with that which is objectively gravely sinful.

Sex Education—*What Must Be Done*

No one can read the writings of Pope Pius XI and Pope Pius XII on the matter of Sex Education, which have been clearly documented in this book, without understanding their absolute condemnation of this modern-day plague.

Considering the gravity of the current situation within the Church on the matter of Sex Education, it is absolutely necessary that the Holy Father address this problem immediately in order that there will be *no misunderstanding whatsoever* that the norms established by his predecessors in this area remain in effect and should be vigorously enforced by all representatives of the Church.

Once and for all, John Paul II needs to let the world know that he is in complete agreement with the teachings of the Council of Trent, Pope Pius XI, Pope Pius XII and our Catholic tradition on the matter of Sex Education, and that he intends to make the eradication of this moral and spiritual plague a keystone of his pontificate.

Summary Statement on Sex Education

Sex Education, that is, the teaching of explicit sexual matters as a formal matter of classroom instruction, either as a separate curriculum or as an integrated part of legitimate courses of study at the elementary or secondary grade level, has a long and tortuous history which is deeply rooted in the Malthusian, Eugenics and Sexual Libertarian Movements of the last half of the nineteenth century.

Philosophically constructed on the denial of the existence of moral absolutes and the Natural Law, Sex Education is by nature and by design intrinsically evil. As a child of Modernism, Sex Education seeks to undermine the teaching authority of the Church by attacking Catholic doctrine on matters of sexual morality, and by replacing sound doctrinal catechesis with a new sexual catechesis that is directed at the destruction of the latency period in the child and the deforming of the young and impressionable conscience.

Only those who are totally ignorant of the nature and objectives of Sex Education, or those who have simply lost the Faith, can fail to appreciate the moral gravity of the Sex Education scandal and its implications for the future of the Church.

In the United States, the principal promoter of classroom Sex Education for Catholic schools has been the Bishops' United States Catholic Conference, which, since its creation in 1967, has promulgated the Modernist agenda of the American Church. On the matter of Sex Education, the USCC has published Sex Education "Guidelines" which have been appropriately dubbed "a kindergarten version" of the 1977 Catholic Theological Society of America study, *Human Sexuality—New Directions in American Catholic Thought,* which was condemned by the Vatican for its Modernist pronouncements on matters of human sexuality.

The confrontation between the Faithful and proponents of classroom Sex Education has been complicated by the proliferation of ill-conceived, ambiguously worded documents on the matter of Sex Education. The issue has also been clouded by attempts to develop a "Catholic" form of Sex Education, which, if one properly understands the nature of the beast, is akin to developing a "Catholic" version of adultery or fornication.

An immediate and universal ban, therefore, on all forms of classroom Sex Education in Catholic schools and CCD programs is necessary for the restoration of moral sanity in the Catholic Church today.

Epilogue

The New Barbarian and His World

The great British essayist Hilaire Belloc has described the new barbarian in unforgettable terms:

> We sit by and watch the Barbarian, we tolerate him; in the long stretches of peace we are not afraid. We are tickled by his irreverence; his comic inversion of our old certitudes and our fixed creeds refreshes us; we laugh. But as we laugh we are watched by large and awful faces from beyond; and on those faces there is no smile.

It has been 2000 years since Christ came into the world. Twentieth century man has difficulty imagining what it must have been like before the dawn of Christianity—to live in a pagan world ruled by fear and superstition, a world without conscience, without mercy, a world where the barbarian waited at the gate to rape and pillage and trample all vestiges of civilization beneath his feet.

Sex Education—The Final Plague is, of course, a book about the New Barbarian who no longer waits at the gate but lives amongst us. He has traded his loin cloth for a white jacket or designer suit, his spear for a degree. He may even wear a smile—or at least the mask of a smile. He tells us what he is all about and what he intends to do—and we tolerate him. We even welcome him into the public square, into the classroom and into our homes. We are not afraid! He tells us he has come for our children, and we give them over to him. We dismiss with disdain those who sound the warning trumpet, calling them the disturbers of the peace. We tranquilize our consciences and we laugh. We are not afraid!

Let us then have our fill of laughter *now,* for when the world of the New Barbarian comes into its complete development, all the laughter will end. We will have entered the "Brave New World"[533] and there will be no turning back.

True to Huxley's prophetic vision, the world of the New Barbarian will be:

> . . . A world of sterile human "hatcheries" and "decanters," of Epsilons, Deltas, and Alphas.
>
> . . . A world of *absolute* sexual license and *absolute* reproductive tyranny.
>
> . . . A world of "soma" and "hyponopaldia," where sleeping children begin their education with forty minutes of indoctrination on Elementary Sex and Erotic Play followed by Elementary Class Consciousness.
>
> . . . A world of Malthusian drills and birth control cartridges—of abortion centers to dispense with young "mistakes"—and death conditioning and crematorium units to dispense with old "mistakes."
>
> . . . A world where the word "mother" is an obscenity and "father" a scatological reference.
>
> . . . A world without family, without fidelity—without heroes and without villains.
>
> . . . A world filled with sensations but devoid of passions.
>
> . . . A world where one must be faithfully promiscuous because "Everyone belongs to everyone else," and one must always "love carefully" lest one commit the unpardonable sin of loving another too much.
>
> . . . A world where thoughts of a Supreme Being have been banished from the human consciousness and replaced by a new allegiance to the Fordships who control the ruling biocracy under the World States' motto—*"Community, Identity, Stability."*
>
> . . . A world where "Truth is a menace" to universal peace, and religion is pornography.
>
> . . . A world where all that matters is one's "comfort and happiness," for which all must pay a small price, that of surrendering one's humanity.
>
> Most importantly, it will be a world of supreme darkness because it will be a world without Love, without Hope, without Christ—who is the Light of the World.

This *was* the description of a futuristic utopia envisioned by Huxley in 1932. This *is* the description of the world which will come to pass shortly unless Christians unite with all men of goodwill to oppose and ultimately to eradicate the scourge of Sex Education, which is preparing our children to enter into and embrace the "Brave New World" of the New Barbarian.

In *Sapientiae Christianae,* Pope Leo XIII admonished the Faithful that,

> To recoil before an enemy, or to keep silence when from all sides such clamors are raised up against truth, is the part of man either devoid of character or who entertains doubt as to the truth of what he professes to believe.
>
> In both cases such mode of behavior is base and is insulting to God, and both are incompatible with the salvation of mankind. This kind of conduct is profitable only to the enemies of the Faith, *for nothing emboldens the wicked so greatly as the lack of courage on the part of the good.* [Emphasis added].

Pope Leo XIII then goes on to offer these words of encouragement:

> Christians are. . .*born for combat,* whereof the greater the vehemence, the more assured, God-abiding, the triumph: Have confidence; I have overcome the world! [Emphasis added].

As we enter the battle *against* Sex Education, let us take courage in the words of Pope Leo XIII. After all, was there ever a more noble task than that of defending holy innocence and purity?

It is my earnest prayer that God will pour forth His graces and consolation on all those who take up Christ's banner in this new Holy War, and that Our Lady of Fatima, to whom this book is dedicated, will keep them under her special protection and grant them the final victory.

—The Author

Notes

Chapter 1 The Nature of Sex Education

1. Geoffrey Marks and William Beatty, *Epidemics* (New York: Charles Scribner and Sons Publishers, 1976), p. xi.
2. Ibid., p. 20.
3. M. Anchell and M. Morris, *A Psychiatrist Looks at Sex Education* (Clovis, California: Up with Families Publishers, 1981), p. 5.
4. Claire Chambers, *Humanist Manifesto II: The SIECUS Circle* (Belmont, MA: Western Islands Press, 1977), pp. 410-417.
5. Washington Star News, May 3, 1973.
6. *Epidemics,* pp. 44-45.
7. Ibid., pp. 70-71.
8. Sidney Ditzion, "Moral Evolution in America," *The Encyclopedia of Sexual Behavior,* Ellis and Abarbanel, editors (New York: Hawthorne Press, 1967), p. 82.
9. Ibid., p. 85.
10. Robert Wood, "Sex Reform Movement," *The Encyclopedia of Sexual Behavior,* pp. 956-966.
11. Ibid., p. 961.
12. Ibid., pp. 960-961.
13. Beryl Suitters, *Be Brave and Angry—Chronicles of the International Planned Parenthood Federation* (London, 1973), p. 217.
14. Bernard Schreiber, *Geheime Reichssage—The Men Behind Hitler,* translated by H. R. Martindale (Mureaux, France: LaHaye, 1973).
15. Ibid., p. 23.
16. Ibid., p. 33.

Chapter 2 The Evolution of the Plague

17. Robert Wood, *The Encyclopedia of Sexual Behavior,* p. 961.
18. Ibid., p. 961.
19. Ibid.
20. Cf. James Reed, *From Private Vice to Public Virtue* (New York: Basic Books, 1978).
21. Ibid., p. 111.
22. Allen F. Guttmacher, M.D., *Margaret Sanger—An Autobiography* (New York: Maxwell Reprint Co., 1970), pp. viii-ix.

23. Beryl Suitters, *Be Brave and Angry* (London: IPPF, 1973) pp. 172-173, 215-219.
24. Ibid., pp. 216-217.
25. Ibid., p. 42.
26. Ibid., p. 245.
27. Ibid., pp. 221-222.
28. Ibid., pp. 217-218.
29. Lester A. Kirkendall, "Education for Family Living," *The Encyclopedia of Sexual Behavior,* p. 700.
30. Ibid.

Chapter 3 The Reactivation of the Plague

31. William B. Ball, *Population Control—Civil and Constitutional Concerns* (Cornell University Press, 1968, reprinted by U.S. Coalition for Life, Export, PA 15632), p. 31.
32. Ibid., p. 1.
33. Cahal B. Daly, *Morals, Law and Life* (Chicago: Scepter Press, 1966), p. 101.
34. Ibid., pp. 101-103.
35. Germain Grisez, *Abortion: The Myths, the Realities and the Arguments* (New York: Corpus Publications, 1970), p. 258.
36. Ibid., p. 243.
37. Herbert A. Otto, Editor, *The New Sex Education* (Chicago: Associated Press/Follett Publishers, 1978), book jacket.
38. Ibid., p. 104.
39. Ibid., pp. 101-116.
40. Kirkendall, *The New Sex Education,* pp. 337-338.
41. Ibid., p. 342.
42. *U.S.C.C. Guidelines,* pp. 91-97.
43. Otto, "Neglected Aspects and Priorities in the New Sex Education," *The New Sex Education,* pp. 247-259.
44. Ibid., p. 251.
45. Ibid., p. 254.
46. Ibid., p. 255.
47. Ibid., p. 257.
48. Ibid., pp. 259-260.
49. *SIECUS Factsheet,* December 15, 1970.
50. George Langmyhr, M.D., "The Role of Planned Parenthood—World Population in Abortion," *Clinical Obstetrics Gynecology,* 1971, Vol. 14, p. 1190.
51. Ibid.
52. Ibid., pp. 1190-1191.
53. Ibid., p. 1196.
54. Chambers, p. 5.
55. *U.S. Catholic,* October 1982, p. 26.
56. Ibid., p. 30. (For complete information on SAR films and materials see

Randy Engel, "The Plague of SAR," *Homiletic and Pastoral Review,* pp. 18-27).
57. *U.S. Catholic,* October 1982, p. 28.
58. Ibid.
59. Ibid., pp. 24-25.
60. Harriet F. Pilpel, "The Abortion Crisis," *The Case for Legalized Abortion Now* (CA: Diablo Press, 1967), p. 108.
61. Ibid., p. 103.
62. Chambers, p. 19.
63. SIECUS Position Statement Sheet, 1978.
64. SIECUS Report, Vol. VI, No. 4 (March, 1978), p. 1.
65. E. James Lieberman, M.D., "Informed Consent for Parenthood," *Abortion and the Unwanted Child,* Carl Rieterman, Editor (New York: Springer Publishing Company, 1971), pp. 77-93.
66. "Sex Education," Catholic Hour, National Council of Catholic Men, May 26, 1968, SIECUS Reprint 56, p. 4.
67. Lester A. Kirkendall, "Sex Education In Nine Cooperating High Schools in Oklahoma," *Clearing House,* 18:457 March, 1944.
68. "Joint Committee on Health Problems of the NEA and AMA Resolutions," *School Health Review,* September, 1969, p. 23.
69. Chambers, p. 153.
70. Otto, *The New Sex Education,* p. 169.
71. Ibid., p. 171.
72. Ibid.
73. Ibid., p. 175.
74. Ibid., pp. 177-178.
75. Barbara Morris, "Sex Education for the World," *The Barbara Morris Report,* May, 1973, Vol. 4, No. 3, p. 2.

Chapter 4 The Collapse of the Opposition

76. W. K. Ahern, "Classroom Sex Education—What Has the Church Always Said?" published by CUF of Canada (P.O. Box 6361, Edmonton, Alberta, Canada, TSB 4K7, $1.00).
77. Pius XII, Address of September 18, 1951 to the French Fathers of Families.
78. Ahern, pp. 13-14.
79. Ahern, p. 8.
80. William Ball, *Civil and Constitutional Concerns of Population Control* (USCC reprint, 1968).
81. Ball, p. 7.
82. Ibid., pp. 44-45.
83. Ibid., pp. 5-6.
84. For additional details on the content of Statement and the Interfaith Commission which drafted the document see: *Engel Critique,* pp. 21-22.
85. For complete quotes and documentation see *Engel Critique,* pp. 19-23.
86. Chambers, pp. 430-432.

87. Suitters, *Chronicles of the IPPF,* p. 252.
88. Testimony of Monsignor James T. McHugh on Family Planning Services and Population Research Act (Title X of PHSA), Subcommitee on Public Health and Welfare, Committee on Interstate and Foreign Commerce, U.S. House of Representatives, 91st Congress, Aug. 3, 4 and 7, 1970, p. 361.
89. Drs. James and Marie Fox, *Life Education: A New Series of Correlated Lessons* (New York: Joseph F. Wagner, Inc., 1970), Grade 8 text.
90. Chambers, p. 370.
91. Monsignor Eugene Kevane, ''Catechesis and Sexuality: What the Church Teaches,'' *Human Sexuality in Our Time* (Boston: Daughters of St. Paul, 1979), pp. 188-189.
92. Ibid., pp. 195-196.
93. Ibid., p. 197.
94. Ibid., p. 198.
95. Engel, p. 14.
96. Ibid.
97. ''State of the Question Regarding Moral Education and Sex Education in the Public School Systems,'' *USCC Memo* (Washington, D.C.: Department of Education, USCC, Nov. 8, 1978).
98. Ibid., pp. 1-2.
99. Engel, p. 69.
100. Fr. Robert Nugent, ''Forum,'' *National Catholic Reporter,* August 14, 1981.

Chapter 5 Chronological Addenda

101. *Education in Human Sexuality for Christians* (Washington, D.C.: Department of Education, USCC, 1981), p. vi.
102. Rt. Reverend Mark J. Hurley, *Commentary on the Declaration on Christian Education of Vatican Council II* (New Jersey: Paulist Press, 1966), p. 26.
103. Ibid., p. 7.
104. Ibid., p. 28.
105. Ibid., pp. 42-43.
106. Ibid., p. 43.
107. Ibid., pp. 50-54.
108. Ibid., p. 53.
109. Ibid., p. 54.
110. Ibid.
111. Ibid., p. 55.
112. Austin Flannery, O.P., *Vatican Council II: Conciliar Documents* (New York: Costello Press, 1975), p. 727.
113. Walter M. Abbott, *The Documents of Vatican II* (New York: American Press, 1966).
114. Hurley, p. 55.

115. Ibid., p. 55.
116. Ibid., p. 88.
117. Ibid., pp. 88-89.
118. Ibid., p. 89.
119. Donald A. Doyle, "NCD is Ambiguous: Clarification From Rome Needed" (St. Paul, Minnesota: *The Wanderer,* September 3, 1981), p 1.
120. Kevane, p. 194.
121. Ibid., p. 199.
122. Ibid., pp. 189-190.
123. Kosnik, pp. 86-87.
124. Ibid., p. 31.
125. Ibid., p. 30.
126. Ibid., p. 59.
127. Ibid., pp. 92-95.
128. Ibid., p. 95.
129. Ibid.
130. Ibid., pp. 229-236.
131. Ibid., p. 232.
132. Ibid., pp. 226-228.
133. Ibid., p. 144.
134. Ibid., p. 149.
135. Ibid., pp. 115-116.
136. Ibid., p. 244.
137. Ibid., p. viii.
138. Ibid., p. xiv.
139. Cf. Reverend William B. Smith, "Morality and Sexuality: What the Church Teaches," *Human Sexuality in Our Time* (Boston: Daughters of St. Paul, 1979), pp. 148-171.
140. Kosnik, p. 237.
141. Ibid., p. 237.
142. Ibid., p. 238.
143. Ibid.
144. Cf. Engel, *Critique,* pp. 19-33.
145. Ibid., pp. 37-41.
146. *Guidelines,* p. ix.
147. Ibid., pp. 6, 10-11.
148. Kosnik, p. 241.
149. *Guidelines,* p. 100.
150. *Guidelines,* p. viii.
151. Ibid., p. vii.
152. Ibid.
153. Kosnik, p. 238.
154. *Guidelines,* p. 3.
155. Ibid., p. 6.
156. Ibid., p. 7.
157. Ibid., p. 13.
158. Kevane, p. 196.

159. Cf. Engel, *Critique,* pp. 45-72.
160. Henry Sattler, Ph.D., *Sex Is Alive and Well and Flourishing Among Christians* (Indiana: Our Sunday Visitor, 1979), pp. 111-112.
161. Ibid., pp. 58-60.
162. *Guidelines,* p. x.
163. Ibid., p. 97.
164. Kevane, footnote ii, p. 202.
165. *Guidelines,* p. 67.
166. Ibid., p. x.
167. Ibid., p. 65.
168. Ibid., p. 92.
169. Ibid., p. 85.
170. Ibid., p. 87.
171. Ibid., p. 95.
172. Ibid., p. 89.
173. Ibid., p. 87.
174. Ibid.
175. Ibid., p. 94.
176. Ibid., p. 74.
177. Ibid., p. 86.
178. Ibid., p. 87.
179. Reverend Robert I. Bradley, S.J., "Sexuality and Marriage in the Teaching of the Church," *Human Sexuality in Our Time* (Boston: Daughters of St. Paul, 1979), p. 135.
180. Kevane, p. 200.
181. Germain Grisez, "Turmoil in the Church," transcript of a speech delivered on September 18, 1983, in Chicago before the Fellowship of Catholic Scholars, pp. 5-6.
182. Sattler, p. 60.
183. For an excellent insight into the phenomenon of phantasmagoria cf. *Keep the Faith* tape series 12/1/88 featuring an interview with Fr. Paul Wickens.
184. Kevane, p. 207.
185. Ibid.
186. Pius XII, address of September 18, 1951.
187. "Statement Concerning: Human Sexuality," NCCB Committee on Doctrine, *Origins,* V. 7, No. 24, 12/1/77, pp. 376-378 (order B-126).
188. For complete text cf. *The Pope Speaks,* 7/13/77, (Protocol Number 553-55).
189. Smith, p. 148.
190. Ibid., pp. 148, 169-170.
191. "Sex Education 'Guidelines' 'Solid,' Official Says," *Our Sunday Visitor,* July 6, 1980, p. 2.
192. "Bishop: Guidelines Not Textbook," *OSV,* January 31, 1982, p. 3.
193. R. Nugent, "Sex Education Guidelines: New Gay Insights," NCR.
194. Ibid., p. 11.
195. Ibid.

196. "Scholars Question USCC Book," NC Register, October 25, 1981, p. 1.
197. D. Dolesh, "Guidelines 'Solid,' " *OSV,* July 6, 1980, p. 2.
198. *Serviam* Newsletter, CREDO Chapter of CUF, Buffalo, N.Y., No. 173, April 1987, p. 4.
199. "Bishop Details Deficiences of 'New Creation' Series," *The Wanderer,* July 23, 1987, pp. 1-6.
200. R. Engel, "Sexology and the USCC," *The Wanderer,* June 4, 1981.
201. D. Dolesh, "Letter to the Editor," *The Wanderer,* June 10, 1981.
202. Engel, *Critique,* pp. 6-12.
203. Ibid., p. 73.
204. D. Carmen, "The Love Doctors," *Plain Dealer* Magazine, February 9, 1986, p. 6.
205. Ibid.
206. Ibid.
207. Ibid., p. 8.
208. Ibid., pp. 17, 8.
209. Ibid., p. 8.
210. Ibid., p. 17.
211. Ibid., p. 8.
212. Ibid.

Chapter 6 The Production of Perverts

213. R. Harper, F. Harper, "Education in Sex," *The Encyclopedia of Sexual Behavior,* pp. 344-349.
214. Ibid., p. viii.
215. Ibid., p. 344.
216. Ibid.
217. Ibid., pp. 344-345.
218. Ibid., p. 345.
219. Ibid.
220. Ibid.
221. Ibid., p. 346.
222. Ibid.
223. Ibid.
224. Ibid.
225. Ibid.
226. Ibid., p. 347.
227. Ibid.
228. Ibid.
229. Ibid.
230. Ibid., p. 348.
231. Ibid.
232. Ibid.
233. Ibid.
234. Ibid., p. 349.
235. Ibid.

236. Ibid.
237. Ibid.
238. Ibid.
239. Chambers, p. 298.
240. Ibid., p. 9.
241. Available from American Life Lobby, Stafford, VA, No. SE 17.
242. M. Anchell, M. Norris, "A Psychiatrist Looks at Sex Education," pp. 1-4.
243. Ibid., p. 5.
244. Ibid.
245. Ibid., p. 6.
246. Ibid., p. 7.
247. Ibid., p. 10.
248. Ibid., pp. 10-11.
249. Ibid., p. 14.
250. Ibid.
251. Ibid., p. 16.
252. Ibid., p. 14.
253. Ibid., pp. 16-17.
254. Ibid., p. 15.
255. Ibid., p. 14.
256. Ibid., p. 15.
257. Ibid., p. 17.
258. Ibid., p. 18.
259. Ibid., p. 19.
260. Ibid., p. 21.
261. Ibid., p. 22.
262. Ibid., p. 21.
263. Ibid., pp. 22-23.
264. Ibid., p. 24.
265. Ibid.
266. Ibid.
267. Ibid., p. 29.
268. Ibid.
269. Ibid.
270. Ibid.
271. Ibid.
272. Ibid., p. 30.
273. Ibid., p. 26.
274. Ibid.
275. Ibid.
276. Ibid.
277. Ibid., p. 27.
278. Ibid.
279. Ibid.
280. Ibid., p. 28.
281. Ibid., pp. 31-32.

Chapter 7 Sex Education in Catholic Drag— An Analysis of *Love and Life*

282. Coleen Kelly Mast, *Love and Life—A Christian Sexual Morality Guide for Teens* (San Francisco: Ignatius Press, 1986).
283. Melvin Anchell, M.D., ''The Case Against Sex Education,'' *A.L.L. About Issues,* Nov./Dec.-1988, p. 50.
284. Ibid., p. 48.
285. Ibid.
286. Mast, *Sex Respect—The Option of True Sexual Freedom* (Golf, Illinois: Project Respect Publishers, 1986), Second Edition.
287. Mast, SR, cover insert.
288. Mast, *AIDS—A Risky Business for Everyone* (Bradley, Illinois: Respect, Inc., 1988).
289. For the reader to understand how this principle of ''neutrality'' is applied in actual practice we can look at Mast's latest work, *AIDS—A Risky Business for Everyone,* designed as a supplement to Chapter 5 of the *Sex Respect* Program.

    In the AIDS Parent Guidebook, parents are told that ''because of the freedom in our country, the public school teacher will not impose his or her moral views about homosexuality in the classroom. . .'' (SR/P9).

    In the Student Workbook, the fact that the origin and transmission of the fatal disease is directly linked to unnatural sodomy is downplayed. The Mast message is that ''Anyone can get AIDS in high risk behavior. . . That means that AIDS can be transmitted after homecoming, at a graduation party, during a picnic or after school.'' (SR/S9).

    Students are told, ''Transmission of the AIDS virus can happen between people who are nice, neat and even very much in love.'' (SR/S8).
290. Gerard V. Bradley, *''Caesar's Religion: The Human Life Review''* (New York: Human Life Foundation, Vol. XV, No. 1), p. 52.
291. Ibid.
292. Ibid., p. 54.
293. Paul C. Vitz, *Psychology as Religion—The Cult of Self-Worship* (Grand Rapids, Michigan: W. B. Erdmans Publishers), p. 109.
294. Ibid.
295. Ibid.
296. G. K. Chesterton, *St. Thomas Aquinas* (New York: Image Books, Doubleday, 1933).
297. ''Love and Life Curriculum Critique,'' *WATCH,* Catholic Caucus Newsletter, Summer, 1987, copies available for $3 from *WATCH,* Anne Arundel County Chapter, Inc., P.O. Box 5, Harmans, Maryland 21077.
298. Ibid, pp. 2 & 3.
299. Ibid., p. 3.
300. Ibid., p. 4.
301. Ibid., p. 5.
302. Ibid., p. 6.
303. Copies of these anti-life publications for review purposes are available

from Ed-U Press, 760 Ostrom Ave., Syracus, N.Y. 13210.

304. Cf. Dietrich von Hildebrand, *The Devastated Vineyard* (Harrison, New York: Roman Catholic Books, 1973), p. 214. Speaking on the use of catchwords or slogans, von Hildebrand notes that while they may be "very effective," they frequently contain "many grave and primitive errors." Describing slogans as a "dangerous intellectual weapon," he states how astonished he is to see how naively and gullibly slogans are accepted—and how easily they can vilify very good things.
305. Cf. Dietrich von Hildebrand's essay, "The Cult of the Positive" in *The Devastated Vineyard.* According to von Hildebrand, ". . . With the catchword 'positive' as opposed to 'negative' the illusion is introduced that the avoidance of a sin is morally much less important than a purely positive moral deed." (p. 165). However, he continues, "One forgets that there is a hierarchy in our duties toward God: our first duty is not to offend God by sin; our second duty is to glorify Him by good deeds." (p. 172).
306. Pope Pius XI, encyclical *Education of the Redeemed Man,* 1929.
307. *Familiaris Consortio,* cf. No. 28, 30.
308. Ibid., (1.).
309. Cf. Rt. Rev. Monsignor Paul J. Glenn, *Ethics—A Class Manual in Moral Philosophy* (St. Louis: B. Herder Book Co., 1947), pp. 97-119.
310. Rev. Robert Bradley, S.J., "Sexuality and Marriage," *Human Sexuality in Our Time* (Boston: Daughters of St. Paul, 1979), pp. 120-131.
311. Ibid., p. 131.
312. *Declaration on Certain Questions Concerning Sexual Ethics* (Vatican: Sacred Congregation for the Doctrine of the Faith, Dec. 29, 1975), No. 4.
313. A. Clemens, "Catholicism and Sex," *The Encyclopedia of Behavior,* p. 232.
314. For an excellent discussion of the virtue of chastity, see Smith, op. cit., pp. 149-153.
315. Rev. John A. Hardon, S.J., "Sex and Sanctity," *Human Sexuality in our Time* (Boston: Daughters of St. Paul, 1979), p. 144.
316. Pope Pius XI, *On the Christian Education of Youth* (1929) (Boston: Daughters of St. Paul, reprint), p. 17.
317. Pope John Paul II, *Familiaris Consortio* (Boston: St. Paul Editions), No. 37.
318. Reverend William B. Smith, S.T.D., "Morality and Sexuality," *Human Sexuality in Our Time,* p. 153.
319. Ibid., p. 150.
320. Ibid., pp. 153-154.
321. Ibid., p. 157.
322. Ibid., p. 160.
323. Anne Muggeridge, *The Desolate City* (San Francisco: Harper and Row, 1986), p. 104.
324. Ibid., p. 51.
325. Ibid., p. 9.
326. Ibid., p. 21.
327. Ibid., p. 9.

328. Bradley, op. cit., 120.
329. Ibid., p. 123.
330. Ibid.
331. Ibid.
332. Ibid., p. 122.
333. Ibid., p. 123.
334. *Declaration on Certain Questions Concerning Sexual Ethics* (Vatican: Sacred Congregation for the Doctrine of the Faith, Dec. 29, 1975), No. 3.
335. Muggeridge, p. 154.
336. Pope Pius V, *Catechism of the Council of Trent for Parish Priests,* translated by John A. McHugh, O.P., and Charles J. Callan, O.P. (Phillippines: Sinag-tala Publishers, 1974), p. 431. (Also published by TAN Books and Publishers, Inc.).
337. Ibid.
338. Ibid.
339. Ibid.
340. Ibid., pp. 437-439.
341. Pope Pius XII, "Allocution to Italian Mothers," Oct. 26, 1941.
342. Cahal B. Daly, M.D., D.D., *Morals, Law and Life* (Chicago: Scepter Publishers, 1966), p. 29.
343. Ibid., p. 34.
344. Ibid., p. 30.
345. Ibid., p. 33.
346. Mast, *Love and Life,* Student Guide, p. 69.
347. "Vatican Guidelines See Extra-Marital Sin as a Deviation From Maturity," *Challenge,* December, 1983, p. 19.
348. Father John G. Arintero, O.P., S.T.M., *The Mystical Evolution in the Development and Vitality of the Church* (London: Herder Book Co., 1949; reprinted by TAN, 1978), Vol. II, pp. 50-51.
349. *A Practical Dictionary of Biblical and General Catholic Information,* edited by Rev. John P. O'Connell (Chicago: The Catholic Press, 1951), p. 112.
350. Arintero, op. cit., pp. 50-33.
351. Vitz, op. cit.
352. Ibid., p. 91.
353. Ibid.
354. Ibid., p. 96.
355. Ibid., p. 79.
356. Ibid., pp. 79-81.
357. Ibid., p. 95.
358. Ibid., pp. 95-96.
359. Ibid., p. 101, see footnoted reference to H. Kohut and O. Kerrberg.
360. Ibid.
361. Cf. *WATCH ALERT,* Spring, 1989 on "Self-Esteem."
362. Melvin Anchell, M.D., A.S.P.P., *Killers of Children, A Psychoanalytical Look at Sex Education,* 1988. Available from American Life League, 188 Onville Road, Stafford, VA 22554, $6.95.
363. Ibid., p. 70.

364. Ibid.
365. Ibid., p. 71.
366. Ibid., p. 72.
367. Ibid.
368. C. Derrick, op. cit., p. 87.
369. Cf. Dietrich von Hildebrand, *The Devastated Vineyard.* Speaking on the totalitarian aspects of sex education, von Hildebrand states, "...The damage is not only enormous from a moral point of view, but also disastrous from a purely human viewpoint. The neutralization of the sexual realm which is already present in virtue of the publicity of the classroom, and especially in virtue of treating this realm as academic subject, is dehumanizing...One of the most deplorable consequences of this dehumanization...is the fact that the feeling of shame is dying out..." p. 28.
370. Daly, op. cit., p. 43.
371. Ibid.
372. Ibid.
373. Ibid., p. 75.
374. Ibid.
375. Ibid., p. 44.
376. Ibid.
377. Ibid., p. 96.
378. For a historic perspective of "family planning" see Samuel Saloman, "Birth Control Hearings," Subcommittee of the Committee on Judiciary, U.S. Senate 72nd Congress, S. 4436, May 1932, 73rd Congress, S. 1842 on March 1, 20, 27. Government Printing Office, Washington, D.C., reprinted in *Child and Family,* Vol. 17, No. 1, 1978, Oak Park, Illinois, Herbert Ratner, M.D., Editor, pp. 47-65.
379. William G. White, M.D., "A Response on the NFCPG Position Paper on Sex Education," *Linacre Quarterly,* Vol. 49, Nov. 1982, No. 4.
380. Rev. Anthony Zimmerman, *"NFP Users Don't Have Contraceptive Mentality,"* Letters to the Editor, *Fidelity,* October, 1985, p. 7.
381. Dr. Herbert Ratner, "Who Should Learn NFP?" Letters to the Editor, *Fidelity,* June, 1986, p. 14.
382. Ibid.
383. Dr. Herbert Ratner, "The Natural Institution of the Family" (Marriage: an Office of Nature), speech delivered at the Tenth Convention of the Fellowship of Catholic Scholars, Sept. 26, 1987, Los Angeles, California, published in *The Catholic Church's Message to United States Citizens of the Twenty-first Century,* Editor Paul L. Williams, Ph.D., Northeast Books, Pittston, Pennsylvania, 1988, pp. 154-168 (for subscription information and complete index of back issues, write *Child and Family Quarterly,* Box 508, Oak Park, Illinois 60303).
384. Ibid., p. 165.
385. Ibid.
386. Rev. Sean J. Donnelly, "Responsible Parenthood and the Multi-Child Family," *Homiletic and Pastoral Review,* October, 1987, p. 30.
387. Ibid., p. 30.

388. Ibid., p. 31.
389. Ibid., p. 30.
390. See Rev. George A. Kelly, *The Catholic Marriage Manual* (New York: Random House, 1958), pp. 57-59.

   In addition to the four indications listed by Pope Pius XII by which spouses may justify the practice of periodic continence (i.e., a serious reason of the medical, eugenical, economic or social order), the practice must be mutually agreed upon and not be a proximate occasion of sins against chastity (p. 58).
391. Suitters, op. cit., p. 1.
392. Cahal Daly, op. cit., p. 85.
393. Ibid.
394. Ibid., p. 96.
395. Ibid., p. 85.
396. Ibid.
397. Ibid.
398. Ibid., p. 86.
399. Ratner, op. cit., p. 165
400. The term "Natural Family Planning," or "NFP," was coined in 1971 at a joint meeting of federal public health officials and international leaders of the nascent NFP Movement, and made its first appearance in print in 1973. Unlike the traditional phrases used by the Catholic Church and Catholic laity to describe the practice of sexual abstinence within marriage for the purpose of postponing pregnancy, such as "rhythm" or "periodic continence," the new terminology "Natural Family Planning" proved to be a mischievous hybrid—i.e., the grafting of the word "Natural," pertaining to a *method,* onto "family planning," pertaining to an *ethic* of family limitation, which the Catholic Church has *never* approved of in principle and which by the 1970's was synonymous with the practice of birth control as defined by the Sangerites. The implications of this unfortunate verbal merger were not lost on the population control establishment, which was quick to publicize the idea that the Church had accepted the concept of "family planning" and that the only remaining area of disagreement was over methodology, that is, "artificial" vs. "natural" means. To date, it appears that the Catholic Church has yet to extricate itself from this morass of the anti-child ethic inherent in any form of so-called "family planning."

   In this writer's humble opinion, the Church would be wiser to leave the matter of the training and instruction on the regulation of births based on natural body rhythms to the lay organizers, and where applicable, the scientific and medical community, which can make its contribution in terms of medical knowledge in this area as envisoned by Pope Pius XII in his 1951 address to the Italian Catholic Union of Midwives. The Church, for its part, would then be free to concentrate on the promotion of traditional familial and marital values which have been systematically desecrated by the Sangerites and their heirs; values which would be not only acceptable but positively good and which would emphasize the spirit of generosity which would make every child not "wanted" but *"welcomed"* into the family circle.

401. "Pope Warns Against Natural Family Planning Abuses," *Sun Times Wire Service,* Sept. 1, 1984, p. 1.
402. Ibid.
403. Suitters, op. cit., p. 242.
404. Ibid.
405. Cf. Pope Pius XI, *Casti Connubii* (1930).
406. Ibid.
407. Daly, p. 151.
408. Ibid., p. 176.
409. Ibid., p. 165.
410. Ibid., p. 166.
411. Ibid.
412. Ibid.
413. Ibid., p. 169.
414. Ibid., p. 168.
415. Ibid., p. 170.
416. Ibid.
417. Ibid., p. 172.
418. Ibid., p. 182, footnote 269.
419. Ibid., p. 172.
420. Ibid., p. 175.
421. Ibid., pp. 175-176.

Chapter 8 The Vatican and Sex Education

422. This specific reference to in vitro fertilization raises some doubt as to whether or not Cardinal Ratzinger himself *ever* reviewed the *New Creation Series* before affixing his signature to the February 23, 1989 letter to Archbishop Kucera which doctrinally exonerated the program, since the document entitled *Instruction on Respect for Human Life in its Origin and on the Dignity of Procreation—Replies to Certain Questions of the Day* issued by Cardinal Ratzinger for the Sacred Congregation for the Doctrine of the Faith on February 22, 1987 and approved by the Supreme Pontiff, John Paul II, contains an absolute condemnation of artificial fertilization (pp. 14-19).
423. Letter of October 1988, from Edouard Cardinal Gagnon, p.s.s., President of the Pontifical Council for the Family, Vatican City (Prot. N. 17/18), to Sister Rose Marie Hennessy, Superintendent of Schools, Diocese of Oakland, California.
424. Edouard Cardinal Gagnon, "Marriage and Family Questions Permeate Every Sphere of Pastoral Activity," Speech of May 10, 1989, Rome, reprinted in *The Wanderer,* May 11, 1989, p. 6.
425. Copies of the Engel Critique are available from the U.S. Coalition for Life, Box 315, Export, Pennsylvania 15632, $7.50 prepaid.
426. "Vatican Congregation for Catholic Education to Issue Guidelines on Sex

Ed. & Schools,'' *Catholic Advance,* Wichita, Kansas, November 10, 1983.

427. ''Vatican Sex Education Guidelines Are a Little Confusing'' (Canada: *Challenge,* December 1983), p. 16.
428. *'' 'Orientamenti educativi sull'amore umano''* (Italian Translation), *Seminarium* (Vatican City: Sacred Congregation for Catholic Institutions, Jan.-June 1984), Vol. 24, No. 1-2.
429. ''Educational Guidance in Human Love'' (English Translation), Sacred Congregation for Catholic Education, Nov. 1, 1983, as reprinted from *L'Osservatore Romano,* Eng. edition (Boston: Daughters of St. Paul).
430. *Catholic Advance,* op. cit., p. 3.
431. Ibid.
432. Ibid.
433. Sr. Mary Ann Walsh, ''Parents Play Key Role in Sex Education,'' NC Vatican City Release (undated).
434. Ibid., p. 1.
435. Ibid.
436. Ibid.
437. Cf. ''New Guidelines Stress Parental Responsibility,'' *The Catholic Accent,* Vol. 23-No. 27, Dec. 8, 1983, p. 1.
438. Cf. ''Document from the Holy See Says Parents Should Control Sex Education,'' *Long Island Catholic,* Dec. 8, 1983, pp. 1-2.
439. Cf. Richard Cowden-Guido, ''Family Coalitions Applaud Vatican Guidelines on Chastity Education,'' *The Wanderer,* Dec. 29, 1983, p. 3.
440. Ibid.
441. Ibid.
442. Howard Hurwitz, ''New York Saturates Public Schools with New Sex Syllabus,'' *New York Tribune,* Dec. 14, 1983, p. 1.
443. Ibid.
444. Cf. *Engel Critique of USCC Sex Education Guidelines* for background on 1968 ''Interfaith Statement,'' pp. 21-23.
445. Hurwitz, op. cit., p. 1.
446. Ibid.
447. Note: In comparison with the *New Creation Series,* 7-Lesson Edition (1988), the NYC Sex Syllabus for grades 1-8 is *less* sexually explicit than its parochial school counterpart.
448. Cowden-Guido, op. cit., p. 3.
449. Ibid.
450. ''Vatican Issues Sex Education Guidelines,'' *Respect Life Report,* NCCB/USCC Committee for Pro-life Affairs, Washington, D.C., December, 1983.
451. Cowden-Guido, op. cit., p. 3.
452. For a copy of the full text of the NCCL seven-page press release of December, 1983 write: NCCL, 433 Front Street, Catasauqua, PA 18032.
453. Cowden-Guido, op. cit., p. 3.
454. E. William Sockey III, ''Holy See Issues Sex Education Guidelines,'' *Lay Witness,* Vol. 5, No. 6, February, 1984, pp. 5-7. Copies available from

CUF, 50 Washington Ave., New Rochelle, NY 10801.
455. Ibid., p. 5.
456. Ibid., p. 6.
457. Ibid., pp. 6-7.
458. Ibid., p. 7.
459. "Vatican Issues Statement on Sex Education," *Issues & Action Update,* Vol. 3, No. 1/Winter 1984, Center for Population Options, Washington, D.C., p. 6.
460. Ibid.
461. Ibid.
462. Ibid.
463. Ibid.
464. Ibid.
465. Father G. Grieco, O.F.M., *"Reazioni della stampa di vario orientamento—Una serene e precisa reposta," Seminarium,* Vol. 24, No. 1-2, January-June, 1984, p. 248, Sacred Congregation for Catholic Institutions, Vatican City 00120.
466. Ibid., p. 253.
467. Ibid.
468. Ibid., p. 250.
469. Ibid., p. 251.
470. Ibid.
471. Ibid., pp. 249-259.
472. Ibid., p. 250.
473. Ibid.
474. Op. cit., p. 6.
475. Grieco, p. 249.
476. Ibid., p. 251.
477. Ibid., p. 250.
478. William Cardinal Baum, Press Release on "Educational Guidance in Human Love," *L'Osservatore Romano,* English translation, Dec. 5, 1983, p. 1.
479. Von Hildebrand, op. cit., p. 6.
480. "Sex Education—the Right of the Family, the Duty of the School," *Our Sunday Visitor,* Huntington, Indiana, Jan. 29, 1984, p. 3.
481. Ibid.
482. Ibid.
483. Ibid.
484. Ibid.
485. Ibid.
486. Robert G. Marshall, *Critique of Benziger Family Life Program,* Second Series, K-8 (1988-89), available from American Life League, P.O. Box 1350, Stafford, Virginia 22554, $10.00 prepaid.
487. Abbott, op. cit., No. 1.
488. In Lewis Carroll's *Through the Looking Glass,* Alice engages Humpty Dumpty in a conversation on the ethics of fair verbal labor practices:
"When I use a word," Humpty Dumpty said in a rather scornful tone,

"It means just what I choose it to mean--nothing more nor less."

"The question is," said Alice, "whether you can make words mean so many different things."

"The question is," said Humpty Dumpty, "which is to be master—that's all."

Alice was too much puzzled to say anything, so, after a minute, Humpty Dumpty, looking very much pleased, began again. "They're a temper, some of them—particularly verbs, they're the proudest. Adjectives you can do anything with, but not verbs. However, I can manage the whole lot of them! IMPENETRABILITY! That's what I say!"

"Would you please tell me," said Alice, "what that means?"

"Now you talk like a reasonable child," said Humpty Dumpty, looking very much pleased. "I meant by 'IMPENETRABILITY' that we've had enough of that subject, and it would be just as well if you'd mention what you mean to do next, as I suppose you don't mean to stop here all the rest of your life."

"That's a great deal to make one word mean," Alice said in a thoughtful tone.

"When I make a word do a lot of work like that," said Humpty Dumpty, "I always pay extra."

"Oh!" said Alice. She was too puzzled to make any other remark...

489. "Vatican Sex Education Guidelines Are a Little Confusing," *Challenge,* Manitoba, Canada, Vol. 10, No. 8, December, 1983, p. 16.
490. Ibid.
491. Leo P. Chall, "A Survey of Advances in Modern Sex Research," *The Encyclopedia of Sexual Behavior,* p. 31.
492. Ibid.
493. For a discussion of this predicament in connection with AIDS education, see "How to Talk to Kids about Homosexuality" by W. R. Coulson, Ph.D., a founder of the Center for Enterprising Families, 2054 Oriole St., San Diego, California 92114, footnote 8, pp. 7-8.
494. Cf. "The History of Childhood Sexuality" by Sterling Fishman, *Journal of Contemporary History,* 17:2, April, 1982, 269-283. According to Fishman, in the twentieth century, childhood sexuality has come into its own and its *suppression* is viewed as contributing to "insanity, criminality and decadence." The author hails the fact that *"State school systems which had been suppressing childhood sexuality are now becoming agencies of sex education..."*
495. Patrick Buchanan, "Sexologist Kinsey: Child Abuse Collaborator," *The Washington Times,* May 20, 1983, p. 2C.
496. Edward W. Eichel, "Heterophobia: A Campaign Against Heterosexuality," A Letter of Complaint to Dr. Theresa Crenshaw, President, AASE(T), N.Y., April, 26, 1987, p. 1.
497. Ibid., pp. 1-2.
498. Ibid., p. 1.
499. Ibid., p. 2.
500. Ibid.

501. Ibid.
502. Ibid.
503. "Vatican Sets Extraordinary High Standards for Teachers of Sex Ed.," *Challenge,* Vol. 10, No. 8, Dec. 1983, p. 18.
504. See *Aldous Huxley,* by Harold H. Watts, Twayne Publishers, Boston, 1969, p. 77, for a discussion on who directs the directors of the hatcheries in Huxley's utopia—*Brave New World.*
505. Edward Eichel, "Chart on the Pansexuality Framework." The partial listing of principal figures, institutions, organizations, mechanisms who form the timbers for the pansexuality framework include New York University, University of Pennsylvania, National Sex Forum, the Institute for the Advanced Study of Human Sexuality (IASHS), and the Society for the Scientific Study of Sex (SSSS).
506. W. R. Coulson, Ph.D., J. D. Coulson, M.S., "Confessions of an Ex-Sexologist," *Social Justice Review,* March/April 1988, p. 44.
507. Ibid.
508. Ibid., p. 47, footnote 6.
509. "Sexual Experimentation Can End in Death" by Gordon Slovut, *Star Tribune,* St. Paul, Minnesota, March 23, 1989, p. 1E.
510. Ibid.
511. Ibid., p. 11E
512. Ibid.
513. Ibid.
514. Ibid.
515. "The Strange Values of Fr. John E. Forliti," *Serviam,* Newsletter of CREDO, Buffalo, N.Y., 1988, p. 4.
516. Ibid.
517. Ibid.
518. Dr. Damian Fedoryka, Speech on Sex Education to the National Coalition of Clergy and Laity, June 25, 1988; Letter of Dr. Fedoryka to NCCL Vice-President, Mr. Richard Lloyd, November 17, 1987, p. 2.
519. Ibid., p. 3.
520. Ibid.
521. Ibid. p. 8.
522. Msgr. William Smith, "Secular Humanism and Sex Education," *Lay Witness,* CUF, N.Y., April, 1984, p. 6.
523. See W. R. Coulson, Ph.D., "Helping Youth Decide," *The New York State Journal of Medicine,* Vol. 85, July, 1985, p. 35.
524. Pope Pius XI, *On the Christian Education of Youth,* N.C.W.C.
525. Josef Pieper, Ph.D., *The Four Cardinal Virtues,* University of Notre Dame Press, Notre Dame, Indiana, 1966, pp. 159-160.
526. Ibid., p. 160.
527. Ibid., p. 197.
528. Dr. Dietrich von Hildebrand and Dr. William A. Marra, *Sex Education: The Basic Issues,* A Roman Forum Tract, N.J., 1969, p. 25.
529. Ibid., p. 24.
530. Ibid., p. 25.

531. Ibid., pp. 24-25.
532. Ibid., pp. 25-26.
533. All references and quotations are taken from Aldous Huxley's *Brave New World,* Bantam Books, New York, 1960 paperback edition.

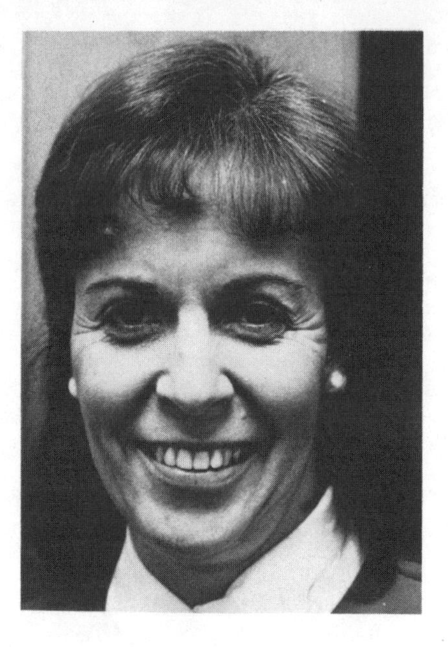

About the Author

Randy Engel has written extensively on a wide variety of Pro-Life issues, including population control, sexual conditioning, eugenic abortion and federal anti-life programs. Founder of the United States Coalition for Life (USCL), she has served since 1972 as National Research Director for USCL. She is Editor of the USCL *Pro-Life Reporter.*

Mrs. Engel has testified numerous times before the U.S. Senate and House of Representatives on various issues. Founder and Executive Director of the International Foundation for Genetic Research/The Michael Fund of Pittsburgh, the author is acclaimed for her work. In 1967, as National Director of the National Vietnam Refugee and Information Services, she received the Distinguished Service Medal for her assistance to South Vietnamese refugees and orphans.